China and India
in
Asia Power Politics

China and India
in
Asia Power Politics

Editor
Rohit Singh

Vij Books India Pvt Ltd
New Delhi (India)

Published by

Vij Books India Pvt Ltd
(Publishers, Distributors & Importers)
2/19 (Second Floor), Ansari Road, Darya Ganj
New Delhi - 110002
Phones: 91-11-43596460, 91-11- 65449971
Fax: 91-11-47340674
web: www.vijbooks.com
e-mail : vijbooks@rediffmail.com

Copyright © 2011, Publisher

ISBN: 978-93-80177-53-3

CONTENTS

PREFACE

China genuinely fears US-India naval cooperation in the Indian Ocean. Beijing's strategy has been to distract India through a policy of fomenting 'contained chaoses in India's neighbourhood — in Nepal, Bangladesh, Pakistan. India never want to be seen as being used by the US as a counterweight to China, but there are subtle ways to signaling that the US is prepared to cooperate in new ways that will deal with the challenge of a rising China.

The visit of US President Barack Obama to India in November 2010 — has proved long enough to accentuate a striking change of course in the US strategic orientation towards Asia in general — and towards China and India in particular. China had closely observed Obama's tour for clues on how far the US goes to project India as a rising 'Asian power' that commands deeper engagement.

The possibility of seeing a higher profile for India in China's neighbourhood in East Asia is additionally giving China some cause for disquiet. Media observations is also taking wary note of Prime Minister Manmohan Singh's visit to Japan, which was embroiled in a bruising maritime dispute with China.

Chinese policy lately in defence of its maritime claims has come close to bullying. In that context, many in the US see India as a potential counterweight against China, and the fact that India is a democracy enhances its reputation in the US. Hope this book will provide a clear view of India's and China's position and their rising power politics in Asia region.

- Editor

1

Introduction

In the 1950s and 1960s, India was an enthusiastic promoter of Asian regionalism. As the second largest country in Asia, in 1967 India even suggested the formation of an Asian Council, believing such "a broad based economic organization of all countries in Asia should be formed so that no single country or group of countries from Asia or outside can dominate any country in Asia". However, India's decision to retain the membership of the Commonwealth after its political independence indicated that India mainly conceived its development in collaboration with the Western world.

Moreover, India's incapacity and economic weakness resulted from its wrong economic policies, such as "an inward-oriented strategy of economic self-reliance through import-substitution and building heavy industries". Moreover, the influence of geopolitics in the Cold War era made it impossible for New Delhi to reach out beyond the Indian subcontinent and develop all-round relations with ASEAN.

As the Cold War ended in the early 1990s and the general trend towards regionalism emerged globally and China's influence increased in Southeast Asia, India again realized ASEAN's importance in terms of politics, economy, and diplomacy, and consequently launched its "Look East" policy, the focus of which was how to become actively engaged in Southeast Asian affairs in the changing post-Cold War era. India's involvement and growing role have brought forth different conceptions of East Asian regionalism, the impact of the India factor on future Sino-ASEAN relations, as well as the significance of China's changing perceptions of India's rise and its role in Southeast Asia, and what approaches China is and will be taking.

INDIA'S NEW POLICIES TOWARDS ASEAN

India's Look East policy was initiated in 1991 after the Cold War when India faced a number of successive strategic and economic challenges which threatened its political survival. The breakup of the Soviet Union deprived India of its main trading partner and source of cheap imported oil. India was forced to purchase oil at market prices which were inflated because of the First Gulf War in 1990. India, therefore, had to realign its foreign policies and implement, what it refers to as a move "towards big power strategy", with the characteristics of a multi-directional foreign policy. Its Look East policy is an important component of this development strategy.

In an attempt to soothe the strategic antagonism between India and ASEAN and enhance ties with the Southeast Asian region, India signaled its intention to join the Asia Pacific Economic Cooperation (APEC) grouping and the Asia Europe Meeting (ASEM) in order to prepare for its eventual leap into the global market as a dominant economic player. During this first phase, India's Look East policy was implemented with the purpose of rebuilding its economic relations with Southeast Asia so as to diversify trade away from its main trading partners in North America and Europe.

The early 1990s also saw the acceleration of economic reforms in India, and a closer economic relationship between ASEAN and India started to look promising to both. ASEAN countries realized that with the rise of India, they can reduce their dependence on Japan, the Western countries, and China in trade and economic relations. They responded positively to India's initiatives and advances, and accepted India as a sectoral dialogue partner of ASEAN in the fields of trade, investment, and tourism in 1992.

In the 1995 ASEAN Summit, Singapore's Prime Minister Goh Chok Tong proposed to elevate India to full dialogue partnership, and this proposal received the consent of all the ASEAN leaders. In 1996, India began participating in the ASEAN Post-Ministerial Conferences and the ASEAN Regional Forum (ARF). This was the first time in 50 years for India to attend a multilateral dialogue on politics and security in the Asia-Pacific region, indicating India's Look East policy had reached an important milestone.

The mid-1990s saw Sino-US relations improve under the Clinton administration in terms of economic cooperation and diplomacy. The US acquiescence in China's transfer of nuclear and missile equipment and technology to Pakistan and its embrace of China during the mid-1990s as a strategic partner confronted India with the prospect not only of US hegemony, but also of US-endorsed Chinese hegemony over it. India has been concerned that China will use its permanent membership in the UN Security Council and its bourgeoning relationship with Washington to block New Delhi from taking its appropriate place in the world stage and in Asia.

In India's case, the issue of an immediate threat from China is less significant, while the widening gap between China and India, as well as its longer-term implications, are deemed to be more crucial. Indeed, India's nuclear ambition might well be driven more by the China factor rather than concerns over Pakistan, which India views as not an equal partner in the balance of power game. After India's nuclear test in May 1998 followed by those in Pakistan, China—exercising its authority as the rotating president of the UN Security Council—actively coordinated permanent member consultations to condemn the tests.

Meanwhile, the United States, Japan, Australia, and some other developed countries unanimously retaliated against India in the form of economic sanctions. ASEAN's concerns over China's rise and dominant role in Southeast Asia could well have tempered the regional association's rather mild response to India's nuclear tests—a factor that has spurred India's post-Cold War engagement in the region. In 1998, Atal Bihari Vajpayee became India's new prime minister, and the Look East policy was hastened. The second phase of India's Look East policy saw greater efforts in forging links with the states of Cambodia, Laos, Myanmar, and Vietnam (CLMV) and marshalling support for India to hold a summit level meeting with ASEAN.

In June 1997, under New Delhi's aegis, a sub-regional grouping called BISTEC (later, BIMSTEC to include Myanmar) comprising three South Asian countries (India, Bangladesh, and Sri Lanka) and two Southeast Asian countries (Thailand and Myanmar) was formed with the aim of creating a free trade zone among member countries before 2017. In 2000, sponsored by India, the "Mekong-Ganges River Cooperation Project" between India and five ASEAN member countries (Vietnam, Laos, Cambodia, Myanmar, and Thailand) was initiated to promote cooperation in tourism, culture, and education in this sub-region.

India is clearly aware that it is not capable enough to compete with China and other big powers in the market of ASEAN's original five members (Indonesia, Malaysia, Singapore, Thailand, and the Philippines), but closer engagement with ASEAN's new members provides it an important access to the whole ASEAN market. So India proposed economic and technical assistance to those new members, including setting up centres for English language training in the CLMV states, and providing unilateral tariff concessions to goods from these countries.

After intensive efforts to achieve parity with China, Japan, and South Korea in the ASEAN scheme of partnerships, India successfully became a summit-level partner in 2002. At the Third ASEAN-India Summit held in November 2004 in Vientiane, India and ASEAN signed the "ASEAN-India Partnership for Peace, Progress and

Shared Prosperity" document, setting out a road map for long-term ASEAN-India engagement.

At the 2005 ASEAN-India Summit, as part of its assistance programme for the new members of ASEAN, India had announced its intention to set up a permanent Centre for English Language Training in each of them and a "satellite-based network" linking India with those countries for tele-medicine and tele-education. In April 2005, with the strong advocacy of Singapore, Indonesia, and Thailand for India's inclusion in the East Asia Summit (EAS), the ASEAN Foreign Ministers endorsed India's participation in the EAS. This was a significant step in India's drive for stronger linkages with East Asia as well as in ASEAN's effort to have India strategically and economically engaged in the affairs of the region, and to play a counter-weight role vis-a-vis China.

BILATERAL ECONOMIC RELATIONS

The launch of ASEAN Free Trade Area (AFTA) in Singapore in 1992 and China's efforts to have a free trade agreement with ASEAN by 2012 added to India's concerns. To counter China's economic initiatives and increasing influence in ASEAN, India hosted the First India-ASEAN Business Summit in the Indian cities of New Delhi and Hyderabad in October 2002. India believes it has the potential to enhance technological cooperation, especially in the information technology (IT) sector with the ASEAN countries.

As bilateral political and diplomatic relations between India and ASEAN improved, bilateral economic relations showed a positive trend, with absolute figures increasing steadily. From 1998 to 2004, the total value of trade between India and ASEAN-5 increased from US$5.6 billion to US$14.5 billion, with India's exports to ASEAN-5 valued at US$6.8 billion, while imports from ASEAN-5 totalled US$7.7 billion. ASEAN has become the third largest trade partner of India, ranking behind European Union and the United States. However, the balance of trade has been in ASEAN's favour, especially since the late 1990s.

Two of ASEAN's largest trade partners with India—
Singapore and Malaysia—accounted for over 60 per cent
of total trade between India and ASEAN. In terms of
investment, from 1991 to 2002, the accumulation of
ASEAN's foreign direct investment (FDI) in India was US$4
billion, or 6.1 per cent of total FDI inflows to India during
this period. ASEAN's FDI to India mainly focuses on
telecommunication, petroleum, and heavy industrial
sectors, with main source countries being Singapore,
Malaysia, and Thailand.

At present, Singapore is the third largest foreign
investor in India, with its investment of US$1.5 billion in
the telecommunication sector and US$2 billion in
technology, finance service sectors, and astronavigation
industry. Malaysia is the tenth largest investor in India,
having completed 21 projects worth an estimated US$1.2
billion. In contrast, as of December 2004, India had invested
in 144 projects worth approximately US$420 million in
Malaysia, mainly in the manufacturing sector.

India-Malaysia trade in 2009 shrunk by nearly a third
to $7.06 billion from $10.52 billion in 2008 after being hit
by the double whammy of a demand slowdown due to the
global financial crisis and fall in prices of major items like
oil. Considering the growth of the Indian economy and its
burgeoning middle class, by 2015 the trade with India and
Malaysia has to grow to the current level of the trade with
China and Malaysia, which is over $50 billion. India-Asean
FTA (Free Trade Agreement) in goods, has been
implemented since January 2010.

FREE TRADE AGREEMENT

Though bilateral trade and investment relations have
made significant progress, the then Indian Finance Minister,
Yashwant Singha was concerned that India's bilateral trade
with ASEAN was mainly limited to only a few economic
sectors and countries, and the balance of trade was in
ASEAN's favour. The issue of bilateral trade was thus

discussed at the First ASEAN-India Summit held in Cambodia in November 2002. At the 5th ASEAN-India Senior Officials Meeting in New Delhi in May 2003, Malaysia, as co-chair of the meeting, emphasized the importance of moving ASEAN-India trade linkages towards a Framework Agreement on Economic Cooperation.

This idea was discussed further at the Second India-ASEAN Summit in Bali, Indonesia in October 2003, and the Framework Agreement on Comprehensive Economic Cooperation between ASEAN and India was signed. It envisages FTA in goods, services, and investment.

Establishing the FTA in goods is targeted for completion by 31 December 2011 for Brunei, Indonesia, Malaysia, Singapore, and Thailand, and India. For the Philippines and the CLMV countries, the target is 31 December 2016. However, negotiations ran into difficulties as India insisted on excluding 1,414 items (including textiles, agricultural products) from the FTA.

Malaysian Prime Minister Abdullah Badawi once said: "ASEAN is concerned on the proposal by India to exclude a substantial portion of trade from the FTA through exclusion of a large number of products from tariff concessions". Countries like Malaysia and Indonesia would want agricultural products like edible oil, pepper and rubber to be part of the FTA.

India's import duties and sectoral FDI caps in telecommunications and aviation are also impeding investments from ASEAN countries. On the part of ASEAN, some countries especially the second tier CLMV, are not ready to open services and IT sectors in which India is more competitive.

The India-ASEAN FTA has come into a stalemate mainly because of the pressure from internal disagreement between the Indian Ministry of Commerce on the one hand, and the Agriculture and Finance Ministries on the other. While the Commerce Ministry has proposed a phased reduction in duty on sensitive products like palm oil, pepper, tea, and coffee, and also proposed to reduce its list of sensitive items to 990, the Agriculture Ministry has raised concerns about the impact of the move on Indian farmers.

Neither is the Finance Ministry in favour of these proposals as they would result in a loss of revenue arising out of tariff cuts under the agreement. Though India's FTA negotiations with ASEAN as a group encountered some difficulties, its talks with some individual ASEAN countries have been proceeding smoothly. India signed a bilateral FTA with Thailand in July 2003, a Comprehensive Economic Cooperation Agreement (CECA) with Singapore in June 2005, and is negotiating another CECA-type FTA with Malaysia.

The India-Singapore CECA is particularly significant for Singapore—a city-state whose development relies heavily on FDI and international trade. After the India-Singapore CECA came into effect on 1 August 2005, Singapore fully eliminated customs duties on all products from India, and India on its part, offered concessions to Singapore on products covering 80 per cent of Singapore's exports to India.

The India-Singapore CECA also includes agreements on avoidance of double taxation, mutual recognition agreements that will establish standards, technical regulations, and sanitary measures in specified sectors in each country; thus trade and investment relations between these two countries are bound to expand greatly. There have been fears that cheap imports from ASEAN member countries will route through Singapore and reach the India market. Therefore, the CECA involves rules of origin, which stipulate that only goods having 40 per cent local (Singapore or India) content will be eligible for tariff concessions.

FACTORS INFLUENCING INDIA'S POST-COLD WAR POLICY TOWARDS ASEAN

STRATEGIC ADJUSTMENTS

During the Cold War period, relying on its leadership role of the non-alliance movement and in the Third World, India played a balancing act between the two superpowers, and created a somewhat significant influence on regional and international affairs. After the Cold War, as the Soviet Union collapsed, India lost a strong ally, together with the military and financial assistance that came with a pro-Soviet orientation. India found itself in a difficult situation, in that it no longer had the leverage that its earlier friendship with the Soviet Union had provided it. Thus its status and prestige ultimately declined in the international arena, and its geopolitical clout decreased dramatically.

India therefore had to readjust and change its foreign policy strategy, and create a new place for itself on the international economic and geopolitical stage. But from a geopolitical perspective, as its arch enemy, Pakistan, is on India's western border, it constitutes a significant geographic obstacle to India's efforts to create and develop relations with West Asia. Moreover, the political situation in the Middle East remains unstable in the long term, while Central Asia and Afghanistan located to the north of India are backward and lack the potential for cooperation.

In the event, the ASEAN countries, as relatively close neighbours of India—both in terms of cultural commonalities and regional interests—have emerged as an attractive proposition in New Delhi's eyes for cultivating closer relations. India realized that if it wanted to have a significant role as a major power, complete its transition from a "South Asian regional power" to an "Asian major power" and eventually become a "major world power", it must develop political and economic relations with ASEAN, using ASEAN as a bridge with which to connect itself to East Asia.

Moreover, the 9/11 terrorist attack was a significant turning point in US relations with South Asia. Besides getting India's possible help and facilities in the fight against terrorism (no doubt because of India's own situation as a long-standing victim of terrorism), India's economic liberalization programme, mutual unease over China's rapid rise, and other factors drove these two sides closer.

DOMESTIC ECONOMIC REFORMS

Apart from the strategic concerns, India's attention to Southeast Asia was based on important considerations. India's main objective after achieving independence in 1947 was to attain self-sufficiency under a planned economic system. But in the first four decades, self-sufficiency remained elusive and the import-substitution policy failed to yield the desired result. Instead, what became obvious was an economy weighed down by inefficiency, stagnation, and poor performance. When Prime Minister P.V. Narasimha Rao assumed power in June 1991, India was experiencing the most serious economic crisis since independence with "a steep fall in foreign exchange reserves to about US$1 billion (equal to two weeks' imports), a sharp downgrading of India's credit rating, and a cut-off of foreign private lending".

In cooperation with the International Monetary Fund (IMF) and the World Bank, the new government started the process of large-scale economic reforms, openly embraced globalization and liberalization with obvious enthusiasm, thus effecting a paradigm shift in its economic posture. Although almost everything needed reforming, the most urgent reforms focused on ensuring rapid economic growth. In order to contain inflation, the government decided to borrow heavily on the market and encourage massive foreign investment rather than "printing money".

To satisfy the demand for capital and maintain economic growth, India not only needs ASEAN's market, but also needs Singapore and Malaysia's technology and investment to ramp up its infrastructure such as airports, roads and power. The current Prime Minister, Manmohan Singh is committed to carrying on this economic reform when he took office in November 2004. He needs new forces from outside to push ahead with his reform policies because "his economic reform plans have been repeatedly stymied by crucial coalition partners and the left parties".

FAILURE OF SAARC

It is evident that one of the facets of post-Cold War regionalism is the trend towards increasing intra-regional and inter-regional economic and political cooperation. The second trend is the concern with enhancing national and regional security especially in the light of 9/11 terrorism. Nevertheless, India's involvement in the South Asian Association for Regional Cooperation (SAARC) as a whole has neither resulted in greater trade nor greater security. The level of intra-regional trade among SAARC countries is low mainly because of the lack of comparative advantages in their economies.

Moreover, the small economies feared that Indian capital and lower-priced goods might flood their markets if they were to liberalize their economies. SAARC countries have resorted to non-tariff policy barriers such as anti-dumping measures to limit trade with India. Contrary to the principles and goals of SAARC, bilateral disputes between India and Pakistan such as over the disputed territory of Kashmir, the issue of water sharing with Bangladesh, the problem of illegal migrants from Nepal, and nuclear weapon tests has together impeded the development of regionalism in SAARC.

India's position is weakened by the fact that Bangladesh, Nepal, Pakistan, and Sri Lanka are all on friendly terms with one another, while all have contentious relations with New Delhi. India has become increasingly concerned and worried that it will be marginalized in the ongoing trend of regionalism and globalization. Although New Delhi has been disappointed with SAARC's lack of political trust and economic progress, India has been duly impressed with the economic progress made by ASEAN and its objective of achieving economic integration for all its members. India is fascinated and drawn to the dynamic of economic integration in ASEAN and its capital surplus, and has been making great efforts to develop and expand its relations with Southeast Asian countries since the early 1990s.

THE CHINA FACTOR IN INDIA-ASEAN RELATIONS

One of the most significant changes in the Asian landscape in the latter part of the 1990s was China's rise and its increasing influence in Southeast Asia. Indeed, China's future role, interests, capabilities, and influence are a major concern to India as it is to ASEAN. India specifically resents China's standing in the international order—not only its UN Security Council seat, but also its clout as a nuclear power. In both these dimensions "India sees itself as a coequal with China, and is at a loss to comprehend why China's role aspiration is acceptable while India's is not".

In the 21st century, India is equally concerned about the competition and "threat" from an emerging China at all levels, from South Asia to Southeast Asia. Since the 1962 Sino-Indian border war, China's relations with South Asian nations, especially Pakistan, developed rapidly. China has made substantial investments in Pakistan, Bangladesh, Sri Lanka, and Nepal, thus opening up these nations for Chinese goods. From 1998 to 2004, China's trade with SAARC rose from US$3.9 billion to US$19.4 billion; China's bilateral trade with India rose from US$1.9 billion to US$13.6 billion.

Similarly, bilateral trade between China and Pakistan has been increasing by 44 per cent on a year-on-year basis, reaching US$3 billion in 2004. In contrast, India's trade with its South Asian neighbours only increased from US$2 billion in 1998 to US$5.1 billion in 2004. Economic relations between India and Pakistan are almost at a standstill as a result of political conflicts, notably the unresolved territorial dispute over Kashmir. India's trade with Bangladesh hovers around US$1.6 billion a year.

Sri Lanka has FTA with both India and Pakistan, but it does not take kindly to India's support for the Tamil Hindu minority in its enduring conflict with the Sinhalese Buddhist majority. India's troubled relations with South Asian nations bolster China's presence in the region. China worked this to its advantage by building a naval port at the Arabian Sea Coast in Gwadar, Pakistan. Similarly, Bangladesh has offered China naval access to its prized Chittagong port, which New Delhi has long sought but to no avail.

India needs access to Chittagong port for its planned natural gas imports from Myanmar for shipment to its northeast region. In April 2005, China also signed a comprehensive agreement with Sri Lanka which provides access to Colombo's prized ports, and thereby to the Indian Ocean. China's increasingly economic and strategic ties with major South Asian nations paved the way for its entry into SAARC as an observer at the 13th SAARC Summit held in Dhaka on 12-13 November 2005. India tried in vain to keep Beijing out of SAARC.

Pakistan saw China's entry into SAARC as an opportunity to "counterbalance India's designs to act as a regional power and dominate SAARC", while for India, "the present impasse in SAARC has forced New Delhi to review its South Asian strategy and progressively shift it away from SAARC". India, however, enjoys a much better situation in Southeast Asia. India's potential as a big power and China's potential threat may have urged ASEAN nations to reassess their relations with India—factors that have encouraged India to increase its presence in the region to compete with China.

During the Cold War, India-Vietnam bilateral relations were close as both shared similar strategic and ideological perspectives regarding the shape and future of post-colonial Asia. In the post-Cold War era, India took the opportunity of developing relations with ASEAN to further enhance its influence in Vietnam. India has deliberately conducted high-profile joint naval exercises in the South China Sea, probably to indicate to Beijing that New Delhi has the ability to impinge on China's traditional strategic area. China has taken countermeasures by providing more FDI and low-interest loans to Vietnam.

The value of its FDI in Vietnam increased from US$7.2 million in 1995 to US$85.6 million in 2004, with the accumulation reaching US$188.7 million during this period. The balance-of-power politics is also obvious in the Sino-Indian rivalry in Myanmar, a buffer state between the two rising Asian powers. China had conducted military sales to Myanmar in the early 1990s, and provided Yangon assistance in the construction of military facilities. The suspected installation of intelligence facilities on Coco Island, and Beijing's alleged interest in establishing a naval presence in the Indian Ocean come into direct conflict with India's national security interests.

Similarly, to counter China's growing links with Myanmar, New Delhi has sought constructive engagement with the military regime, and has not only agreed to take steps to ensure peace and tranquility along the India-Myanmar border but also inaugurated the Tamu-Kalemyo-Kalewa highway, which provides a cross-border link and "is expected to promote economic development, cross-border trade and tourism in the region". At the sub-regional level, sponsored by India, the "Mekong-Ganges River Cooperation Project" between India and ASEAN-5 (Vietnam, Laos, Cambodia, Myanmar, and Thailand) was initiated in 2000.

India is also a member of BIMSTEC (Bangladesh, India, Myanmar, Sri Lanka, and Thailand Economic Cooperation). These projects underline cooperation in tourism, culture, and education; emphasize links between Indian traditional culture and ASEAN's culture, thus underscoring New Delhi's intention to elbow out China's influence from this area. Involvement in infrastructure projects in ASEAN also aided India in countering the influence of China in this sector.

In September 2004, Vajpayee declared in New Delhi that India would cooperate with ASEAN to build a railway from New Delhi to Hanoi, cutting through Myanmar, Thailand, Laos, and Cambodia. Some analysts considered this as India's response to China's proposal to build a "Pan-Asian Railway". Obviously, India's intention is to open up a new trade corridor in the Mekong sub-region, thereby enhancing its clout in the Mekong sub-regional economic cooperation and competition. At the military level, India was concerned that China has persisted in transferring military equipments and technology to Myanmar.

To curb China's growing military influence in Southeast Asia, India and selected ASEAN countries began holding joint military exercises. The Indian navy has conducted joint exercises with Singaporean, Vietnamese, Japanese, and South Korean navies to ensure the safety of strategic waterways in the region such as the Straits of Malacca. In this context, India's Look East policy, launched in 1991 primarily due to economic concerns, has now taken an added security dimension. In sum, ASEAN's economic success and mutual unease over China's rapid rise are among key factors bringing India and ASEAN closer to each other.

Indeed, it is arguable that India's effort to enhance its economic linkages with ASEAN is part of its overall strategy to work with ASEAN to balance the increasing influence that China might wield in its FTA with Southeast Asia. This was clearly reflected in the perspective of India's Ministry of External Affairs, whose goal was to ensure that "engagement with the Southeast Asian region was in line with India's strategic policy to meet the growing threat of China in the region".

THE INDIA FACTOR IN SINO-ASEAN RELATIONS

In the 1970s and 1980s, for several reasons including the India-Soviet alliance and India's recognition of the People's Republic of Kampuchea (PRK) regime under Heng Samrin propped up by Vietnam in July 1980, India was not necessarily seen in a positive light as a promoter of Southeast Asian interests. However, this perspective changed following the collapse of the Soviet Union in 1991 and the rise of China—two major events that fundamentally transformed the Asian landscape at the end of the 20th century. The Southeast Asian countries became worried about China's military power, mainly because of China's nuclear tests, its exclusive claim to sovereignty in the South China Sea and its aggressive attitude towards the Taiwanese elections in 1996.

Fearing that the collapse of the Soviet Union could lead the United States to withdraw from strategic locations in Asia and free China from its previous constraints, Southeast Asian countries were eager to ensure the safety of vital sea lanes of communication, such as the Taiwan, Malacca, Sunda, and Lombok Straits. In this context, ASEAN countries could well regard India as a useful partner to balance China, given the former's nuclear capacity and its naval forces, the largest in the Indian Ocean. At the Manila summit in July 1988, some ASEAN countries (Singapore, Vietnam, Malaysia, and Indonesia) consistently recommended a more benign attitude towards India despite the imposition of sanctions on India by the United States, Japan, and Australia.

Considering ASEAN's changed attitude towards India and the closer engagement between these two sides, will the India factor adversely affect the present status of Sino-ASEAN relations? Probably not. Firstly, both India and ASEAN have their own intentions and different goals in engaging with each other. India's engagement with ASEAN was only part of its Look East policy, ultimately aiming at acquiring the "big power" status which has been pursued by successive Indian leaders ever since its independence in 1947. Indian elites believe that ASEAN would serve as a springboard for its participation in the APEC forum and the annual Asia-Europe Meeting (ASEM) to expand economic gains that would ultimately conduce to India's big power pursuit.

For ASEAN, however, its intention of developing relations with India is primarily aimed at balancing its relations with the big powers, so as to promote peace, stability, and prosperity in Southeast Asia. In view of India's past history and goal of pursuing regional hegemony in South Asia, ASEAN countries are still wary of New Delhi's "imperial" ambitions and expansionist policies. Secondly, the economic linkage between ASEAN and Northeast Asian countries has been far closer than that between ASEAN and South Asia.

According to ASEAN Trade Statistics Database, between 2001 and 2004 the trade volume between China and ASEAN-6 (Singapore, Malaysia, Thailand, Indonesia, the Philippines, and Brunei) expanded on average 32 per cent, reaching from US$31.5 billion to US$72.5 billion, accounting for 7.5 per cent of the total volume of ASEAN-6 trade with the outside world (US$975.2 billion); whereas trade between the ASEAN-6 and India expanded on average 25 per cent, from US$9.7 billion to US$17.1 billion, accounting for less than 1.7 per cent of total ASEAN trade. In terms of FDI from 1995 to 2004, the accumulated value of China's FDI in ASEAN was US$1,018 million, accounting for 0.42 per cent of the total FDI inflows (US$241,826.4 million) into ASEAN.

Japan accounted for US$32,071.3 million (13.3 per cent); Asian NIEs (excluding Singapore) recorded US$20,009.6 million, accounting for 8.3 per cent, whereas FDI from India was US$736.8 million, accounting for only 0.3 per cent of the total FDI inflows into ASEAN during the same period. In real terms, ASEAN has been drawn into a thick network of trade and investment with Northeast Asia, as is reflected in the capital flows and intra-industry trade between China, ASEAN, and other Northeast Asian countries.

A closer look at the behaviour of Japanese multinational firms (MNFs) in East Asia reveals that 96 per cent of the exports of Japanese MNF affiliates were destined for their parent companies, while 83 per cent of their imports from

Japan came from their parent companies, contributing to intra-industrial trade between these companies in East Asia of 59 per cent of their total trade within this region. Many corporations of Asian newly industrialized economies (NIEs) are setting up similar production networks in China and ASEAN countries.

Much of what is "made in China" in fact contains large doses of value-added created in Japan, South Korea, Singapore, and other Western countries, mainly inputs of more advanced technology and capital-intensive products that are shipped to China for final assembly before being exported to ASEAN. The MNFs in China accounted for 60.6 per cent of China's total trade with ASEAN in 2005; at the same time this sort of trade also accounts for a high percentage of ASEAN's exports to China.

This production chain coupled with China's accession to the World Trade Organization (WTO) gives ASEAN ample opportunities and stimulus for expanding trade with China. In contrast, although India has a comparative advantage as a business outsourcing hub and very good economic growth in recent years, its persistent economic weakness (the Indian economy was valued at US$660 billion in 2005, standing at less than one-third of China's economy of US$2.2 trillion), backward infrastructure has contributed to the reluctance of MNFs from Northeast Asia and ASEAN to locate some parts of their value-chain in India.

Lastly, the impact of the India factor on the future of Sino-ASEAN relations may well depend upon the extent to which India's economic potential can be translated into political and strategic influence. India is still relatively weak in terms of economic and political power, while its broader geopolitical ambitions have to some extent been held in check by its rivalry with Pakistan. Even in the post-9/11 era, India would find it difficult to translate economic power and potential into political and strategic influence.

With regard to post-Cold War ASEAN-China relations, both entities have concentrated on strengthening constructive engagement, not simply creating economic interdependence, with the overall aim of strengthening cooperation in international and regional affairs. For instance, in multilateral fora such as APEC and the ARF, China and ASEAN have found themselves virtually de facto allies, articulating an "Asian way" in organizing regional interactions.

China and ASEAN are strong proponents of the principle of nonintervention, sharing perspectives that regional cooperation should adopt an informal, flexible, gradualist, consensus-based approach, rather than the more structured and binding format favoured by the West. In the circumstances, India has a long way to go in competing with China in Southeast Asia where economic and political relations are hugely tilted in Beijing's favour.

CHINA'S APPROACHES

For years, China and India have looked at each other with a mix of apathy and suspicion. As India's economy opened up in the early 1990s and exchanges between these two countries increased China's perceptions of India changed to become more positive and China's attitude more cooperative. India's recent economic performance combined with its growing importance in international affairs has led to a reassessment in Beijing of India as a "comprehensive national power", acknowledging that its rise is beneficial to Asia and the world. An article in Beijing Review notes that "with its 1.1 billion populations, seventh largest land mass and strategic location on the Indian Ocean rim, India has everything necessary to become a major power".

Chinese scholars also hold that China and India share many common views on international affairs, and that "while their politicians both dislike American hegemony, particularly in Asia, they have no intention to challenge the existing international order led by the United States, because both of them are developing countries and need a stable international system for their domestic construction". China and India have every reason to be headed towards greater pragmatic cooperation.

In affirming this view, China's ambassador to India, Sun Yuxi cited earlier remarks made by the former senior statesman and leader, Deng Xiaoping that "only when China and India develop well, can one claim that the century of Asia has come. If China and India strengthen cooperation, Asian unity, stability and prosperity will be very hopeful; the world will be in peace and make more progress".

On India's role in East Asia, China initially viewed India's involvement with a measure of apprehension. Beijing feared that this would enable New Delhi to win recognition as a political and military power in Asia, thus complicating the political situation in that region.

China was also concerned that the United States might manipulate India's evolving relations with ASEAN in order to contain China or "smother" China's attempt to exert its influence in the region.

As China's policy towards multilateralism changed from initial caution to one that is more confident, so too has it become more confident in viewing India's evolving role in providing new momentum for East Asian cooperation, and thereby strengthening the trend towards multipolarity in Asia and the Asia Pacific. China believes that multilateralism is a much safer and better way to expand its international influence and protect its national interests.

For example, ASEAN-sponsored multilateralism in East Asian security and economic affairs has offered China the opportunity to develop a counterweight to America's dominant role in the Asia-Pacific region, and to argue against Japan's EAC (East Asian Community) design based on the creation of a Japan-ASEAN axis and Tokyo's more prominent regional political-military role. As one Indian analyst pointedly observes: "as two major countries in the emerging multipolar global order, the simultaneous development of India and China will have a positive influence on the future international and regional systems".

It was in light of this recognition that China raised its relations with India to "Strategic and Cooperative Partnership for Peace and Prosperity" in the year 2005 when Chinese premier Wen Jia Bao visited New Delhi. This implied that the relationship has been upgraded from a merely bilateral level to a global level, signalling an important shift in China's policies towards India. China's increasing recognition of India's big power status and growing influence was further verified by Chinese president Wu Jin Tao during his visit to New Delhi in November 2006 when he candidly stated that China welcomed India's rise and supported a greater role for it in international affairs.

China has looked at India as a potential rival whose growth momentum and involvement in East Asia cannot be contained, and hence must be engaged in a constructive way that is good for business on both sides. China seems to have taken this approach towards New Delhi, taking more specific steps and separating political issues from economic relations. China believes that economic interdependence may encourage the two countries' peaceful ascent and restrain conflict escalation. To date, bilateral trade between China and India has been growing rapidly.

China has become India's second largest trading partner, with bilateral trade. Chinese Premier Wen Jiabao said "We have set an objective (in the joint statement) to increase the two-way trade volume from 13.6 billion dollar at present to 20 billion dollar...we plan to take it to 30 billion dollar by 2010." Moreover, in recent years China and India have forged a new alliance in the energy sector—one in which both sides require security for exponentially growing domestic demand. They have worked out new synergies in acquiring overseas energy assets:

      (a) in December 2004 China and India have worked jointly in Syria and Sudan, and won a joint bid to buy PetroCanada's 37 per cent

stake in Syrian oilfields for US$573 million;
(b) in March 2006, China Petrochemical Corp and
India's state-owned Hindustan Petroleum Corp
Ltd. signed a preliminary agreement for
projects in India, China, and elsewhere;
(c) in August 2006, China Petrochemical Corp
and India's Oil and Natural Gas Corp formed
a joint-venture company and invested US$850
million to buy a 50 per cent stake in Omimex
de Colombia Ltd., which has oil- and gas-
producing assets in the South American
country and is owned by US-based Omimex
Resources Inc.

China hopes to develop further this model of
cooperation in Southeast Asia to promote their common
interests. Nevertheless, it cannot be denied that some
divergent perceptions and interests are apparent between
China and India with regard to their respective relations
with ASEAN. The long-standing geopolitical rivalry
between the two coupled with the almost simultaneous rise
to world prominence ensures that these two big countries
will be competitors for ASEAN's favours from the tangibles
of trade and investment for their domestic modernization
to the intangibles of cooperation and support for their
increasing international influence.

In the context of exports to ASEAN, the share of
electronic products in China's exports to ASEAN increased
from 43.1 per cent in 2001 to 50.2 per cent in 2004, while
that of India's decreased from 21.3 to 1.9 per cent. Although
India's IT sector is more competitive than China's—in 2001,
India's IT exports reached US$7.8 billion, while China's
was only US$0.72 billion, the IT sector accounts for only 3
per cent of India's GDP. In order to eradicate domestic
poverty and realize industrialization, India will be making
efforts to develop its industrial sector.

While on the part of China, in order to create more
jobs for its large population and maintain social stability, it

will continue to develop its manufacturing sector. Thus, both countries will be competing with each other to be the world's manufacturing centre. This competition is the logical extension of their search for potential markets and political influence, and will continue in the near future. Moreover, Indian Prime Minister Manmohan Singh once said that India's strategic footprint as a "super regional power covers the region bounded by the Horn of Africa, West Asia, Central Asia, Southeast Asia and beyond, to the far reaches of the Indian Ocean".

China is conscious of New Delhi's intentions in Southeast Asia, as well as its ambitions to project its power into and beyond the Indian Ocean. India's ambitious geopolitical expansion strategy and its economic potential might not only turn India and China into competitors over oil supplies, but also increase their desire to maximize "relative economic gains" in the short term, especially when weighed against the threat of increased geopolitical competition in the long term. In this sense, China and India are rivals in Southeast Asia.

CHALLENGES AND PROSPECTS FOR INDIA-ASEAN-CHINA TRILATERAL COOPERATION

Generally speaking, there exist some common views and understandings of the current state of international political and economic relations among the key players in the region, namely, China, India, and ASEAN. These three entities have similar perspectives on regional integration in one form or another.

Globally, China, India, and most ASEAN countries have roughly similar positions on international trade negotiations, including opposition to the inclusion of human rights and environmental standards in international trade agreements. They advocate narrowing the inequities perpetrated by globalization, supporting the democratization of international relations, the harmony of international society, a just and equitable world order and a multipolar world.

China, India, and ASEAN are generally committed to preventing hegemonism in Asia, regardless of whether it is internally or externally generated. Such a convergence of strategic interests in the first decade of the new millennium augurs well for trilateral cooperation in many areas including the political, economic, and security dimensions. There are good indications that such cooperation has already begun. Indeed, Chinese as well as Indian leaders have made concerted efforts not only to widen and deepen their economic interaction beyond political issues but also to seek out new avenues of potential cooperation in Asia and elsewhere. Thus, a greater emphasis on improving links is evident in economic and trade cooperation.

Recent visits by top leaders on both sides are indicative of this new trend in bilateral relations. Similarly, the working out of bilateral synergies in acquiring overseas energy assets and the setting up of joint ventures reflect positive trends in business relations between these two countries, indicating that one-time rivals can become partners and "stakeholders". However, domestic politics and internal disagreements on both sides can influence "whether this positive trend will continue or whether it will descend into fierce and antagonistic economic competition".

On the part of India, Prime Minister Manmohan Singh said recently that "the world is large enough to accommodate the growth of India and China", and he believes most constraints to further cooperation with China are inherently internal. It is true that there exist deep-seated suspicions in the bureaucracy about China that go back to the 1962 Sino-India border war, and it must be recognized that China and India both aspire to great power status; hence there inevitably will be undercurrents of competition and conflict of interests in Southeast Asia. India is certainly concerned over ASEAN's trade diversion in China's favour. Given the geopolitical and economic realities of Southeast Asia, and the determination of Beijing and New Delhi to gain influence in this region, long-term reconciliation of their strategic interests can prove to be elusive.

The recent thaw in bilateral relations is unlikely to reduce their continuing and long-term competition for regional influence in the ASEAN region. Balance-of-power politics will continue to inform Sino-India rivalry in Myanmar, Vietnam, and other ASEAN countries. In this context, India is a potential opponent and competitor to China in the Southeast Asian market, and consequently China would be best advised to invest more time and resources into strengthening bilateral relations with both India and ASEAN. With greater transparency and a clearer identification of shared interests in Southeast Asia, there is scope for even better relations and constructive engagement among China, India, and ASEAN.

President Pratibha Patil on May 31, 2010 said that she had accomplished her goal of enhancing "trust, friendship and understanding" between the two countries. Citing the support of the Chinese leaders on several crucial issues, including India's bid for membership of the UN Security Council and correcting the trade imbalance now heavily in favour of China, Patil said that Sino-Indian relationship has gone beyond purely bilateral aspects and had acquired a global dimension. On her way back home from Shanghai at the conclusion of her six-day state visit, the first by an Indian President in a decade, Patil recalled her "constructive, wide-ranging and fruitful" talks with President Hu Jintao and Premier Wen Jiabao.

2

India Security Building In The New Century

Confidence- and security-building measures (CSBMs) are practical actions aimed at creating attitudes of cooperation. The primary objective of this concept is to generate confidence between rivals (enemies) or nations in competition—the sense that cooperation is both possible and is better than confrontation. Scholars working in this area argue that national interests can be promoted when two countries use political and diplomatic means to defuse mutual tension and that conflict can be avoided if fair steps are taken by both sides and that a win-win strategy is better than a zero-sum game, where the gains of one party result in losses for the other.

In their most general sense, CSBMs are instruments for the prevention of war and conflict and for the resolution of existing conflicts between regional neighbors or parties to the kind of long-standing confrontation, exemplified by the Cold War, in which normal channels of communication are weak or have broken down. The utility of CSBMs is perceived to derive from their gradual creation of an atmosphere of mutual trust, transparency, and predictability in slow and incremental steps in order to provide alternatives to confrontation and conflict where differences between states recur or have been inflamed or where new points of contention have arisen. Thus, CSBMs are a complex phenomenon. They have been useful, however—primarily in constructing new forms of military and civilian relationships to change the nature of hostility and mutual misperceptions.

Moreover, in the absence of strong political commitments, peace activists and security institutions have proposed CSBMs as a starting point for a process of mutual familiarization and willingness to move beyond confrontation and competition to cooperation and reconciliation. CSBMs are a conceptual and procedural tool based on the assumption that parties to a conflict have a mutual interest in pursuing at least some cooperative solutions in order to realize a shared goal.

The rationale underlying CSBMs is that a gradual process of confidence building is the key to overcoming obstacles on the way to realizing a mutually beneficial goal. Many of the international structures of the Cold War have been dismantled, much of the world is heading toward regional integration, market economies are said to be reshaping a new world, and democratic forces are replacing many repressive regimes; relations nevertheless remain very chilly in South Asia, which remains one of the most volatile and explosive regions in the world. Not only is South Asia one of the poorest regions in the world but it is also the region where the probability of an accidental nuclear war is greatest. South Asia covers approximately 4,468,000 square kilometers (about 1,725,000 sq. miles).

The inhabitants of South Asia number more than one billion (one-fifth of the world's population), making this one of the world's major population clusters. It has the world's biggest concentration of poverty-stricken people and is dominated by heavily militarized and bureaucratized polities thriving on regional confrontations and state-sponsored terrorism. After fifty years of independence, increasing numbers of people are still suffering from hunger, illiteracy, and preventable diseases. The worst affected are children, who should be the hope for the future.

The majorities are suffering from malnutrition; millions are engaged in labor, and many are afflicted with lung diseases and brain deformities related to poisonous emissions and the physical hazards at workplaces. According to one survey, by almost every measure of human development most of the people of India and Pakistan are poor, illiterate, malnourished, and disadvantaged. India has nearly one-half of its population living in absolute poverty and has an illiterate population more than 2.5 times that of sub-Saharan Africa. More than one-half of India's children over the age of four are malnourished.

India's nuclear explosions on 11 May and 13 May 1998 in Pokharan seriously disrupted the trend of normalization in India-China relations that had been developing steadily since Rajiv Gandhi's visit to China in 1988. More than the explosions themselves it was the manner of their justification — references to a "threat" from China to India's security — that offended China. Indian Prime Minister Atal Bihari Vajpayee's letter to President Clinton, which was leaked to the *Washington Post* and published on 13 May 1998, cited the threat to India's security environment from a country, armed with nuclear weapons since 1964. Vajpayee noted that India was invaded in 1962 by a neighboring nuclear power.

This neighbor, he implied, should be blamed for the deteriorating security environment in the region. The reference was obviously to China. A few days before the nuclear explosions, India's Defence Minister George Fernandes delivered the V K. Krishna Menon Lecture on India's security in which he described China as the "potential threat number one."

This statement, taken together with the letter to President Clinton, betrayed a certain hostility toward China by India's Bharatiya Janata Party (BJP)-led government. The Chinese government reacted sharply. High-level visits were suspended between India and China and the meeting of the Joint Working Group (JWG), which was to have convened in Beijing in 1998, did not take place, (There was one preparatory JWG meeting in June, but this reportedly produced no result.) China also made its position clear to India in the way it reacted to Pakistan's nuclear explosions on 28 May: the Chinese government expressed regret rather than a condemnation of the tests. The deadlock in India-China relations persisted through 1998, although academic and cultural visits between India and China continued to take place.

The BJP-led government's policy did not get full support from the other political parties of India, however. The opposition parties, namely the Congress-I, the Janata Dal, and the Communist Party of India (Marxist) (CPI[[M]), severely criticized the BJP-led government for having disrupted the carefully developed normalization process in India-China relations and even in India-Pakistan relations On several occasions the Chinese Ambassador in New Delhi affirmed the long-term interests of the two countries 'in forging constructive and cooperative relations into the twenty-first century.

A high point of the mutual exchange of cordial greetings was reached in December 1998 when Chinese Foreign Minister Tang Jiaxuan sent a message of greetings to Jaswant Singh, India's newly appointed Minister for External Affairs. Singh replied: "India seeks friendly, good-neighbourly, constructive and cooperative relations with China on the basis of Panchasheel," the "Five Principles of Peaceful Coexistence" that India and China jointly formulated in 1954. He referred to their meeting in Manila in July at the Asean Regional Forum and stated that he looked forward to "continuing our interaction to further mutual understanding, cooperation and friendship, so essential for our two countries and people."

The process of India-China normalization during the 1980s had followed the lines of the Panchasheel principles of peaceful coexistence. These principles had been crafted during Jawaharlal Nehru's visit to China in 1954 and were reaffirmed during Deng Xiaoping's meeting with Rajiv Gandhi in 1988. China and India both felt that the Panchasheel principles were the most appropriate framework for guiding international politics in the new era. The five principles are these:

(1) mutual respect for sovereignty and territorial integrity;
(2) mutual non-aggression;
(3) non-interference in each other's internal affairs;
(4) equality and mutual benefit; and
(5) peaceful coexistence.

These principles were evidently not based on unity and solidarity — in the mold of fraternal or "Bhai-Bhai" relations — but were rather in the nature of a realistic framework of interaction based on mutual respect and cooperation according to agreed-upon terms. The question arises whether the new nuclear equation will irrevocably destroy the Panchasheel effort. Or will the pressures of objective and subjective forces restore the process of normalization between India and China? By the close of the year, indications were that India and China would be back on the course of Panchasheel sooner rather than later.

As large, populous developing countries, India and China both have to cope with serious problems of unemployment, poverty, and other basic human needs. Peace is a prerequisite for dealing with these problems. The two countries need the framework of a cooperative relationship in order to promote peace and guarantee a tension-free environment in the region. Otherwise India's South Asian neighbors may seek Chinese assistance in order to balance pressure from India. China too may find a hostile Vietnam forging close relations with India or Russia to keep pressure on China.

The potential of Chinese assistance to the insurgents in Northeast India and Indian assistance to Tibetans (to create political and military problems for China, thus fomenting trouble for both countries) already exists. Finally, the two countries become more vulnerable to a big power link-up whenever they are in tension with one another. Around the time of Rajiv Gandhi's visit to China in 1988, a consensus had emerged in India, cutting across political parties, in favor of the Panchasheel framework of normalization and supporting the resolution of outstanding differences with China through peaceful negotiations. It is widely believed that friendly relations between India and China may not only contribute to peace in Asia and the world but that their joint efforts may also democratize the world process and create conditions for a just and equitable world order.

CHINA'S REACTIONS TO THE TESTS

It is instructive to compare the two statements that the Chinese government made after India's two sets of nuclear tests in 1998. At a press briefing after the three explosions on May 11, China's Foreign Ministry spokesman Zhu Bangazao responded to a request for a comment on India's nuclear tests, saying that the Chinese government was "seriously concerned about the nuclear tests conducted by India." This was not a condemnation, though he added that the tests went "against [the] international trend and [were] detrimental to the peace and stability of the South Asian region."

At that point China was generally making its position known, noting that progress had been achieved in prolonging the Nuclear-Non Proliferation Treaty (NPT) indefinitely and in working out an agreement regarding the Comprehensive Test Ban Treaty (CTBT). The reference to the negative effects of the tests on the South Asian region was conspicuous. Perhaps this level of reaction from China would have stabilized had the letter from India's prime minister to President Clinton not obliquely mentioned "the China threat" as a justification for the tests.

Prime Minister Vajpayee's letter to President Clinton, the publication of which coincided with the second round of nuclear tests by India on May 13, provoked a strong condemnation from the Chinese government the next day. Couched in strong language, a statement from China's Ministry of Foreign Affairs declared that the Chinese government was "deeply shocked" and wished to express its "strong condemnation" of the test. This language was reminiscent of statements made in 1971 during the war between Pakistan and the Indian Army-supported liberation forces in what was to become Bangladesh.

The statement had three components. First, it referred to India's going against the international trend for nuclear disarmament: "This act of India is nothing but an [expression of] outrageous contempt for the common will of the international community for the comprehensive ban on nuclear tests and a hard blow on the international effort to prevent nuclear weapon proliferation." This line of thinking was prominent in deliberations among the five permanent members of the UN Security Council (the so-called P-5) and in the resolution that the Security Council issued in early June 1998.

The second element in the Chinese statement was the charge that India's desire to seek "hegemony in South Asia" was triggering a nuclear arms race in the region. "Hegemony" is a term that the Chinese government uses with care. For many years during the 1970s Beijing had condemned Soviet hegemony; but since 1982, China has avoided using the term in reference to any particular country. They spoke only of the phenomenon of hegemonism and power-politics in the contemporary world.

Mao Zedong's statement "never seek hegemony" is frequently invoked in China's foreign policy statements as a way of saying that China will not seek hegemony. Thus the characterization of India's nuclear explosions as hegemonic definitely conveyed a strong Chinese denunciation. The tests might also have added a new element in Chinese policy considerations inasmuch as China now had to deal with an emerging military power.

The third component of the Ministry of Foreign Affairs statement was a refutation of India's reference to the nuclear threat from China as a justification for the tests. China called this excuse "malicious" and "groundless," noting that "ever since China possessed nuclear weapons, it has advocated the complete prohibition and thorough destruction of nuclear weapons and has unilaterally and unconditionally undertaken not to use or threaten to use nuclear weapons against non-nuclear weapon states and [against countries in] nuclear free zones."

The May 14 statement maintained that India-until recently a non-nuclear state — was not threatened by China's nuclear weapons. Moreover, it was noted that during the past two decades China had been totally preoccupied with economic reconstruction and was engaged in developing friendly relations with all its neighbors in order to create an international environment conducive to economic development. Read against this backdrop the Chinese statement had a special meaning.

The statement insisted that "this gratuitous accusation by India against China is solely for [the] purpose of [India] finding an excuse for the development of its nuclear weapons." The concluding sentence had a threatening tone: "The Chinese government will continue to closely watch the development of the situation."

A spate of articles and commentaries appeared in the Chinese press in the weeks following the tests. A commentary in the *People's Daily* on May 15 discussed Defence Minister Fernandes's assertion that China was the number one potential threat to India, noting that statements by other political figures in India showed that India's operations were prompted by its distrust of neighboring states. (This was a reference either to Indian Home Minister L K. Advani's statement that there had been a change in the strategic balance in the subcontinent or to Parliamentary Affairs Minister Madan Lal Khurana's assertion of India's right to use nuclear bombs to liberate Pakistan-occupied Kashmir.)

The *People's Daily* commentary, noted the decline in China's military spending in proportion to its Gross Domestic Product (an assertion that many in India found difficult to believe) and it cited the recognition by the international community of China's efforts for peace and disarmament. The commentary also pointed out that in April, while receiving the visiting chief of staff of China's People's Liberation Army, Defence Minister Fernandes had expressed satisfaction with the peace and tranquillity that prevailed on the India-China border. (His reference to the "China threat" just a month later was therefore not convincing.)

Statements made by Indian leaders in April and early May had "hurt" the feelings of the Chinese people and undermined Sino-Inthan friendship, according to the newspaper commentary. Indeed the' perception had spread in China that Indian leaders considered China to be an enemy (*diren*). Thus the edifice of trust — at the government-to-government level and also at the popular level — was seriously affected by this action. The fact that Fernandes had not used. the term "enemy" — nor had he said "threat" but only "potential threat number one" — was missed in the popular discourse.

The Indian government refuted China's statements with matching sentiments. Newspapers in India carried numerous commentaries rejecting Chinese accusations. The Indian government's Ministry of External Affairs (MEA) stated on 16 May 1998 that China's charge that India seeks hegemony in South. Asia is "baseless" and "unwarranted." Ministry officials pointed out that India was committed to the process of greater regional cooperation and economic integration in South Asia. Echoing the justification mentioned in Vajpayee's letter to Clinton, the statement said that "India cannot but take into account the offensive nuclear weapon and missile capability in neither our region nor the well-documented history of proliferation through clandestine accusation taking place in our neighbourhood."

Both allegations were clearly stated. One, China's nuclear weapons and missiles were considered a threat by India, and two, that China had assisted Pakistan to develop its nuclear program, in violation of the non-proliferation regime. One press report even declared that China had nuclear weapons stationed in Tibet and targeted towards India — a charge that China has denied repeatedly and that no authoritative Western strategic analyst has been able to confirm. But the fact that China has deployed nuclear loaded missiles in different parts of the country cannot be denied.

The MEA statement on May 16 also questioned why China, itself a nuclear power, should object to India's exploding bombs for security reasons. The statement pointed out that between 1964 and 1996 China had conducted forty-five nuclear tests, including twenty-three atmospheric explosions. China's forty-fifth test was conducted on the eve of finalizing the CTBT. In fact, the United States and France also conducted tests in the months prior to the conclusion of the CTBT.

India, on the other hand, took twenty-four years after its first test in 1974 to conduct an underground test to check the technical aspects of its nuclear capability. In its statement on May 16, the: Indian government expressed its commitment to the "total elimination of nuclear weapons in a time bound framework on a comprehensive, universal, non-discriminatory and verifiable basis." Furthermore, the government declared that India was committed to a process of dialogue with China in order to resolve outstanding differences and wished to develop "[a] friendly, cooperative good neighbourly and mutually beneficial relationship with China, our largest neighbour."

Responding to India's criticisms, China said that it had conducted nuclear explosions in 1964 for reasons that could no longer be used to justify India's going nuclear. First, China was beleaguered at that time by a U.S.-led embargo and it faced an array of U.S. nuclear weapons targeted against China. Second China's tests were conducted in a cold-war situation in which military tensions were high. Third, far from advancing the nuclear disarmament process, tensions in the region increased with Madan Lal Khurana's discussion of India's right to use nuclear bombs to liberate Pakistan-occupied Kashmir.

The *People's Daily* commentary (cited above) concluded that India could have continued to pursue normalized relations with Pakistan and China — to reduce mutual perceptions of threat — rather than deciding in favor of the nuclear explosions. Exchanges between the Chinese and Indian governments in spring 1998 heightened tensions between the two countries, vastly changing the climate of goodwill and dialogue that had existed prior to Pokharan-II. The press in the two countries reprinted acrimonious statements about the India-China border dispute and the war of 1962. In this atmosphere, as noted above, when Pakistan tested its nuclear devices on May 28 China expressed "deep regret" rather than condemnation.

The Chinese foreign ministry, spokesperson commented in a routine briefing that the Chinese government was deeply worried and felt uneasy, about the present nuclear race in South Asia. The spokesperson added that "the current nuclear arms race in South Asia [had been] triggered by India single-handedly because Pakistan nuclear tests were conducted as a response to the Indian threat." From its side, India censured China, though not naming it in formal statements, for assisting in the development of Pakistan's nuclear and missile program.

CHINA AND PAKISTAN'S NUCLEAR PROGRAM

As of December 1998 China had not joined the Missile Technology and Control Regime (MTCR). China's official position is that it is studying this international treaty although it did not participated in the formulation of the MTCR. "China has promised to observe some criteria and indices of MTCR and will never go back on its commitment," Zhu Bangzao said on 2 June 1998. Referring to the transfer of nuclear and missile technology to Pakistan, Ambassador Zhou Gang said in an interview in July that the two friendly sovereign countries had cooperated in various fields, including nuclear power generation, in a manner that was fully consistent with International Atomic Energy Agency (IAEA) stipulations.

According to him China had offered to collaborate with India in a similar manner. China even supplied India with "heavy water" for a nuclear reactor on one occasion. Prior to China's acceptance of the NPT in 1992 US intelligence agencies were reporting that China had provided a nuclear weapons design to Pakistan along with adequate amounts of weapons-grade uranium for two nuclear weapons. In 1986 China supplied enriched uranium and also tritium gas to Pakistan — enough to produce ten nuclear weapons. Chinese scientists working in Pakistan reportedly assisted in the development of Pakistan's nuclear program and scientists from Pakistan allegedly participated in the Chinese nuclear test in Lop Nor in 1989.

The landmark nuclear cooperation agreement entered into by China and Pakistan in 1986 was noted in India with serious concern. Following the signing of this agreement, Rajiv Gandhi (then Prime Minister) conducted a full-scale review of India's nuclear policy and ordered the development of a weapons program in 1987. China denies that it is engaged in nuclear proliferation and insists that its nuclear cooperation with Pakistan has been purely for peaceful proposes. In 1993, China and the IAEA signed an agreement to apply IAEA safeguards to a nuclear power station built with China's assistance in Pakistan.

In 1994 China is reported to have refused a Pakistani request to correct some problems with Pakistan's nuclear weapons. U. S. agencies feared that the 40-megawatt reactor at Khushab, which had been constructed with Chinese assistance, could provide plutonium for Pakistan's weapons program. In late 1995 the export of about 5,000 specially designed ring magnets from the China Nuclear Energy Corporation to a Pakistani laboratory was reported in the world press — a report denied by both China and Pakistan.

On 10 May 1996 the U.S. State Department announced that it would not impose sanctions on China in exchange for a Chinese pledge not to provide nuclear assistance to unsafeguarded facilities in Pakistan. In August-September 1996 there was a report, which was also denied by China, that China had supplied a special industrial furnace and diagnostic equipment to a Pakistani nuclear facility. In a 1997 report the director of the U.S. Central Intelligence Agency charged that China was "the primary, source of nuclear-related equipment and technology [supplies] to Pakistan."

The U.S. Arms Control and Disarmament Agency said in its annual report in 1997 that it was unclear whether or not Beijing had ceased sending supplies for Pakistan's nuclear weapons program. China and Pakistan have affirmed that their nuclear cooperation efforts are entirely legitimate and are for peaceful purposes only. Undoubtedly, the A.Q. Khan Research Laboratory (at Kahuta) and the Khushab Nuclear Facility (in Khushab) have received a significant measure of technological assistance, raw materials, and equipment from China. The Kanupp Pressurised Heavy Water Reactor and the Chashma Pressurised Water Reactor have also received Chinese assistance, but have been put under IAEA safeguards.

Some of these facilities may be capable of dual use: for weaponization programs and for the production of nuclear energy for peaceful purposes. Whether China has assisted Pakistan's missile program or not is a matter of continuing controversy. During a visit to India in December 1997 Chinese Communist Party (CCP) Politburo Standing Committee member Wei Jianxing denied published reports that had supplied Pakistan with M-11 missiles capable of carrying nuclear weapons. However, a U.S. Defence

Department report on proliferation in November 1997 states that "China remains Pakistan's principal supplier of missile-related technology and assistance."

These reports and this body of evidence have contributed to the way in which India views its own nuclear program. Even though the U.S. government was aware of China's assistance to Pakistan's nuclear program it did not make this an issue to the extent of imposing sanctions on China. U.S. leaders reportedly took up this question in their periodic dialogues with China, but China ignored these informal pressures. Meanwhile, the United States had its own reasons for maintaining balanced relations with China. U.S. corporations wanted stable U.S.-China relations so that their investments and businesses in China would be secure.

Was the development of Pakistan's nuclear weapons program — taken together with Pakistan's successful testing of a new medium-range surface-to-surface Ghauri missile on 6 May 1998 — reason enough for India to conduct its nuclear explosions in May 1998? Was China's assistance to Pakistan's nuclear program the reason for the Indian government's justification for its explosion (the so-called "China threat")?

These elements no doubt played a part in the government's thinking, but it became clear as the days went by that domestic political considerations were behind the BJP-led government's decision to test the weapons. Conflicts among the partners in the BJP coalition pushed the government to take this step in order to mobilize nationalist political sentiment in its favor. As a matter of fact, the BJP had advocated a strong, nuclear India right from the party's inception as Jana Sangh.

They declared as much in their 1996 and 1998 election manifestos and in 1996 they even considered conducting a test of India's nuclear weapons. The test never materialized because Vajpayee's thirteen-day-old government could not muster enough support in the Lower House. The political gamble of May 1998 did not pay off for the BJP, however.

Even in the by-elections of June 1998, the BJP did not do well. Meanwhile, the economic situation in the country has worsened, with prices of essential commodities soaring. In the Assembly elections of November 1998 the BJP lost power in the states of Delhi and Rajasthan and it failed to defeat the incumbent Congress regime in Madhya Pradesh.

CHINA, THE BIG POWERS, AND INDIA

In its response to India's nuclear tests, China reaffirmed its special relationship with Pakistan and, at the global level, it expressed support for the position of the other permanent members of the UN Security Council. India portrayed its nuclear test as a challenge to the nuclear monopoly of the five big powers, explaining its decision as an effort to assure a degree of security for India in the subcontinent and in the Asian region. On both fronts, however, there were doubts. Even with its nuclear weapons, India remains dependent on Western capital and technology.

The seven rounds of talks (May-December 1998) between Jaswant Singh, who later became Foreign Minister of India, and U.S. Deputy Secretary of State Strobe Talbott exposed the paradox of the Clinton administration imposing sanctions on India (in response to India's nuclear tests) at the same time as it was trying to establish friendly relations with India and insisting that India sign the CTBT and roll back its nuclear program. As to achieving security in the subcontinent, Pakistan's nuclear explosions on May 28 shifted the regional balance and increased insecurity for both countries. In terms of security vis-à-vis China, there is a clear imbalance not only in nuclear and missile capacity — with China enjoying considerable superiority — but also in the realm of economic development in which China has achieved an enormous advantage over India.

Despite these disadvantages, India went ahead with its tests, propelling China to actively campaign against this decision in global fora. In the China-European Union summit in London on May 26 a pattern of international condemnation of India's actions began to emerge. On June 4 the Foreign Ministers of the P-5 countries met in Geneva. China presided over the meeting, but reportedly left it to the United States and Russia to work out a compromise line. France and Russia wished to take a moderate stance, but the United States wanted to denounce India firmly.

The final statement expressed deep concern about the nuclear situation in South Asia and called upon India and Pakistan to stop further tests and to sign the CTBT. The UN Security Council's final resolution, issued on June 6, denounced both India and Pakistan, echoing worldwide concerns over the nuclearization of South Asia. (India was satisfied that the resolution made no reference to self-determination in reference to Kashmir. The Chinese delegate who had earlier brought up the need to work out a solution to the Kashmir problem according to the principles of the UN resolutions did not insist on its incorporation in the final resolution.)

When the G-8 industrialized countries met in London on June 12 the pattern of condemnation was the same. The Sino- U. S. linkup in this context was a significant development. On the eve of his visit to China: President Clinton said in several interviews and talks that "China and the United States should be partners for security and stability in Asia." He noted that China had played a positive role in the P-5 talks on South Asia and had taken the lead in "preventing a nuclear race in that region."

The climax of this process came with the signing of the "Sino-U.S. Presidential Joint Statement on South Asia" on 27 June 1998, at the conclusion of Clinton's visit to China. Avoiding the use of words like "condemn" and "denounce," the statement described the tests as a "source of deep and lasting concern for both of us." The two leaders agreed to work closely "to prevent an accelerating nuclear and missile arms race in South Asia, strengthen international non-proliferation efforts, and promote reconciliation and the peaceful resolution of differences between India and

Pakistan," They called on India and Pakistan to stop all further nuclear tests, adhere immediately and unconditionally to the CTBT, and refrain from weaponization and the deployment of missiles.

The leaders of China and the United States reaffirmed their own commitment to the NPT and CTBT and urged India and Pakistan to participate in negotiations for a multilateral treaty banning the production of fissile material. Finally, they offered "to assist, where possible, India and Pakistan to resolve peacefully the difficult and long-standing differences between them, including the issue of Kashmir."

A sharp reaction to the Sino-U.S. joint statement followed in India. The Ministry of External Affairs declared: "India categorically rejects the notion of these two countries arrogating to themselves jont or individual responsibility for maintenance of peace, stability, and security in the region." India claimed that: the Sino-U.S. moves reflected a "hegemonistic mentality of a bygone era." The Indian government used the occasion to criticize China and the United States for aiding and abetting Pakistan's nuclear program.

The Ministry of External Affairs statement stated; "It is most ironical that two countries that have directly and indirectly contributed to the unabated proliferation of nuclear weapons and delivery systems in our neighbourhood are now pressuring to prescribe norms for non-proliferation." The press in India was full of critical articles on this subject. An editorial in one leading Indian daily, entitled "Munich 1998", condemned the statement as one made between China-the-nuclear-proliferator and the Unites States-the-acquiescent-power.

The suggestion that China and the United States could help resolve Indo-Pakistan tensions was rejected by India. India had always taken the stand that all issues between India and Pakistan should be discussed bilaterally between the two countries under the Shimla Agreement of 1972, and even China's President Zemin, visiting India and

Pakistan in 1996, had called resolution' of outstanding problems between India and through peaceful dialogue between the two countries. Sino-U.S. statement was seen as an act of interference by powers in the region and hence a departure from Chin before the Pokharan blasts.

The international discourse on the May 1998 nuclear tests developed other dimensions, with France indicating its willingness to accept India as a nuclear weapons state and Russia's only that it regretted India's nuclear tests. When Clinton visited Moscow in September 1998 he wanted Russian President Boris! Yeltsin to sign a joint statement on South Asia similar to the one issued by China and the United States. But Yeltsin refused. Their joint statement, signed on 2 September 1998, contained only an appeal to India and Pakistan to forego further tests. Yeltsin also rejected Clinton's demand that Russia terminate military deals with India, especially the impending supply of a nuclear reactor and S-300 advanced air Defence system.

Russian Premier Yevgeny Primakov's visit to New Delhi in December 1998 — in the aftermath of U.S.-British bombing attacks on Iraq — established a "new and heightened level of strategic friendship between India and Russia. The relationship between China and Russia is also warm — as was evident from President Jiang Zemin's visit to Russia in November 1998 and the growing economic, technical, and military cooperation between the two countries and with the Central Asian Republics. But clearly a post-Soviet Russia wants to establish a firm and long-lasting bond with India in order to balance its relations with China and deal with U.S. pressures at the global level.

CHINA AND POST-NUCLEAR INDIA

Addressing the National Defence College in New Delhi in September 1998 Ambassador Zhou Gang said that India and China were bound to get beyond the current phase of setbacks in their relationship and build a constructive and cooperative partnership in the twenty-first century. But the

Chinese government leaders blamed India for the setbacks. Quoting a Chinese proverb the ambassador said in an earlier interview that "the doer must untie the knot." The Chinese expect that India will take substantive steps to build a climate of trust vis-à-vis China. Some Indian leaders did respond to China's concerns, but belatedly. Speaking in the Lok Sabha on 4 August 1998, Prime Minister Vajpayee announced India's nuclear doctrine and also declared his intent to resuscitate India-China relations.

He recalled that it was he as India's Foreign Minister in 1979 who had started the normalization process with China. He announced a voluntary moratorium on nuclear tests, though he reserved the right to review this decision in the future. He also announced that India would not use nuclear weapons against non-nuclear states and that it would not be the first to use nuclear weapons against any country. China should see these announcements as positive signs from India. The clearest signal from India came in the press conference by Brajesh Mishra, Principal Secretary to the Prime Minister of India, on 27 November 1998. Mishra stated that India did not consider China to be a potential threat.

Beijing did not react to this statement, however, since it was not in the nature of a high-level official communication to China. In the meantime, efforts to fix the next (the eighteenth) meeting of the Joint Working Group were going on. There was a deadlock here too: India was asking Beijing to set a firm date for the meeting, while China was pushing for a preparatory session before the actual forum. Since the JWG is the forum which economic, cultural, and technical agreements are renewed, the deadlock meant that bilateral relations would be more or less frozen until the end of 1998. Important academic events took place during this period. Two major seminars took place 'in Beijing in October 1998.

One was hosted by the Chinese Association for International Understanding, commemorating the birth centenary of the late Professor Tan Yunshan, the founder of Cheena Bhawan (China Hall) at Shantiniketan, the Viswa Bharati University founded by Tagore in India. The other seminar was hosted by the China Institute of Contemporary International Relations on the theme of India-China relations. The Indian participants included senior academics, well-known journalists, and a former ambassador to China. Equally significant were two international events in India in November. One was a conference in New Delhi on regional development in India and China, with a focus on Southwest China and Northeast India.

Organized by the Institute of Chinese Studies and the Indira Gandhi National Centre for the Arts, the conference 'included five scholars from the Sichuan Academy of Social Sciences and ten scholars from the Yunnan Academy of Social Sciences and the Institute of International Studies. This was followed by a seven-country' conference on the topic "Shared Ecology of the Himalayas" at the Indira Gandhi National Museum of Mankind at Bhopal. Twenty-two scholars from China participated. The exchange of students and teachers under earlier agreements had also continued even though almost half of the slots were not filled.

Economic deals between India and China continue to be in force, but new initiatives have not been undertaken since May 1998. A Chinese delegation led by the former Chinese Ambassador to India Cheng Ruisheng participated in the Track-II Sino-Indian Dialogue organized by the Centre for Policy Research in New Delhi on 25-28 January 1999, engaging in a dialogue at the non-official level that was reportedly "frank and friendly." Ambassador Cheng met with Defence Minister Fernandes and was received by President K. R. Narayanan in a meeting that was prominently reported on by China's *People's Daily* on 29 January 1999.

The *People's Daily* report quoted President Narayanan as saying, "China is not a threat to India and India is not a threat to China either. A prosperous and strong China will be of great support to India as well as to other developing nations, besides being of importance to world peace." The BJP-led government's disruption of the consensus in Indian foreign policy has been widely criticized by other political parties and by democratic opinion in India. With the exception of the BJP and George Fernandes's Samata Party all other parties hope for friendly relations with all of India's neighbors, especially China and Pakistan.

The Congress-I has particularly emphasized the need for returning to the path of normalization. The euphoria that was seen in the media in India right after the nuclear explosions soon died down and a sober atmosphere prevailed after a few weeks. Public opinion favors a rational foreign policy based on a peaceful relationship with India's neighbors, along with independence and non-alignment in world affairs. India's isolation during the Non-Aligned Movement (NAM) summit in Durban, South Africa, in July 1998, was a stark reminder of the decline in India's influence in world politics.

The economic crisis deepened in India in the second half of 1998 with price hikes on essential commodities and a drop in India's credit rating in the international market. The BJP-led government paid for these declines in its electoral losses in November 1998. This reality compels Indian leaders to reassess the post-nuclear trends.

Restoration of the Panchasheel course of India-China relations requires action by both India and China. India has to convey its sincerity and trust by establishing high-level contacts with China. In fact, India has yet to reciprocate (as of December 1998) for the high-level visits by Qiao Shi, then chair person of the National People's Congress Standing Committee, President Jiang Zemin, Politburo Standing Committee member Wei Jianxing, and Fu Qianyou, the chief of the People's Liberation Army. In late December, there were indications that the Congress-I was preparing to accept an invitation from the CCP to send a high-level delegation to China, led by either President Sonia Gandhi herself or by Sharad Pawar, the party leader in Lok Sabha.

Congress may indeed take the credit for revamping the India-China relationship ten years after its leader Rajiv Gandhi took bilateral relations to a new plane. The signing of the "Agreement on Maintaining Peace and Tranquillity along the Border," during Prime Minister P. V Narasimha Rao's visit to China in 1993, and the "Agreement on Confidence-building Measures," during President Jiang Zemin's visit to India, has carried the process of normalization further. At the same time, China must convince India that it is not part of the big power maneuvers in South Asia. China is in the unenviable situation of being part of the P-5 as well as part of the third world.

In fora like APEC and meetings of the Asia-European Union, China acts more like a powerful country, distancing itself from India. On other occasions, such as negotiations for entering the World Trade Organization as a developing country, it takes a different stance. China should appreciate that the Government of India has refrained from supporting the Dalai Lama's political moves since it considers Tibet to be an integral and autonomous part of China. Prior to Pokharan China's Pakistan policy had moved in a direction tolerable to India. Indeed, China should encourage bilateral dialogue between India and Pakistan with the aim of solving outstanding problems such as the Kashmir conflict.

China should also allow member nations in the South Asian Association of Regional Cooperation (SAARC) to collectively resolve their common problems and take concrete steps for economic development of the poverty-stricken region. A joint strategy, that gives China and the United States responsibility for peace and stability in South Asia is likely to do just the opposite. It would transplant an Iraq-like situation into South Asia, provoking all sorts of tensions in a region that is already volatile with ethnic strife and mass upheavals. If Asia is to become an autonomous zone of peace and prosperity, all the countries of the continent have to respect one another within the framework of Panchasheel and reduce their vulnerability to pressures by the NATO countries led by the United States.

For some time China had acquiesced in the face of U.S. military involvement in East Asia. Remnants of that thinking will continue to provoke tensions in the continent. Countries in Asia are currently engaged in democratic transformations in an effort to achieve autonomy and dignity at every level — regional, national, and sub-national. China and India have to adopt policies consistent with this historical trend. With that end in view peaceful and cooperative relations between India and China are imperative for the sake of a democratic and egalitarian world. Setting a course in this direction will leave the tensions of the nuclear summer of 1998 far behind.

3
China And India: Theories Of Development

The rapid and parallel rise of China and India on the world stage has resulted in rife critical comparisons of the two Asian giants. However, an exploration of potential scope for Sino-Indian cooperation to their mutual benefit may prove a more fruitful exercise. Whether in the economic or strategic sense, or whether pertaining to aspirations towards global power status, Sino-Indian interests are certainly converging. Already, progressively deeper Sino-Indian interactions signal a ripening of mutual trust. This could pave the way for the establishment of specific platforms of mutual collaboration, lesson-learning and aid which would not only be useful in themselves, but may serve as important confidence building-measures for the future.

China and India represent two of the greatest civilizations in the history of the human race. These two nations have in common not only great ancient histories, but have also arguably mirrored each other to some extent in the modern day: India and China both established new states within a similar period of time, and also implemented revolutionary economic reform just outside a decade from one another. But more importantly, the reform undertaken by both countries has resulted in a surprising parallel rise on the world stage that has elicited much excited comment and criticism.

In particular, many analysts have postulated that the recent but rapid renewal of friendly relations between the two giants now signals the beginning of a new economic world order. In October 2003, Goldman Sachs economists Dominic Wilson and Roopa Purushothaman released a now-famous report which predicted that within 40 years, the economies of India and China, added to those of Brazil and Russia (the BRICs) would be larger than that of the US, Germany, Japan, Britain, France and Italy combined. China would overtake the US as the world's largest economy and India would be third, outpacing all other industrialised nations. Similarly, in 2004, a report by the US National Intelligence Council compared the rise of China and India in the 21st century to that of Germany and the US in the 19th and 20th centuries, respectively.

But, at the same time, the rapid growth of both nations cannot eclipse the fact that both are facing colossal difficulties on the home front. China has to deal with, for example, its relatively weak private sector and increasing levels of unemployment, while India's problems include difficulties with its cumbersome bureaucracy and poor infrastructure. However, partial solutions for these dilemmas may well come from new and innovative alliances between the two countries. The recent normalisation of Sino-Indian relations has resulted in several cooperative ventures between the two, such as the Greater Nile Project in Sudan, an increase in interaction across economic sectors in general.

However, this is but the beginning of what could prove to be a long and fruitful relationship. Sino-Indian interactions have rapidly expanded from simple economic cooperation to progressively more complex projects and collaboration on the world stage. But more than that, the success of these ventures is giving birth to a tentative strategic political partnership, indicative of growing mutual confidence. It is argued here that given this burgeoning mutual cooperation and support between China and India, there is scope for the emergence of platforms for lesson-sharing and mutual policy exchange that will extend relations even further, and accelerate the further growth and development of both economies.

It has become apparent that both are uniquely placed to lend a hand to each other. This is especially so because of the complementary nature of each nation's strengths and weaknesses. This chapter has two main purposes. Due to the hype surrounding this new phenomenon, the first purpose is to place the current evolution of Sino-Indian relations within a balanced historical context.

The second is to put forward the idea that the progressively deeper and more complex interactions taking place signal a ripening of bilateral trust, and that this growing Sino-Indian confidence could act as a springboard for the creation of more specific forms of mutual collaboration, lesson-learning and aid. India and China both have the potential and need for the formation of such policy-exchange platforms in which integrated cross-sectoral lesson-learning and support can take place. Even so, the beginnings of this form of exchange are being formulated in the information and communication technology (ICT) sectors of both countries. It will be suggested that this is a useful model that can be formalised across many areas.

WARMER SINO-INDIAN RELATIONS

Amidst both overly optimistic and overly pessimistic media reportage of Sino-Indian relations, it is important to try to put the bilateral ties within a balanced historical context. The relationship to date has been characterised by several specific issues of contention and conflict, with very marked upturns and downturns.

However, while many of the contentious issues between the two Asian giants are not only serious but on-going, there is always some sense of political will for peace between the two, and, as in the case of the border war of 1962 for example, this amicable political will seems to appear at the most critical junctures.

THE TIBET ISSUE

The first major modern Sino-Indian disagreement was over Tibet, a geographical and political buffer zone between the two countries over which India had been given special privileges during the British colonial rule. In 1950, China reasserted its control over Tibet by force. In keeping with a policy of friendship with China, and in an attempt at pacification, mixed with no small amount of condescension, Indian Prime Minister Nehru assured Chinese leaders that India had neither political nor territorial ambitions, and did not want to seek special privileges in Tibet, but that traditional trading rights must continue.

Through India's encouragement, Tibetan leaders signed an agreement in May 1951 recognising Chinese sovereignty and control while at the same time ensuring that the existing socio-political systems in Tibet would be allowed to continue as before. Furthermore, in April 1954, India and China signed an eight-year agreement on Tibet that set forth the basis of their relationship in the form of the Panch Shila, literally five principles of mutual respect, mutual sovereignty, mutual non-interference, mutual benefit and peaceful co-existence. This effectively settled the Tibet issue in the short term, but was to be one of several major Sino-Indian conflicts to come.

China on May 2010 raised the Tibet issue with visiting Indian President Pratibha Patil and sought reassurance from New Delhi that no anti-China activities are allowed to take place by Tibetans living in exile in India. Senior Chinese leader Jia Quinglin, during his talks with Patil, raised the Tibet issue and sought a reassurance from India.

THE 1962 BORDER WAR

Up to 1959, despite border skirmishes and contentions over lines of delineation on territorial maps, Chinese leaders had amicably assured India that there was no territorial dispute along the border. However, the situation began to come to a head with the discovery of a completed Chinese road cutting across the Aksai Chin region of the Ladakh District of Jammu and Kashmir by an Indian reconnaissance team.

To exacerbate matters, in January 1959, Chinese Premier Zhou Enlai wrote to PM Nehru rejecting the Indian Prime Minister's contention that the border was based on treaty and custom, asserting instead that China had never accepted the 550 mile McMahon Line drawn up during the 1914 Simla Convention which defined the eastern section of the border between India and Tibet, a demarcation which Zhou Enlai termed "a product of the British policy of aggression" against China.

A second cause for bilateral friction at that time was the fact that the Dalai Lama had sought sanctuary in Dharmsala, Himachal Pradesh, in March 1959, and thousands of Tibetan refugees settled in northwestern India, particularly in Himachal Pradesh. China accused India of expansionist intentions in Tibet and responded by claiming 104,000 square kilometres of territory over which India's maps showed clear sovereignty. Zhou's brazen proposal was that China would relinquish its claim to most of India's northeastern territory on the condition that India abandon its claim over Aksai Chin.

The Indian government, swayed by dominant domestic public opinion, took the stance that the idea of a settlement based on uncompensated territory loss would be unfair, not to mention humiliating. Chinese forces launched an attack on India on 20 October 1962. However, although it was clearly winning the war, having successfully pushed back Indian forces and occupied key areas in Ladakh, China declared a unilateral cease-fire on 21 November.

This unusual move proved that the situation was more a demonstration of Chinese military strength than a will to claim territory, and could even be construed as unwillingness on the part of the Chinese to cause irreparable damage to relations with its South Asian neighbour. However, the 1962 war rankles in Indian historical memory and at various levels still impedes the increasingly warm relations between India and China to this day.

CHINA AND PAKISTAN

Sino-India relations continued to worsen during the rest of the 1960s and the early 1970s in inverse proportion to the warming Chinese-Pakistani relations, and were exacerbated by the deterioration of Chinese-Soviet relations. The crunch came when China backed Pakistan in its 1965 war with India. Further- more, between 1967 and 1971, an all-weather road was built across Indian- claimed territory, linking China's Xinjiang Uygur Autonomous Region with Pakistan. India could only express its displeasure as it watched the situation unfold.

Stopping short of using force, China launched an indirect attack against India on several other fronts, including the initiation of an active propaganda campaign against India on one hand while supplying ideological, financial and other assistance to anti-Indian dissident groups—especially to tribes in northeastern India—on the other. However, despite this, diplomatic contact between the two governments remained at a bare minimum and was never formally severed, even when in August 1971, India signed its Treaty of Peace, Friendship and Cooperation with the Soviet Union and the United States, and China sided with Pakistan in its December 1971 war with India.

Some semblance of desire to engage amicably still remained, as evident in renewed bilateral efforts to improve relations after the Soviet Union invaded Afghanistan in December 1979. China indicated some measure of goodwill by moderating its pro-Pakistan stand on Kashmir and by refraining from taking action either on the issue of India's absorption of Sikkim or on its special advisory relationship with Bhutan.

China's leaders also agreed to open up for discussion the boundary issue as a signal of a positive change in posture towards India. In 1981 Chinese Minister of Foreign Affairs Huang

Hua accepted an invitation to visit India, which acted as a catalyst to eight rounds of Sino-Indian border negotiations between December 1981 and November 1987, but no successful outcome was achieved. However, China's construction of a military post along the border in 1986 and India's granting of statehood to Arunachal Pradesh (formerly the North-East Frontier Agency) in February 1987 resulted once more in the deployment of troops to the area by both parties, once again raising tensions and fears of a second border war.

But by the summer of 1987, both sides had once more backed away from conflict and even readily denied that military clashes had ever occurred in the first place. Thus, although Sino-Indian conflicts have been at times very serious, resulting even in war, there has never been a full unleashing of aggression. Rather, both sides have always managed to exhibit some, albeit often small, measure of restraint in their dealings with each other.

SINO-INDIAN RAPPROCHEMENT

A more genuine warming in relations was facilitated by Rajiv Gandhi's visit to China in December 1988, the first by an Indian Prime Minister to China since Nehru's visit in 1954. This historic occasion saw the separation of ongoing difficulties in border negotiations from the other aspects of expanding relations between India and China. This trend of isolating the more volatile bilateral issues was to continue with Jiang Zemin's visit to India in 1996 which was to result in the de-linking of China's Pakistan policy from its India policy.

Gandhi's visit was also marked by a joint communique issued by China and India that stressed the need to restore friendly relations, once again on the basis of the Panch Shila. India and China also agreed to broaden bilateral ties in various areas.

Critics have observed that there occurred from this time forward an overt shift of emphasis away from the assertion of huge territorial claims and high moral principles. Instead there ensued an increased rhetoric concerning the need for "mutual concessions" and "accommodation" on the part of the Chinese, and an increased emphasis on historical, legal, geographical realities on the part of the Indians.

Both parties now called for a "fair, reasonable and mutually acceptable" compromise solution to their boundary question. There was a display of determination by both China and India to resolve the border issue. The two governments agreed to hold annual diplomatic consultations between their respective foreign ministers, set up a joint ministerial committee on economic and scientific cooperation and establish a joint working group on finding a solution to the boundary issue.

Between December 1988 and June 1993, no less than six rounds of talks by the Indian-Chinese Joint Working Group on the Border Issue were held, and border tensions were reduced through confidence-building measures which included mutual troop reductions, regular meetings of local military commanders, and the advance notification of the commencement of military exercises. A visible sign of the improved Sino-Indian bilateral relations was the resumption of border trade in July 1992 after a hiatus of more than 30 years.

Consulates were also reopened in Bombay (Mumbai) and Shanghai in December 1992 and in June 1993 the two sides agreed to open an additional border trading post. Good relations and mutual confidence were high on the agenda when, during Sharad Pawar's July 1992 visit to Beijing— the first ever by an Indian minister of defence—the two militaries agreed to develop not only academic, scientific and technological exchanges, but also military exchanges and a Chinese naval vessel was scheduled to make a visit to an Indian port.

The People's Republic of China does not appear to have come out so far with any official reaction on the subject;

interesting however is that the same theme of India's 'two front war', worded a bit differently as 'two front mobile warfare' has figured in an in-depth authoritative Chinese evaluation of India's defence strategy, done as early as November 2009; it raises a question whether or not Beijing already knew about India's reported revision of its defence strategy. This apart, it would be important to have a close look at what has been said in that analysis, for drawing meaningful conclusions. What follows is an attempt in that direction.

1998 NUCLEAR TESTS

While the determined but slow improvement of relations in the 1990s could not forefend the May 1998 Indian nuclear tests (Pokhran II), which once again brought Sino-Indian bilateral relations to a new low, it may have played a part in ensuring that the fallout of this with regards to Sino-Indian ties was less dire than it could have been, although there was indeed enough good reason for fresh hostility. Indian Defence Minister George Fernandes unequivocally declared China to be India's "potential threat number one" and Beijing's choice to interpret India's nuclear tests as part of India's containment policy towards China in its quest for regional hegemony only further exacerbated the matter.

It is worth noting though, that while the Chinese Government was clearly offended and exerted much pressure on New Delhi to recant its rhetoric on the China threat, some critics contend that Beijing was not unduly concerned by the nuclear tests as any real threat per se. It is against this historical backdrop of alternating friction and goodwill that the latest phase of growing trust in China-India relations must be viewed. However, it must be underscored that the most recent warming in Sino-Indian relations is unique and cause for optimism.

As previous bilateral hostilities stopped just short of prolonged war, the goodwill phases of Sino-Indian relations had also stopped just short of true or sustained rapprochement. The singularity of the newest upturn in Sino-Indian ties lies in the fact that it is accompanied by forays into joint ventures, various types of cooperation and even tentative beginnings of a strategic partnership (discussed below) as both governments begin to recognise opportunities for mutual benefit. The most recent phase of good relations between China and India was ushered in by the successful visit of Indian Prime Minister Atal Behari Vajpayee to China in June 2003, during which he and Chinese Premier Wen Jiabao signed a Declaration on Cooperation as well as nine protocols on bilateral cooperation, thereby fully normalising Sino-Indian relations.

Both leaders had pledged that their countries would work together for regional peace and stability, and progress was made even with regards to the long-standing Sino-Indian boundary dispute: the two leaders reaffirmed their commitment of 1993 and 1996 to maintaining peace and tranquillity along the border, and to take steps to codify the Line of Actual Control (LAC). There have also been six rounds of talks held between designated Special Representatives from both countries on the border issue. This is significant in that it has raised the level and stakes of border talks from the foreign secretary level of before.

Seen in the context of the unsuccessful border talks of the 1980s as well as the 15 rounds (to date) of meetings under the auspices of the Joint Working Group, it is indicative of the renewed commitment on both sides to find a viable solution to the border issue, despite the fact that a political framework for solving the problem still proves elusive. A significant aspect of the June 2003 agreement was that India reiterated its recognition of Tibet as part of Chinese territory, and made a pact not to support separatist activities by Tibetan exiles in India. China, on its part, agreed to open a point for border trade in Sikkim, thus indirectly accepting Sikkim's status as part of India.

This was given even clearer emphasis by the deliberate publication of a new map in 2005 which includes the new delineations. In short, there is definitely room for growing optimism that these one-time adversaries are becoming, if not friends, at least productive partners.

Following the change of government in India from May 2004 onwards, the leaders of both countries have met again several times, including at the bilateral summit in New Delhi in April 2005, and are expanding relations on many fronts, not least the economic one. As Indian Prime Minister Manmohan Singh was quoted as saying recently, "Who could have imagined that China would emerge as [India's] second-largest trade partner?"Now it seems that past predictions of an "Asianism" in which India and China would come together to a prominent position on the world stage is emerging as a distinct possibility.

Both nations have, to date, ostensibly put aside their hostile past in favour of the benefits that friendly relations may bring. Indeed, accompanying their parallel rise is an inexorable sense that for India and China, whether in the economic or strategic sense, or whether pertaining to their aspirations towards global power status, their interests are certainly converging.

On May 2010, India's President Pratibha Patil was invited by her Chinese counterpart Hu Jintao and her visit coincides with the 60th anniversary of the establishment of diplomatic relations between India and China. Patil and Chinese leaders reached consensus on many major issues. She focused attention on India's aspiration for permanent seat in a reformed United Nations Security Council. President Hu (Jintao) and Premier Wen (Jiabao) were understanding and supportive for India's desire.

FROM RAPPROCHEMENT TO COOPERATION

The first fruits of the recent Sino-Indian rapprochement are most evident, and naturally so, in the gargantuan growth in bilateral trade. While just a decade ago, it amounted to a mere $1 billion, bilateral trade in 2004 jumped to $13.6 billion. More recently, between July to October 2005 alone, China's trade with India reached $6 billion. There are indications that this growth may be a sustained trend rather than one likely to fizzle out. This mutual economic gain has helped melt away much of the previous fear and hostility between the two nations, and as Swaran Singh has demonstrated, trade can indeed be a powerful confidence-building measure between countries.

The rapid growth in bilateral trade is also indicative of a change in mutual perceptions by these two Asian giants, not just on an official level, but also in the less official business world. China and India are learning to see each other as opportunities. In the three years 1999/2000 to 2002/3, India's exports to China increased at an average of 50.2 per cent per year, and imports from China at an average of 26.6 per cent per year. However, it would be injudicious to be taken in by effusive speculations of unfettered friendship between the two countries. While bilateral trade in real terms has increased significantly, bilateral trade with China still only accounted for 5 per cent of India's total foreign trade in 2004 and China's trade with India, a mere 1.1 per cent of its total foreign trade.

Chinese attempts to initiate a Free Trade Agreement (FTA) with India during Wen Jiabao's visit to India in April 2005, while not completely rejected, were nonetheless met with reservations, especially since Indian analysts believe that a Sino-Indian FTA would be more advantageous to China than to India, owing largely to the fact that since China already has fairly low tariff barriers compared to the rest of the world, no serious market benefits can be expected by Indian producers after the creation of an FTA where tariffs are significantly reduced.

While prospects for continued warm relations between India and China are certainly not out of place, in terms of trade at least, it has been more a case of steady expansion rather than a no holds barred scenario. But that which is most spectacular about current China-India ties is not so much the depth of their warming relationship but rather the breadth of it. From the energy sector, to the ICT sector, and teamwork on the multilateral stage to strategic partnership, China and India are finding more and more common space in which to occupy well together.

THE ENERGY SECTOR

It is no surprise that rivalry in the oil sector between these two developing giants is aggressive, since India is just as hungry for supplies as China. The two are battling each other in the search for oil from Sudan to Siberia as they try to secure the resources to fuel their vast economies. Recently, the Chinese seem to be winning. The board of PetroKazakhstan, a Canadian- owned company with oil fields in Central Asia, accepted a $4.2 billion take- over bid by state-owned China National Petroleum Corporation (CNPC) on 22 August 2005.

The CNPC had surpassed a $3.6 billion offer from India's own state-owned giant, Oil and Natural Gas Corporation (ONGC), and in 2006, the Chinese National Offshore Oil Corporation again beat India's ONGC to buy a 45 per cent stake in a Nigerian oil and gas field for $2.3 billion. Both of Asia's largest rising powers desperately need energy, especially oil. China today imports roughly half of its oil. Consumption rose by 15 per cent last year, 2009 and is forecast to jump by an additional 9 per cent this year. By 2025, according to projections made by the US Energy Department, China will be requiring 14.2 million barrels a day, double this year's level.

India's oil imports are expected to rise to some 5 million barrels a day by 2020, up from around 1.4 million barrels now. However, scope for cooperation in this cut-throat competition for oil has also already been demonstrated. A good example of the broadening spirit of cooperation between India and China is in Sudan's Greater Nile project, in which Indian ONGC Videsh Limited (OVL) and CNPC are working in a cooperative partnership: While China built a refinery in Khartoum, India was responsible for building a product pipeline from the refinery to the port of Sudan. India's Petroleum Minister Mani Shankar Aiyar has remarked, "there are enormous prospects for India and China to work together. Our interests are complementary."

He visited China on 12-13 January 2006 and signed not only a government-level Memorandum of Understanding (MoU), but also several MoUs between Indian and Chinese oil companies. Also in December 2005, China-India successfully launched their first ever joint venture, Himalayan Limited, that has already won its first bid of about $700 million, buying a 38 per cent stake in a Canadian company's operations in Al Furat, Syria's largest gas and oil fields. With the current success of the Greater Nile cooperation, Mr Aiyar's continued optimism seems warranted.

SINO-INDIAN COOPERATION WITHIN A MULTILATERAL CONTEXT

While straightforward cooperative projects have acted as effective bilateral confidence-building measures, they have had the follow-on effect of paving the way for other collaborations. The beginnings of this are already being hinted at. For example, in the energy sector, Mr Aiyar would like to build on the international cooperation of the Greater Nile Project. He asserts, "In Sudan, both India and China have been working together in perfect harmony.

There has been not a single incidence [sic] of dispute ... this model of cooperation can be replicated in Iran, Africa, Latin American, north and Central Asia ... we want to learn and replicate Chinese success in energy and other sectors." But more than that, this cooperation may be expanding into a multilateral framework. On 6 January 2005, India hosted oil ministers from China, Japan and South Korea— as well as eight OPEC producers—to discuss creating a loosely named "Organisation for Oil Importing Countries" to ensure a stable, equitably priced energy supply for Asia.

India also hosted the first Round Table of Asian Oil Ministers on 25 November 2005, where oil ministers from Russia, Kazakhstan, Uzbekistan, Turkmenistan and Azerbaijan along with principal Asian oil and gas consuming countries—Japan, South Korea, China, Turkey and India—agreed on a 13-point action plan for the development of the Asian oil and gas economy, including the Indian proposal to study the exploration of all alternative linkages by land and sea, especially the alternative of linking the Caspian basin to South Asian countries.

By teaming up, former Indian Oil Minister Aiyar suggests China, and India as well as South Korea and Japan can cut a better price deal from OPEC producers through collaborative bidding. Wenran Jiang, an expert on Asian energy at the University of Alberta postulates that "if these [Asian] countries collaborate and influence the Arab nations on energy, they will be a formidable new energy bloc". Simple bilateral cooperation is being successfully built upon, and even now, a semblance of solidarity between India and China in the international arena is beginning to form. Moreover, this is also happening within the more formal context of international institutions.

It had already been clearly demonstrated early on that when India, China and other developing nations band together, outcomes can be influenced. At the fourth WTO meeting in Doha, Qatar in November 2001, leading developing countries (DCs), namely, Brazil, India, China and South Africa, formed a group of 20 (G-20) members to articulate and negotiate on behalf of all the developing countries (DCs) at the meeting. At the ministerial meeting at Punta del Este in 1986 which launched the Uruguay Round, a similar group of ten DCs led by Brazil and India was also formed. But this latter group in effect disintegrated at the meeting. At Cancun, however, the G-20 were able to hold their position until the end.

Analysts have suggested that China—as the world's fifth largest exporter and sixth largest importer, in joining forces with India's market size, combined with the other members of G-20—had a lot to do with why G-20 was taken far more seriously at Cancun than the G-10 was in Punta del Este in 1986. But more than that, India and China also share the common interest of preserving their own comparative advantage in various economic sectors. For example, while working together in the textile and clothing sector increases their leverage in the international arena, it does not adversely affect their individual national interest since both have comparative advantages in the production of different goods.

China has a relatively high advantage in woven textile, knit/crochet fabric and made-up textile articles while India's advantage lies in its export of textile yarn and woven cotton fabrics. Thus, working together could ensure a win-win outcome for both parties. The prospect of continued and increased cooperation at the WTO seems likely, and a joint statement has already been issued to this end, pledging a regular exchange of views on major international and regional issues as well as a strengthening of cooperation "in the WTO and other international multilateral organisations".

Nations such as Brazil, India, South Africa and China are increasingly acknowledging that they share not only common social and economic challenges, but also common goals in international held in Hong Kong in December 2005, India and China, along with Brazil trade negotiations. Most recently, in the sixth round of Doha WTO talks and other developing countries are together pushing the idea of protection against "biopiracy" that would prevent corporations from using native plants or animal matter to make pharmaceuticals and other products without financial compensation to the original country.

These countries are coming to realise more and more that the chances of achieving goals in the multilateral arena increase significantly if they act together. At the same time, multilateral cooperation has gone beyond trade to the realm of science and technology. The recent signing of agreements between these countries, ranging from biotechnology to AIDS treatment is a reflection of this trend. Such collaboration need not end. The sharing of experience can take place across any number of fields whereby the weaknesses of one country can be bolstered by aid and technology from another. More than any other developing countries, India and China are uniquely well-placed for bilateral collaboration since they share similar problems with regards to energy needs, environmental issues and large populations.

FROM ECONOMIC COOPERATION TO STRATEGIC PARTNERSHIP

The latent potential in the Sino-Indian engagement does not end with joint economic or even collaborative action on the world stage. Germane to sustainable peaceful relations is mutual understanding and consensus on the security front. Tentative forays into the formation of a strategic partnership have already been made. Couched within Chinese Prime Minister Wen Jiabao's historic visit to India in April 2005 and the ensuing agreements, is the possibility of a strategic partnership between the two nations—one that would eventually "reshape the world order". India's Foreign Secretary, Shyam Saran has alluded to the "global and strategic" implications of the new Sino-Indian partnership.

It is possible that China and India, who have been critical of American unilateralism, may join together in "balancing" the current hegemon. For instance, one critic has postulated that they might take action in opposing the US plan for the weaponisation of outer space. The two rounds of bilateral strategic dialogue that have been held to date attest to the fact that at the very least, both countries are able to see beyond their ongoing disagreements, whether over the border issue or the Dalai Lama, to acknowledge the value of cooperation on the strategic front. They have come a long way from hostile posturing and outright war, to economic cooperation and the tentative beginnings of a productive security partnership.

CHINA AND INDIA'S SHARED INTERESTS AND COMPLEMENTARITIES

The fact that India and China are willing to extend their interaction from the economic sector into the political arena is indicative of the beginnings of maturing confidence between the two, but more than that, both are beginning to recognise the similar issues and concerns that they share. During former Indian Defence Minister George Fernandes' meeting with Chinese Minister Wen Jiabao in 2003, both came to the conclusion that their main domestic problems included unemployment, regional disparities and the enduring poverty of farmers, which led Fernandes, who was once famous for his hostility towards China, finally to concede, "we are both sailing in the same boat".

However, it is these surprising parallels between the two countries that make an even deeper form of cooperation advantageous. Both have embarked on radical economic reforms which have, to date, lifted their respective economies far beyond expectation. However, the two also share massive populations with correspondingly huge resource demands, especially for land, water and energy. Furthermore, environmental decay and high HIV infection rates are problems common to both. In terms of security, both face similar dilemmas: for China, its dispute with the US over Taiwan, and for India, the ongoing dispute with Pakistan over Kashmir.

While broad parallels and similarities between these two vastly different countries do not necessarily count for much, there is a worthwhile point to be made in that in some significant ways, both are brought together by their shared interests. Clad has suggested that these two countries' similarities can be viewed in terms of their "common predicament" as well as their "common responses" in the face of global trends and pressures. Thus more than just cooperation, lesson-learning and policy exchange can be even more profitable between India and China. One sector in which lesson-learning is already taking place is in the all important IT industry, where China's hardware sector is a complement to India's thriving software industry.

LESSON LEARNING IN THE IT SECTOR

There are four features of China's industrialisation which have been particularly impressive: a 43 per cent domestic savings rate, astounding progress in building infrastructure, surging foreign direct investment and a vast reservoir of hard- working, low-cost labour. As Luce and Kynge point out, "whether it is China's cheaper, more reliable power supply or the more rapid turn-around at its ports, China remains an incalculably better environment for most manufacturing than India, which is slowly waking up to this".

However, China is still very deficient in most services— especially retailing, distribution and professional services such as accountancy, medicine, consultancy and the law. India's economic development has also been impressive. Its success in services is a testament to its greatest strengths which include a highly skilled workforce in the scientific, technical, managerial and professional arenas, information technology competency, English-language proficiency as well as a significantly positive response from private enterprises to economic reforms and the globalisation process.

This winning combination has turbo-charged India's IT-enabled services—software, business process outsourcing, multimedia, network management and systems integration—which have enabled India to fill the void left by chronic deficiencies in industrialisation. Critics have estimated that India is five to seven years ahead of China in the software sector, primarily because of the lack of English language skills among the Chinese and the absence of experienced project managers. However, India's IT sector has been held back by weak infrastructure, high administrative and regulatory barriers to business, as well as a relatively low ability to attract foreign direct investment.

India attracted FDI equity inflows of US$ 1.2 billion during March 2010 as compared to the US$53 billion that poured into China in each of the last two years. However, both countries are beginning to grow cognisant of the fact that their complementary strengths and weaknesses make collaboration a win-win choice. A prime example of Chinese-Indian collaboration in the IT sector is the Hwawei-Wipro cooperative venture. On 31 July 2002, Bangalore-based Wipro ePeripherals (WeP) had announced its new venture with China-based Huawei Technologies in selling Huawei's high-end networking products under the WeP brand.

The goal here is for WeP to take on rivals in the routers and switches market. Besides providing Huawei a direct channel and presence in India, the Huawei-Wipro venture has also proven to be a successful platform for research and development. The company's R & D operations, which employ 160 Chinese and about 200 Indians, is handling around 50 projects and growing fast. Meanwhile, many foreign software developers are attracted by low-cost skilled labour, tax breaks and government policies favouring locally developed software to be found in China.

A number of Indian firms have also announced new or expanded China operations recently. According to Indian press reports, major Indian software companies Mphesis and Infosys, are tapping into China, and another important Indian firm, Satyam, has also recently announced it would set up operations in Shanghai. Indian outsourcing company Tata Consultancy Services (TCS), launched a subsidiary in Shanghai in June 2004 and has since set up offices in Beijing and Hangzhou. For Indian firms, which rely heavily on the outsourcing business, China presents a unique opportunity.

On the one hand, the traditional skills of Indian companies, in terms of management and ability, to tackle complex projects are complementary to the weaknesses of Chinese developers. On the other hand, the local and language-specific expertise of Chinese professionals, meanwhile, will allow Indian firms to reach the domestic market as well as others in the region, especially those of Japan and South Korea. While India can help China expand its base of ICT skills and participate in the global knowledge economy, India too can benefit from this developing talent stream.

It is predicted that Indian ICT companies will be the largest procurers of Chinese programming talent over the next few years, once the country has created relevantly skilled professionals. Indian ICT professionals are also moving into higher-end segments such as project management, systems integration, consultancy, analysis, design, R&D, solutions architectures and product development, and will source programming material from China. Besides which, China can provide India with a model for infrastructure development.

For even though China remains weak in terms of HR resources, it has built up its strengths in the area of infrastructure, an important prerequisite for the success of the ICT sector.

Chinese cities such as Shanghai, can thus offer ICT investors some of the more advanced physical and telecom infrastructure—roads, highways, airports, land line, internet and mobile connectivity—that is currently available anywhere.

At the same time, China also appears keen to learn from the Indian ICT trade advances in its quest to become a knowledge-based economy. As Singapore's Minister Mentor Lee Kuan Yew has observed:

The Chinese are keen to develop a services sector like India's.... The Chinese want to attain international standards for the software outsourcing industry and learn how to deal with US and European clients as India is doing.

The recent appointment of Vijay Thadani, the CEO of NIIT (one of India's most renowned ICT firms specialising in ICT training), as Economic Adviser for western China's largest city, Chongqing, reiterates China's desire to gain from the Indian ICT experience.

To facilitate this goal of mutual learning, the Confederation of Indian Industries (CII) signed an MoU in June 2004 with the Shanghai-Pudong Software Park to promote Sino- Indian co-operation in software and facilitate the move of Indian firms into the park. The sharing of resources and lessons will strengthen both countries' positions in the ICT industry. Chinese Premier Wen Jiabao has already acknowledged this fact.

During his visit to India's southern technology hub of Bangalore in April 2005, he compared India and China's ICT sector to "two pagodas (temples), one hardware and one software", and that, "combined, [India and China] can take the leadership position in the world". But this is not the end of the story. The ICT sector is but one of many avenues in which policy and lesson exchange platforms will be beneficial to both India and China.

POLICY-EXCHANGE AND LESSON LEARNING IN THE FUTURE

With the recent warming of Sino-Indian relations and the confidence gained through successful cooperative projects, it seems very plausible that both China and India may reach their shared goal of development (especially economic) more quickly if they choose to deepen their mutual interaction, exchange and aid, especially given that in many sectors, one country's strengths are the other's weaknesses and vice versa.

Steps have already been taken towards this end. In the joint statement issued in Delhi on 11 April 2005, India and China agreed to further promote cooperation in education, science and technology, healthcare, information, tourism, youth exchange, agriculture, dairy development, sports and other fields on the basis of mutual benefit and reciprocity, as well as to strengthen air and sea connectivity, having established an MoU for the major liberalisation of civil aviation links between the two countries.

In fact, 2006 was declared the Year of Friendship between India and China during Wen Jiabao's visit to New Delhi in April 2005. India and China have also decided to establish a China-India Steering Committee on Scientific and Technological Cooperation chaired by their respective ministers for science and technology, and are starting consultation rounds for an agreement on mutual recognition of academic certificates and degrees. Furthermore, the two sides announced the launching of regular youth exchange activities. China is planning to invite 100 Indian youths to China and hold an exhibition on advanced and applicable technologies in India.

All of this bodes well for a more formal bilateral lesson-sharing approach to augment growth and development. In time, these exchanges may develop into formal policy exchange platforms which, besides being a highly positive end in themselves, may also prove to be further steps forward in confidence- building. This may prove all important, since despite efforts to put issues of contention on the back burner, bilateral irritants continue to surface between the two countries. Historically, booming trade relations and even formal agreements on strategic issues may have served to mute the consequences of bilateral hostilities, but have not been able to completely forestall them.

For example, in 1999, Sino-Indian trade rose to a remarkable USD1.16 billion as compared to the mere USD2.5 million in 1977, and in 1994, both parties signed protocols granting the other Most Favoured Nation Status. On the security front, agreements such as the nine point "Agreement on Maintenance of Peace and Tranquillity along the Actual Line of Control" was signed between Prime Ministers Narasimha Rao and Li Peng in 1993, and another similar agreement was signed during President Jiang Zemin's visit to Delhi in 1996.

However, none of these efforts successfully put a stop to India's decision to hold nuclear tests in 1998 which were in part aimed at sending a warning to China. What can be done differently this time round is the creation of non-official platforms of exchange which can facilitate the lesson-sharing across a variety of sectors for which India and China are particularly well-placed. While there is room to be optimistic that the warming of relations between India and China will be long term, it would be wrong to assume that there are not difficult issues that still need to be resolved.

Added to the ever present disagreement over the border issue, India's nuclear intentions, China's alleged assistance to Pakistan in the nuclear arena, is the growing sense that the US will use India on the frontline as part of its strategy to contain China.

The recent signing of a 10-Year Defence Agreement between the US and India in June 2005, aimed at expanding security-related bilateral cooperation on many fronts, as well as the contentious US-India nuclear cooperation may be indicative of just such a possibility.

More than ever there is a need to step up and strengthen confidence-building platforms of mutual exchange between these global giants, which may go some way in building a store of political capital that could be drawn upon in the future. It is crucial that more scholarly research and dialogue take place encouraging further bilateral collaboration between China and India. For the first time in the modern era, the world's two most populous countries (by a huge margin) are becoming major global players in their own right. The international community must play its part in responsibly fostering and facilitating the stable and sustainable development of both these global giants, for in time to come, China and India may indeed prove to be the two "major arbiters of all our futures".

4

India's Security Policy

India's domestic resources and efforts were sufficient to cope with the Pakistani threat and internal security threats. The Chinese threat, however, required support from allies. In its efforts to cope with this threat, the Indian political leadership carefully forged a relationship with the Soviet Union in the 1960s and the 1970s. The Soviets, keen on limiting both Chinese and American influence in South Asia, supported India's position on the Kashmir issue, supplied India with a range of sophisticated weaponry at highly favorable rates and opened markets to a plethora of Indian consumer goods. The end of the Cold War abruptly loosened many of these familiar moorings of Indian Defence policy. Russia saw little need to perpetuate the strategic nexus that had linked India and the former Soviet Union.

Accordingly, it was no longer willing to provide India with weaponry at highly concessional rates. Nor was it ready to unequivocally support its position on the Kashmir question. Having failed to anticipate the sudden collapse of the Soviet bloc, India's political-military leadership suddenly found itself in uncharted territory as the long-familiar anchors had suddenly disappeared from the international arena. As early as 1989, Indian policymakers started to improve relations with China. New Delhi had to make disproportionate concessions to obtain Chinese cooperation.

Indian diplomacy, although unable to neutralize the Chinese threat, nevertheless succeeded in reducing it to more manageable proportions as the two sides agreed on mutual troop withdrawals and a series of other confidence and security-building measures. Even though India's policymakers had demonstrated dexterity in reducing tensions with China, they did not display similar skill in improving relations with India's long-standing adversary, Pakistan. Nor did they show much ingenuity in coping with a variety of internal conflicts. On the contrary, the policies adopted in the domestic realm promoted and exacerbated incipient conflicts. Consequently, three threats remained at the end of the Cold War: the Pakistani irredentist claim to Kashmir, the Chinese capability threat and internal conflicts.

THE CHALLENGES AHEAD

As India approaches the end of the century, what then are the principal threats to its security and how is it gearing up to cope with them? This chapter will seek to address these questions.

PAKISTAN'S TERRITORIAL CLAIMS

Pakistan remains India's principal adversary. Although a variety of other issues divide the two states, the principal source of discord stems from the disputed status of the state of Jammu and Kashmir. Pakistan's claim to Kashmir is irredentist. Its leaders have long argued that Pakistan remains "incomplete" without Kashmir because of its predominantly Muslim composition and its territorial contiguity. India has held half of Kashmir with a tenacity equal only to Pakistan's hold of the other half of the region.

Initially, India sought to demonstrate Kashmir's secular status, but later it claimed the imperatives of retaining all of Kashmir for the purposes of state-building and national cohesion. Unbridled escalation of the conflict within Kashmir could conceivably draw India into another war with Pakistan. Since their emergence as independent states from the detritus of the British Indian Empire, India and

Pakistan have fought each other in three wars, in 1947 to 1948, 1965 and 1971. The origins of the first two conflicts can be traced to Pakistan's attempts to forcibly seize Kashmir from India. The first Indo-Pakistani war of 1947 to 1948 left Pakistan in control of one-third of Kashmir.

The second Indo-Pakistani war of 1965 resulted in some critical Indian territorial gains including the capture of the strategic Haji Pir Pass. Most of these battlefield gains were ceded to Pakistan, however, at the Soviet-sponsored talks in Tashkent, Uzbekistan, as part of the post-war settlement. The third IndoPakistani war was fought in 1971. This resulted in the breakup of East from West Pakistan and the creation of the independent state of Bangladesh. After the war of 1971, the conflict over Kashmir remained largely dormant. It was not until 1989, when an ethno-religious insurgency abruptly erupted in the Kashmir valley, that Pakistan found a new opportunity to re-open the dispute.

The roots of the 1989 insurgency are quintessentially indigenous and can be traced to the exigencies of Indian domestic politics. However, systematic Pakistani training, material support and the provision of sanctuaries have greatly escalated the level of violence in Kashmir. Recently, at least two major crises, in 1987 and 1990, have punctuated Indo-Pakistani relations. Since the onset of the conflict in 1989, India has pursued a counterinsurgency strategy, based upon its extremely successful experiences in the other parts of the country It has deployed approximately 400,000 security personnel in Kashmir, including troops of the Central Reserve Police Force, the Border Security Force, the Rashtriya Rifles (National Rifles, a specially constituted counterinsurgency force drawn from units of the Indian Army) and the Indian Army itself.

The strategy involves the extensive use of numerically superior paramilitary forces and the Army's efforts to torment the insurgents. Given that it took close to two decades to quell the Naga and Mizo insurgencies in the northeast, the Indian authorities assume that time is on their side with this strategy. When the will of the insurgents to continue fighting eventually wanes, the government offers to negotiate with them and hold elections. As long as former insurgents agree to uphold India's territorial integrity, they are allowed to participate in local elections and even assume political office.

Unfortunately, this strategy may not work as well in Kashmir because there are a number of critical differences between India's northeast, the Punjab and Kashmir. In the northeast, the Indian Army used force against the rebel Nagas and Mizos with impunity. Today, Indian forces are operating in Kashmir under the glare of foreign journalists and human rights observers who have documented numerous cases of torture and indiscriminate use of force. Consequently, the security forces have had to exercise more restraint than they demonstrated elsewhere, such as the northeastern states that were indisputably part of India.

Finally, in the northeast and especially in the Punjab, only small numbers of the local population were disaffected from the Indian state. Despite the holding of a very successful and largely fair election in Kashmir in August 1997, large numbers of Kashmiris still remain alienated from the Indian state. India may have no alternative but to use force against those insurgents who remain intransigent. However, the newly elected government of Chief Minister Farooq Abdullah will have to devise a variety of other options and measures to restore the fractured rule of law in the state and win back the trust and confidence of the Kashmiris.

CHINESE POWER

The other external security threat that India faces is from China. After various attempts to negotiate a territorial settlement, talks finally collapsed in 1960. The Chinese eventually resorted to force against India in 1962. The Indian forces, grossly unprepared and poorly equipped for mountain warfare, suffered their most dramatic defeat in the post-independence era. At the end of this brief but brutal conflict the Chinese came to successfully occupy 14,000 square miles of territory before declaring a unilateral cease-fire. In the wake of the Sino-Indian border war India undertook a major effort to build up its military forces.

The army's sanctioned strength was raised to a million soldiers, including the creation of 10 new divisions equipped and trained for mountain warfare. The air force sought to expand to 45 squadrons equipped with modern jet aircraft. Plans were also made for the modernization of the navy. Despite some minor attempts at improvement, Sino-Indian relations remained largely frozen through the late 1970s. A serious border skirmish took place in 1967 near the Nathu La Pass.

Additionally, China, although failing to assist Pakistan with material during the 1971 Indo-Pakistani War, expressed political opposition to India. More recently, in 1986, the two militaries clashed at Sumdurong Chu near the China-Bhutan-India border. Today, while India's conventional forces along the Himalayan border surpass China's military prowess, the latter excels in developing and deploying missiles and nuclear weapons and will most likely continue to do so for the foreseeable future.

Furthermore, despite significant improvements in bilateral relations since the late 1980s, the Sino-Indian border dispute remains unresolved. At a political level, both India and China perceive themselves as great powers. Yet, they have markedly different political systems; they have sought divergent foreign policy goals and support disparate causes. For example, India has watched with growing alarm Chinese attempts to penetrate Myanmar (Burma). Furthermore, Indian maritime security specialists have expressed misgivings about the Chinese development of an electronic eavesdropping facility a mere 30 nautical miles from the Indian-controlled Andaman Islands chain in the Bay of Bengal.

INTERNAL THREATS

India also faces myriad internal security threats. They include the continuing insurgency in Kashmir, the seemingly dormant insurgency in the Punjab, the Bodo insurgency in Assam, the Naga-Kuki violence in the northeastern state of Nagaland and the Uttarkhand agitation in the northern state of Uttar Pradesh. Some of these conflicts, particularly those in Kashmir and Punjab, stem from two intertwined sources: the centralizing propensities of the national government in New Delhi and the dramatic growth of political mobilization in India. As political awareness and mobilization proceeded apace, various regional parties sought to voice the real and imagined grievances of local populations and ethnic groups.

Most central governments, especially during the time of Prime Minister Indira Gandhi, tended to see these movements as potentially secessionist demands. Accordingly, the central government resorted to extra-constitutional and repressive measures to contain these demands. These steps, far from curbing discontent, frequently ignited a process of escalating demands that culminated in nationwide violence. The other conflicts, such as those in the northeast, could be traced to the increasing political awareness of newly enfranchised ethnic groups. An increased sense of political efficacy has also raised fears among these ethnic minorities that their distinctive cultural practices and traits will be effaced over time. Consequently, their demands have frequently been expressed in terms of the preservation of group rights and privileges.

When these demands were expressed in secessionist terms, for example by the Nagas and the Mizos, the response of the Indian state was harsh and clear-cut: their demands would not be tolerated. Once the insurgents dropped their secessionist demands, the Indian state proved more than willing to address their grievances. Accordingly, former Naga and Mizo separatist insurgents now occupy prominent elected positions in the states of Nagaland and Mizoram.

In addition to these regional conflicts, India also now faces a renewed nationwide outbreak of Hindu-Muslim violence. This constitutes a serious security threat because often local police and even paramilitary forces fail to quell these riots. Moreover, they have even taken sides in the fighting at times. As a result, thousands—usually minorities—have died in the ensuing violence. Unable to contain the violence, the civil authorities have had to call in regular army units to restore law and order on a number of occasions.

Hindu-Muslim violence reached its apogee in recent years, when in 1992, several thousand Hindu fanatics who were affiliated with the right-wing Hindu organizations, the Rashtriya Swyam Sevaks and the Bajrang Dal, attacked and destroyed the Babri Masjid, a 16th century mosque. The mosque was allegedly built on the ruins of a Hindu temple that consecrated the birthplace of Lord Rama, a significant member of the Hindu pantheon.

In the wake of the destruction of the mosque, widespread rioting broke out through much of northern India and even extended to the metropolitan centers of Calcutta in the east and Mumbai in the west. Several thousand people, principally Muslims, lost their lives in the riots. Hindu-Muslim relations are currently at their lowest point in India since the partition of the country in 1947. Thus, the country remains fraught with the renewed possibility of Hindu-Muslim violence.

COPING WITH THREATS

India possesses one of the more formidable military forces anywhere in the world. It also has the distinction of having one of the most professional of military services in the developing world. The Indian Army has 980,000 men and is equipped with 2,400 main battle tanks of Soviet and domestic origin. The Indian Navy has a fleet of 25 main surface combat assets and 19 submarines manufactured in the Soviet Union and Germany. The Indian Air Force (IAF) has 37 squadrons of modern fighter aircraft purchased from the former Soviet Union, France and Britain. Despite the existence of these weapons, the armed forces have played little or no role in the formulation of Defence policies.

Their role largely remains confined to the operational aspects of Defence policy and not to its evolution and formulation. Decisions on Defence and security issues remain largely within the purview of bureaucrats in the Ministry of Defence (MOD). Unlike most advanced industrial states, where career bureaucrats develop substantive expertise in specific functional areas, most personnel of the MOD are not especially knowledgeable about security and Defence issues. They are frequently rotated from other ministries and do not spend extended periods of time in the MOD. Consequently, they rarely have occasion to develop more than a rudimentary knowledge of Defence and security-related issues. This lack of specialized expertise has contributed to a lack of long-term planning and a critical absence of an overall strategic doctrine.

This absence has made Indian security decisionmaking and weapons acquisitions reactive and ad hoc. In addition to these institutional limitations, other constraints also hobble India's ability to meet national security challenges. The most significant constraint that it currently faces is fiscal. Since 1991, in the wake of a major liquidity crisis, India has been engaged in a tortured attempt to restructure its national economy. This process seeks to dismantle a long-existing web of regulatory constraints that stifled economic growth.

As part of this effort at economic reform, the Indian exchequer has also attempted to trim government in an attempt to reduce India's fiscal deficit. Accordingly, growth in the Indian Defence budget has been cut. In the fiscal year 1996 to 1997, the nominal increase in the Defence budget was 3.2 percent. However, according to government estimates, annual inflation was about 4.5 percent,

Consequently, there was a decrease in real terms. The most recent budget (fiscal year 1997 to 1998) looks somewhat better for the armed services.

The budget is increased by 23 percent in nominal terms. Salary increases for military personnel will absorb a substantial portion of the increase, leaving the Defence services still short on capital expenditures. In effect, India's ability to cope with the extant threats will be significantly constrained by its fiscal limitations. Yet, the armed forces face a number of important needs. The Indian Navy, a long-neglected service, now faces further constraints on its capabilities. The Second World War vintage aircraft carrier, INS Vikrant, has been retired, leaving the Navy with a single small aircraft carrier, the INS Virat. Currently, the government is in the midst of negotiations to buy a used aircraft carrier from either France or Russia.

Furthermore, the Navy lacks the necessary resources to upgrade and modernize its submarine fleet. The necessity for upgrading these forces stems from three important security concerns. First, there is a need to protect India's extensive shoreline, and more specifically the 200-mile exclusive economic zone. Second, the presence of the Chinese Navy is growing in the Indian Ocean. The Chinese Navy's efforts to obtain base facilities in Myanmar forces India to maintain and modernize its naval capabilities. The growth of a Chinese naval presence in the Indian Ocean assumes increasing importance in light of the need to protect India's expanding sea-borne trade links with the nations of Southeast Asia.

Finally, India would like to possess the requisite naval capabilities to carry out peace-keeping missions in the Indian Ocean littoral. The IAF also faces significant constraints on its capabilities. It desperately needs an advanced jet trainer and needs to upgrade its fleet of 125 aging MiG-21s. In March 1996, the IAF entered into an agreement with the Russian Moscow Aircraft Production Organization to upgrade the MiGs. Under the terms of the agreement, the MiG's will be fitted with advanced airborne radar and air-launched missile capabilities. Yet bureaucratic bungling and a paucity of funds has slowed down this urgent project.

While the wrangling over the upgrade of the MiGs continues, the government is finally proceeding with the purchase of some 40 Su-30 multi-role fighter aircraft from Russia. Other problems of weapons acquisition continue to plague the IAE After a number of desultory discussions, India has now chosen not to purchase the British-made Hawk on the grounds of technological obsolescence. Instead it is now entering discussions with Germany to purchase the new AT-2000. Finally, India's efforts to develop an indigenous Light Combat Aircraft (LCA) is years behind schedule. The hopes of indigenous production of the LCA are proving to be little more than a mirage.

Fiscal constraints have also taken their toll on the Indian Army and its plans for modernization. Specifically, General Krishnaswami Sundarji, the Chief of Army Staff in the late 1980s, outlined an ambitious and elaborate plan for increasing the strength of the army from 34 to 45 divisions. These would include four tank divisions, eight mechanized infantry divisions, seven Reorganized Army Plains Divisions and two Air Assault Divisions. Most of these plans were either shelved or dramatically decelerated due to the fiscal constraints that emerged in the early 1990s. Furthermore, the recruitment and training of technical personnel has also suffered.

Even though the three armed services are cash-strapped and short on resources, India's nuclear and ballistic missile programs are proceeding apace. Formal denials notwithstanding, for all practical purposes India is an incipient nuclear-weapons state. It conducted its first and only nuclear test at Pokhran in the Rajasthan desert in May 1974. A plethora of long-term and proximate factors explain the decision to conduct a nuclear test in 1974. The long-term factors included India's aspirations for great power status, its desire to consolidate its standing in the subcontinent after the 1971 war with Pakistan and its misgivings about China.

The more immediate precipitant of the decision to conduct a nuclear test arose from the particular exigencies of India's domestic politics. In the aftermath of the OPEC-induced oil crisis of 1973, the Indian economy was in a tailspin. Furthermore, the first Congress party government of Prime Minister Indira Gandhi seemed incapable of coping with the varied socio-political challenges with which the Indian polity was beset.

The nuclear test, at least momentarily, bought the regime in New Delhi some minor respite. The drama of the nuclear explosion led to a fleeting surge of popularity. New Delhi, however, encountered considerable international disapprobation. Specifically, both the United States and Canada cut off all nuclear assistance. The United States also took the initiative to form the London Supplier's Club, a set of arrangements among the major industrial countries to prevent the export of dual-use nuclear technologies. Faced with this sharp and adverse international reaction, India chose not to conduct any further tests.

It nevertheless proceeded apace with its civilian and military nuclear programs. India's desire to emerge as a great power, combined with a long-term and deep-seated fear of Chinese power, continued to drive the nuclear weapons program. India's nuclear strategy remains one of calculated "strategic ambiguity" India's official spokespeople continue to deny that India possesses any nuclear weapons. However, they are also quick to point out that India could develop a nuclear weapon should it choose to do so. It is entirely possible that this strategy, in concert with Pakistan's acquisition of nuclear capabilities in the late 1980s, contributed to a form of crude deterrence between India and Pakistan.

The first test of this deterrent relationship probably took place during a crisis in Indo-Pakistani relations in 1990.

The likely origins and evolution of this crisis have been described and analyzed at considerable length elsewhere. Briefly, in early 1990, the insurgency in Kashmir peaked. As widespread violence racked the Kashmir Valley, Indian intelligence agencies obtained incontrovertible evidence of Pakistan's involvement in organizing, training and supporting many of the Kashmiri insurgent groups.

Yet, Indian security forces were unable to prevent the percolation of the insurgents across a highly porous and mountainous border from so-called Azad Kashmir (Pakistani controlled Kashmir) into the Kashmir Valley Faced with this seemingly untenable situation, Indian political and military authorities considered strikes into Pakistan-controlled territory. Accordingly between January and May of 1990 the Indian political leadership issued a series of stern warnings and veiled threats to the Pakistanis. The Pakistani political and military leadership responded in kind.

The rejoinders left little doubt that Pakistan would resort to the use of nuclear weapons to forestall an Indian attack into the Pakistani heartland. American intercession may well have played a vital role in defusing this crisis. The precise motivations for the U.S. diplomatic mission to Islamabad and New Delhi led by Deputy National Security Advisor Robert Gates remain unclear.

It is well known, however, that in Islamabad, Gates cautioned the Pakistani decisionmakers against supporting terrorism in Kashmir. In New Delhi, Gates advised Indian officials against attacking Pakistani training camps within "Azad Kashmir" (literally "free Kashmir"), arguing that such an incursion could lead to nuclear escalation. A number of factors may contribute to the breakdown in the future of the crude deterrent relationship that has emerged between the two countries. Misperception and organizational errors could lead to inadvertent conflict.

The Indian acquisition of ballistic missiles capabilities and Pakistan's efforts to match them may also undermine stability In tandem with the quest for nuclear weapons, India embarked on a program to acquire the necessary delivery vehicles for a nuclear weapon. In 1983, India launched the Integrated Guided Missile Development Program under the aegis of the Defence Research and Development Organization (DRDO). The DRDO sought to manufacture a complete range of short-, medium- and long-range missiles.

These missiles included the Nag (a short-range, anti-tank missile), the Trishul (a surface-to-air missile), the Akaash (a surface-to-air missile), the Prithvi (a 250-kilometer range, surface-to-surface missile) and the Agni (a surface-to-surface, intermediate-range ballistic missile with a range of 1,500 and 2,500 kilometers). Additionally, India is reportedly developing the Surya (another ballistic missile) and the Sagarika (a submarine-launched ballistic missile). The Agni and the Prithvi have attracted the most attention from Western Defence analysts and policymakers.

The Agni is an intermediate range ballistic missile capable of striking targets throughout Pakistan and significant portions of southern China. The Prithvi, which has undergone extensive field trials and is ready for serial production, can primarily strike targets within Pakistan. In the view of most analysts, the deployment of the Prithvi along India's western border could be highly destabilizing, inciting Pakistan to uncrate and deploy the M-11 missiles received from China. Already, Pakistan has deployed the domestically built Hatf I and Hatf II missiles which can strike targets at distances of approximately 100 and 150 kilometers, respectively It is reportedly at work on a third missile, the Hatf III, with a range of 600 kilometers.

The mutual deployment of short-range missiles along a highly volatile border would increase the importance of pre-emptive strategies. Such strategies could greatly undermine the prospects of crisis stability as each side would have considerable incentive to suppress the other's offensive capabilities in the event of a crisis. The decline of mutual commitments to confidence and security building measures in the region enhances the misgivings about the erosion of stability. The development and potential deployment of the Agni, in turn, has also caused considerable concern in the West, especially in the United States.

The deployment of the Agni would challenge the U.S.-sponsored Missile Technology Control Regime guidelines, which seek to prevent the proliferation of missiles with a payload of 500 kilograms and a range of 300 kilometers. It appears that persistent American pressure may have prevented the actual induction and deployment of the Prithvi, and possibly additional tests of the Agni. Specifically, in December 1996, Prime Minister Deve Gowda announced that further tests of the Agni were indefinitely shelved unless a changed security environment warranted renewed efforts.

Nevertheless, the scientific, technological and bureaucratic momentum behind these weapons programs will continue to drive their research and development. In December 1995, there was widespread speculation in the American press that India was on the verge of conducting a second nuclear test. Apparently; U.S. reconnaissance satellites had picked up signs of activity near the test site. These developments had prompted U.S. intelligence agencies to warn of an impending Indian nuclear test. It cannot be stated with any certainty that India was indeed planning a second test.

The government of Prime Minister Narasimha Rao simply initiated some work at the test site in an attempt to obtain domestic political mileage and to gauge international reactions. Even in the absence of clear-cut corroborating evidence, this argument can be supported on the basis of inference and attribution. Domestically, the Rao government was increasingly coming under fire from the jingoistic, predominantly Hindu party; the Bharatiya Janata Party (BJP), for its putative weakness on issues pertaining to India's national security Raising the possibility of conducting a nuclear test would enable the regime to fend off these criticisms.

Simultaneously; the government may also have been interested in assessing the response of key states in the international community to an Indian nuclear test shortly before the conclusion of the Comprehensive Test Ban Treaty (CTBT) negotiations in Geneva. If any plans for conducting a nuclear test did exist, the sharp international reaction quickly squelched them. Even though India did not carry out a nuclear test, it adamantly refused to sign the CTBT. More importantly, it went to the extent of attempting to prevent the treaty from being reported out of the Conference on Disarmament in Geneva for a vote at the United Nations General Assembly in New York. The Indian intransigence on the CTBT, at one level, was quite puzzling.

As early as 1954 India had first sponsored a resolution in the General Assembly calling for a cessation of all nuclear testing. More recently, in December 1993, India again co-sponsored a resolution in the U.N. General Assembly calling for a comprehensive test ban. There are three factors that explain India's about face—operating at multilateral, bilateral and domestic levels—that were significant in changing India's long-standing position on the CTBT. In 1995, to the surprise of Indian decision-makers, the United States and its allies successfully built a substantial coalition of countries in the U.N. General Assembly to ensure the "indefinite and unconditional" extension of the Nuclear Non-Proliferation Treaty As India had not been a party to the Treaty, it chose not to participate in the deliberations.

In the end, only three states—India, Israel and Pakistan—remained outside the ambit of the Treaty. The Indian strategic community realized that Israel's special relationship would ensure that the United States would exert little, if any, pressure on it to accede to the Treaty. Consequently, India and Pakistan became the central focus of U.S. nonproliferation policy not surprisingly; hawkish Indian strategists urged the government to firm up its stand on the nuclear question. As leverage with Pakistan on the nuclear issue, the United States lifted some of the sanctions that it had earlier imposed.

Accordingly, in February 1996, the U.S. Congress, at the behest of the Clinton administration, passed the Brown Amendment to the Foreign Assistance Act. This provision diluted the terms of the Pressler Amendment of 1985, which had prohibited all arms assistance to Pakistan unless the president of the United States could certify that it did not possess nuclear weapons. The Indian strategic community viewed the passage of this legislation with considerable dismay. Many construed its adoption as a sign that the United States was interested in renewing a strategic relationship with Pakistan at the end of the Cold War.

The perceived shift in the American stance led to a hardening of India's position on issues pertaining to nuclear weapons. Indian domestic politics also conspired to a toughening of the Indian stance on the CTBT. Prime Minister Narasimha Rao, facing an election in April 1996, sought to outbid the hard-liners in the opposition BJP. Accordingly; he adopted a tougher posture on the CTBT issue. Even though India was completely isolated in the U.N. General Assembly (only Bhutan, whose foreign policy India controls, voted against the CTBT), its position was, with marked exceptions, warmly endorsed at home.

The vast majority of India's political commentators applauded India's lone position at the U.N. General Assembly. It is unlikely that its position will change in the foreseeable future. Any government that seeks to publicly shift its stand on this issue will face a firestorm of criticism from a large segment of attentive electorate.

Nonetheless, it is equally unlikely that India will resume nuclear testing. Instead it will attempt to continue its research and development efforts in the areas of nuclear weapons and ballistic missiles while avoiding any overt deployment of its capabilities. Barring a dramatic and unforeseen contingency posing a fundamental threat to its security, Indian Defence policy is likely to remain largely rudderless. Since the end of the Cold War, Indian policymakers have been unable to articulate a new strategic vision for the country.

Consequently, policymaking has been largely reactive, ad hoc and idiosyncratic. The decline of political institutions in India and the level of regime instability is likely to ensure continued drift in Defence policymaking. Consequently, a combination of internal bureaucratic pressures and the perceived threats from Pakistan and China will drive the direction of future Defence policy.

In the immediate future, Pakistan and China will remain India's two principal adversaries. Improvements in Indo-Pakistani relations will hinge on three distinct factors: the prevailing political conditions in Kashmir, the degree of political stability within Pakistan and the ideological proclivities of the regime in New Delhi. The warming trend in Sino-Indian relations will, in all likelihood, continue, since both sides are keen on avoiding another border conflict. Nevertheless, the growing Chinese naval presence in the Bay of Bengal and China's willingness to supply missiles and nuclear components to Pakistan will remain important sources of discord in the relationship.

Beyond its security preoccupations with Pakistan and China, will India be able to take on the mantle of leadership in South Asia? Two closely intertwined factors, in large part, will determine the answer to that question: the viability of India's political institutions and the nation's prospects of achieving economic development. The brittle quality of India's political institutions and its failure to promote rapid economic growth has placed important constraints on India's emergence as a great power.

The inability of its political institutions to move forward has exacerbated a range of internal conflicts and has led various governments to rely on coercive mechanisms to maintain political order. Slow and limited economic growth has placed constraints on its ability to devote adequate resources to maintain the quality, alertness and capabilities of its armed forces. Consequently, India's ability to play a meaningful role within the subcontinent and beyond will depend upon restoring the efficacy of its political institutions and generating rapid economic growth. In terms of the subcontinent, a politically stable, economically prosperous and strategically secure India may acquire the requisite confidence to deal with its smaller neighbors on more magnanimous terms. An India that is both secure and solvent may also serve as a viable counterpoise to the growth of Chinese military power and potential adventurism in the region in the next century.

Prime Minister Dr. Manmohan Singh on April 9th, 2010 expressed that Nuclear Summit hosted by US President Barack Obama to focus on nuclear terrorism and proliferation of sensitive nuclear materials and technologies.India has a well-developed indigenous nuclear energy programme, which dates back six decades. He said that We have an impeccable record of security, safety and non-proliferation, which reflects our conduct as a responsible nuclear power". The Prime Minister said that India has been a consistent advocate of complete and universal global nuclear disarmament.

5

India ASEAN Relations

India which launched the Look East Policy in 1991 has crossed another milestone in its decade long journey towards growing strategic and economic relations with the South East Asian countries. Leaders of the ten-member ASEAN and Prime Minister Manmohan Singh who incidentally was the Finance Minister in the Narasimha Rao Government when the latter launched the Look East Policy inked a historic Partnership pact for Peace, Progress and Shared Prosperity at the just-ended third India-ASEAN summit in the Laotian capital, Vientiane. The four-page pact and the nine-page Action Plan signed at the end of the summit outline a long-term vision for boosting trade, investment, tourism, culture, sports and people-to-people contacts.

The document calls for taking full advantage of the geographical contiguity of South East Asia and India in implementing the Free Trade Pact by 2011 for the ASEAN and India and progressively bringing in its fold other member States by 2018. the document's Plan of Action touches upon the entire gamut of political and security cooperation, including food, human and energy, finance, science and technology, IT and communication technology, human resource development, health, and agriculture. At the Indo-ASEAN summit, Dr. Singh's reasoned argument and exposition on giving a huge push to economic development in the ASEAN region and beyond stirred the leaders. His idea of an Asian Economic Community on the lines of the European Union, first unveiled at an India-ASEAN conference in New Delhi found many backers, notably Japan, another summit partner of the ASEAN, because of its own reasons.

The importance of common market and free trade agreement within Asia cannot be ignored when regional trading agreements such as the EU and NAFTA have led to higher trade and investment while Asia continues to lag behind. A trade bloc comprising India, China, South Korea and the ten ASEAN nations would represent a giant free trade zone.

It would negate the impression created by Western countries at the Cancun Summit (Mexico) that the developing countries were unwilling to open up their economies. At the second India-ASEAN summit in Bali (Indonesia) in October, 2003, India and the ASEAN had signed three documents, two of which were: a Framework Agreement on Comprehensive Economic Cooperation leading to the creation of a free trade area by the year2011 and India's accession to the Treaty of Amity and Cooperation in South East Asia.

The third document was on cooperation to combat international terrorism. India's accession to ASEAN's Treaty of Amity and Cooperation spoke of a growing closeness with South Asia and was seen as another step towards India's Look East Policy. But of greater significance was the framework agreement aimed at creating a Free Trade Area in ten years as provided in the agreement on comprehensive economic cooperation. This pact for comprehensive economic cooperation with the ASEAN is complemented by bilateral and sub-regional attempts towards cooperation.

These include the bilateral free trade agreements with Thailand and Singapore. India, Thailand and Myanmar along with a couple of South Asian countries are partners in BISMTEC, a sub-regional grouping that is becoming active with the adoption of a free trade area plan. To further deepen the India-ASEAN economic ties and promote tourism, India went beyond the envisaged cooperation with the grouping at the second India-ASEAN summit in Bali, 2003 [New Delhi will host the India-ASEAN summit in 2012]. The then Prime minister, Atal Bihari Vajpayee who headed the Indian delegation to the Bali summit offered to provide "fast track" tariff concessions unilaterally and also offered the ASEAN countries to run daily flights to major Indian cities including New Delhi, Kolkata, Mumbai and Chennai.

The ASEAN Senior Economic Officials' Preparatory Meeting (SEOM) was held in Hanoi, Vietnam, on 6th April, 2010. Under the chairmanship of Vietnam, the meeting reviewed the progress in implementing the blueprint on the implementation of the ASEAN Economic Community in 2015 and discuss directions to deepen the economic integration in ASEAN in terms of trade in goods, trade in services and investment..., aiming to establish the ASEAN Economic Community in 2015. Its worth to mention that a proposal made by India at the Bali summit for a car rally bore fruit. Coinciding with the 2004 ASEAN summit in Laos, Prime Minister Manmohan Singh had flagged off the car rally from Guwahati. The rally was promoted to emphasize the connectivity of India and South East Asia through a land route. In the past, India's engagement with much of Asia, including South-east and East Asia was built on an idealistic connection of Asian brotherhood based on shared experiences of colonialism and cultural ties.

The rhythm of the region today is determined, however, as much by trade, investment and production as by history and culture. That is what motivated the decade old Look East Policy. India's relations with the ASEAN which was launched in 1967 began when it was given the status of a sectoral partner way back in 1992. In 1996, India was recognized as a full Dialogue Partner. India was then made a member of the ASEAN Regional Forum (ARF) after a lot of hiccups and some objections. India encountered some difficulty for entry into the ARF because at least three of the seven ASEAN (which has since been expanded to ten members) countries had some reservations.

Countries like Malaysia, Indonesia and Brunei did not want to let down Pakistan which was also seeking the Dialogue Partner status and entry into the ARF. But, much of the spadework was done by Singapore which, of all the other Asean members, had the closest of relations with India. Until the Narasimha Rao Government successfully set in motion the "Look East Policy" of cultivating the long-neglected neighbours of India in 1991, New Delhi was really not interested in the East except perhaps Japan. Its attitude towards the ASEAN during the early years of its birth was ambivalent.

The ASEAN came into existence when the US was escalating the Vietnam war. With the acceptance of the Zone of Peace, Freedom and Neutrality (ZOPFAN) in November, 1971, India felt that it could find commonality of interests with the ASEAN. In 1973, India made the first explicit reference welcoming the ASEAN initiative. However, the Indo-Soviet Treaty, India's ambivalence on the question of Soviet invasion of Afghanistan and finally the recognition of the Heng Samrin government in Cambodia in July 1981, all these led to estrangement between India and the ASEAN. So, period between 1980 and 1984 proved to be the most frigid in the Indo-ASEAN relations.

New Delhi's attitude towards the Kampuchean crisis as a direct consequence of its assessment of Sino-Vietnamese differences and the security threat posed to Vietnam by the Pol Pot regime. After a short honeymoon, the relations once again came under strain when India undertook the Pokhran II nuclear tests in 1998 and the Kargil war got India's Look East Policy out of focus. Three years of political instability, the slow down of reforms and economic meltdown in East Asia made India's trumpet in Asia an uncertain one. India's nuclear tests and its increased political tension with the US, Japan and China put it in a difficult position vis-a-vis Asia.

Renewed hostilities with Pakistan over Kargil reinforced the traditional image of a perennially nibbling subcontinent that few in South East Asia have the desire to get entangled in. But a string of high-level visits from the ASEAN and the visits by some Indian Ministers to that region helped restore the earlier warmth in bilateral relations. The Look East Policy was launched in response to growing recognition that Asia was emerging as a centre of gravity with rapid speed.

In support of the policy, it was argued that India and the ASEAN nations have strong civilisational linkages in addition to geographic proximity and political and strategic convergence. Both have neither any territorial disputes nor any conflict of strategic interests. They also have similar political value systems. The intensification of the economic linkages with the ASEAN has quietly led India into a second phase of its "Look East" policy. Phase-I of the policy was characterized by trade and investment linkages. Phase-II is marked by arrangements for free trade areas and establishing institutional economic linkages between the countries of the region and India. In Phase-II, India has a larger geographic scope of the initiative - from the initial focus on South East Asia to include East Asia and the South Pacific.

It is characterized by an expanded definition of the "East" extending from Australia to China and East Asia with the ASEAN as its core. South Korea has emerged as a major economic partner of India while economic ties with Japan need to be upgraded and the potential with Australia and the South Pacific remains to be tapped fully. The broader agenda of Phase-II also focuses on security cooperation, including joint operations to protect sea lanes and pooling resources in the war against terrorism.

The military contacts and joint exercises that India launched with ASEAN states on a low key basis in the early 1990s are now expanding into full fledged defence cooperation. India has quietly begun to put in place arrangements for regular access to ports in South East Asia. India's defence contacts have widened to include Japan, South Korea and China. Never before has India engaged in such multi-directional defence diplomacy in Asia. The other features identified as unique to Phase-II of India's Look East Policy include the pursuit of physical connectivity to South Asia through transport linkages.

As part of its road diplomacy India is now actively building transport corridors to the region. These include trilateral highway projects involving Myanmar and Thailand and the proposed rail link between New Delhi and Hanoi. India and ASEAN trade has multiplied four-fold from $3.1 billion in 1991 to about $12 billion in 2002. In October 2009, India signed a Free Trade Agreement (FTA) with the ASEAN members in Thailand. Under the ASEAN-India FTA, ASEAN member countries and India will lift import tariffs on more than 80 per cent of traded products between 2013 and 2016. There are four meetings scheduled between January and July and the deal is expected to be finalised by August 2010.

Top on the list of growth areas listed is India's IT enabled services, financial services industry, pharmaceutical industry and infrastructure development like the upgradation of highways, bridges, ports and airports in India. India-ASEAN relations thus hold a very bright future. Much has been achieved in the three summit-level meetings so far and much more would hopefully be achieved. The Prime Minister Manmohan Singh has given top priority to improving relations with the Association of South East Asian Nations (ASEAN).

India's Look East policy is much less controversial and contentious than India's engagement with the countries of West Asia. The Eastern part of India is a growth area, while the Western part is an area of enormous energy resources. To maintain the current rate of economic growth New Delhi needs to maintain and enhance its cooperation with both the dynamic economies of the East and the oil producing countries of the West.

However, India appears to be more successful in its oriental economic and political ventures. During the Cold War days, most of East and South-East Asia, including China, was pro-US oriented. India maintained cordial ties with Indo-Chinese countries and North Korea and was thus viewed with suspicion by the majority of the countries of this region. In addition, the relatively restricted economic policy of India failed to engage the dynamic and rapidly growing economies, such as South Korea, Singapore, Taiwan, Malaysia and a few others.

The end of the Cold War coincided with India's economic reforms. The expansion of the ASEAN to include the three Indo-Chinese countries of Vietnam, Laos and Cambodia, improvement in Indo-US relations and Sino-Indian cooperation all contributed towards a transformed and more positive image of India in the ASEAN. India's status was enhanced from a sect oral dialogue partner to a full dialogue partner. Also, India's inclusion as a member of the ASEAN Regional Forum and the Indian efforts to devise a new foreign policy strategy of Look East brought dividends.

Sooner than later, New Delhi became a founding member of East Asia Summit a larger Asian initiative to forge regional cooperation in a much wider area than ever before contemplated. India's first Prime Minister Jawaharlal Nehru dreamt of an Indian role in the Asia-Pacific while in prison during the freedom struggle. He also tried to lead a new initiative in forging Asian regional cooperation by calling for such a mechanism at the Asian Relations Conference in 1947 and 1949. However, regional events in South Asia then overtook such a grand initiative and India spent more time and energy in dealing with bordering enemies.

Not until the collapse of the Soviet Union and wide ranging economic reforms could India revive Nehru's dream of engaging in wider regional cooperative efforts in the Asia-Pacific region. The Look East policy announced with much fanfare by the Narashimha Rao Government failed to take off due to a variety of reasons. First of all, India got stuck with another grand plan to forge regional cooperation in the Indian Ocean Region IOARC— and a smaller version of sub-regional cooperation known as BIMSTEC. The nuclear test of 1998 and the Kargil War of 1999 also had a role in the lackluster performance of the Look East strategy. The UPA Government led by Prime Minister Manmohan Singh has invested substantial diplomatic and political capital to broaden and deepen India's economic and political cooperation with the ASEAN countries.

What is the likely outcome of India-ASEAN emerging initiatives? Several factors will influence the course of this emerging relationship. First of all, India's continued economic performance alone can promote closer cooperation with the ASEAN. The Americans, Europeans and the Japanese have begun to focus attention on the growing Indian economy. So are the ASEAN member countries.

While India has been able to increase its trade with the ASEAN considerably to the tune of $30 billion, it is small change compared to China's trade with this region. Can India's economy successfully integrate with that of the ASEAN? New Delhi was initially reluctant to join this grouping. The ASEAN later gave a cold shoulder to India both because of political reasons the Cold War considerations and the Pakistan factor. Both these factors are non-existent now. But the absence of political hurdles is not enough. Political will is essential to make the best use of the opportunity.

The current leadership appears to have had the will and it is all reflected in the efforts to sign a free trade agreement with the ASEAN. Secondly, India needs to do some catching up with China in the fields of economic performance, diplomatic skill as well as military modernization to be able to play an influential role in the ASEAN. The South-East Asian leaders will not talk about it, the Indian leaders will avoid comments on this, but it is widely understood. Japan and the US maintain traditional influence in the ASEAN. China is already influential. India is still regarded as a country of potentiality.

Japan's lackluster economic performance and China's hyper activities have generated an expectation in the region that India would play a moderating influence for the Asian balance of power. New Delhi needs to consciously and conscientiously work on this. Thirdly, the positive Indo-US engagements will go a long way to assist Indian efforts to be a role player in the Asia-Pacific. The American hegemony in this region is real, accepted in the region and privately appreciated by many. China at one time sought to be a revisionist power, but no more. The US makes China richer by more than $200 billion by buying more Chinese goods and selling less.

China has prospered under the US hegemony and quietly desires it to stay. Some Indian leaders and analysts still conjure up negative images of the US role to the complete exclusion of its positive influences. More regrettably, Indians do not discuss how to benefit from the existing system that is unlikely to be replaced in the near future. All this is partially reflected in the discussion on the Indo-US nuclear deal. Instead of focusing on what India can gain and whether India can gain sufficiently, the opponents of the deal went to the extent of name calling. This already has negative diplomatic consequences in the larger region.

But the bottom line is: India is incapable of playing the role of a revisionist power now. It needs to take care of the above-mentioned points to be able to emerge as a meaningful partner of the ASEAN the most successful regional cooperation arrangement in Asia. The tumultuous relationship with Pakistan affected India's policy considerations as India looked to develop and maintain good relations with the Western world, so that they supported India's views on Kashmir.

The Non-Aligned Movement (NAM) afforded a greater degree of interaction between India and many countries which it had neglected in the immediate years after its independence. India supported the anti-colonial movement in Southeast Asia—the convening of the Asian Relations Conference in 1947, a special conference on Indonesia in January 1949, Chairmanship of the International Control Commission on India-China in 1954 and the sponsoring of the Bandung Conference—all these reflected India's deep involvement in the freedom struggle being waged by the countries of the region.

But the growing pro-Soviet tilt in India's foreign policy drove a wedge between India and the Southeast Asian nations. Malaysia, Indonesia, Thailand, Singapore and the Philippines were strongly anti-communist. India's proposal for a security arrangement in the region also did not go down well with the ASEAN countries as it was seen to be part of the Soviet Union's attempts to bring the region under its influence. ASEAN also did not support India's cause during the 1971 Indo-Pak war. The resolution of the Cambodian conflict brought about a change in Indo-ASEAN relations.

The then Prime Minister Rajiv Gandhi's path-breaking visit to China in 1988 also marked a tremendous shift in Sino-Indian relations and had a bearing on Indo-ASEAN relations as well. With the launching of India's economic liberalisation programme in 1991, ASEAN came to be identified as being pivotal to India's policy in the Asia-Pacific region. ASEAN also decided to expand its membership to include all countries which are geographically part of Southeast Asia. A quantum jump in Indo-Asean relations came with the effort to forge closer links with the Southeast Asian countries after 1991.

This period saw the beginning of its Look-East Policy which was intended to reach out to the countries of East and Southeast Asia which had been neglected by India in spite of cultural, religious, geographical proximity and historical links. The Association of Southeast Asian Nations (ASEAN) was formed in 1967 by Indonesia, the Philippines, Malaysia, Singapore and Thailand. The changed global circumstances forced India to adapt itself to the new emerging world order. India began an overhaul of its foreign policy and it was felt that ASEAN could be of much help to India in this exercise. India extended support to ASEAN's efforts in establishing peace in Cambodia and bring the warring factions to the negotiating table at the Jakarta Informal Meet (JIM I and JIM II) and later co-operated with the United Nations Transitional Authority in its efforts to bring peace to Cambodia.

It was in the wake of the failure of SAARC that India decided to "Look-East" as India already had deep-seated cultural, religious and political links with the Southeast Asian countries. But there were many factors which impeded India's efforts in this process. The ASEAN countries were pro-West in their outlook and projected Vietnam as their common threat as opposed to India's views on Vietnam and Cambodia.

The booming economies of the Southeast Asian countries also attracted India. ASEAN was also on the lookout for new partners and untapped markets. The break-up of the erstwhile Soviet Union, its withdrawal from Cam Ranh Bay and the American withdrawal from the Subic Bay naval base created a security vacuum in the region. India's close relations with the Soviet Union acted as a dampener. India's position on the Soviet presence in Afghanistan and the recognition given to the Heng Samarin regime in Cambodia also hindered the development of close ties with ASEAN. However, India ultimately succeeded in becoming a sectoral- dialogue partner of the ASEAN in 1992 and a full-dialogue partner in 1996.

The end of the cold war marked a turning point in India's relations with ASEAN. India becoming a full-dialogue partner has brought it closer to the ASEAN member- countries. The other full dialogue partners are: Australia, Canada, China, the European Union, Japan, New Zealand, the Republic of Korea, Russia and the US. With the inclusion of Myanmar, India and ASEAN now share a 1,600-km land border. Despite the economic crisis that plagued the region in the late 1990's, Indo-ASEAN relations have been continuously on the upswing. The second Indo-ASEAN summit at Bali in Indonesia in October 2003 was a big leap forward in their mutual relations.

Two broad agreements, for comprehensive economic co-operation and combating terrorism were signed. The former Prime Minister Atal Behari Vajpayee also offered a unilateral "open skies" policy to designated Southeast Asian airlines which would be free to operate daily flights to the Indian metros outside of any bilateral aviation pact. Vajpayee also talked about the possibility of holding an India-ASEAN motor rally, which has become a reality now with the flagging-off of the Indo-ASEAN car rally from Guwahati. It is basically seen as a means of recharging the trade routes that had existed between India and the Southeast Asian countries in the not too distant past. India also acceded to the ASEAN Treaty of Amity and Cooperation. The framework agreement aims at creating a free trade area within 10 years.

During the same month India and Thailand also signed a number of agreements including the landmark free trade agreement. The proposed Free Trade Agreement (FTA) will lead to free trade in goods by the year 2010 and in services and investments by 2006. The FTA slashed tariff on 84 items from March 1, 2004. The Bali meet set its sights on creating a single Southeast Asian market, covering 500 million people, involving an annual trade of USD 720 billion.

At present, the level of two-way trade between India and ASEAN stands at USD 12.5 billion a year which is projected to rise to USD 30 billion by the year 2007. But the larger aim remains the creation of an ASEAN-India Free Trade Area in the next 10 years, developing an Asian

Economic Community by 2020 on the lines of the European Union and eventually creating a single currency for Asia. The next three years will witness the exchange of tariff concessions and elimination of tariffs on a list of 105 items based on full reciprocity between India and the ASEAN countries, viz., Thailand, Indonesia, Brunei, Malaysia and the Philippines.

India has mooted a trilateral highway project involving Myanmar and Thailand and also a rail link between New Delhi and Hanoi. Another economic grouping is the BIMSTEC which has brought together five nations of the subcontinent—Bangladesh, Bhutan, India, Nepal, Sri Lanka together with two countries from Southeast Asia, Myanmar and Thailand. An ASEAN - India Eminent Persons' Lecture Series has been launched for the furtherance of ASEAN-India relations. The initiative for ASEAN integration (IAI) was launched by ASEAN to bridge the intra-ASEAN development gap, especially between the four new ASEAN entrants, viz., Cambodia Laos, Myanmar, Vietnam and the other six.

India has been very keen to help ASEAN in this regard. After India became a sectoral dialogue partner of the ASEAN in 1992, an ASEAN-India Business Council (AIBC) was established to advance business opportunities. ASEAN emerged as a major actor in the politics of the Asia Pacific region after the end of the cold war. It was felt that India needed a long term partnership with the ASEAN countries in the interest of its stability, security and development. India's major issues are insurgency in the Northeast, smuggling of narcotics, border disputes and access to the Southeast Asian economies.

India's main exports to ASEAN include gems, jewellery, meat and meat preparations, cotton yarn, fabrics, made ups, engineering goods, transport equipment, machinery and instrument, electronic goods, marine products, fruits and vegetables, rice, drugs and pharmaceuticals and chemicals. Imports are comprised of artificial resins, plastic materials, natural rubber, wood and wood products, electronic goods, non-ferrous metals, metali-ferrous ores, metal scrap, organic chemicals, edible oils, coal and fertilizers. ASEAN-India trade in 2001-02 stood at USD 7.8 billion. India's exports to ASEAN stood as USD 3.5 billion while imports stood at USD 4.3 billion. ASEAN, especially Malaysia, Singapore and Thailand have become a major source of Foreign Direct Investment in India. Though it was a pittance in 1991, the cumulative approved FDI between January 1991 and May 2002 from ASEAN stood at over Rs 14,000 crore.

In the area of Human Resource Development, India has earmarked 100 seats in various training courses at reputed Indian institutions for students from the ASEAN countries. 50 of these will be for IT while the rest will be divided between management, banking and finance, urban development, educational planning and labour relations. The dialogue process with ASEAN is meant to complement and augment India's bilateral relations with the Southeast Asian neighbours. There is much more that can be achieved. It is up to India and ASEAN to seize the initiative. The potential is huge and as they say, the sky is the limit.

6
Perspectives On The Rise Of China

The unprecedented rise of the People's Republic of China (PRC) is a global reality. From one of the world's least developed countries in the 1970s, China had developed one of the largest economies in the world by the late 1990s. The World Bank and the International Monetary Fund (IMF) reported that from 1979 to 1997, China's gross domestic product (GDP) grew at an average rate of 9.8 percent. This phenomenal economic growth has spilled over to China's Defence budget, with military spending rising to 17.6 percent of China's outlays, an equivalent of $3 billion in March 2002 alone.

Because of the burgeoning economic and military power of China, there are enormous worries about the idea of a "China threat." The United States has particularly expressed strong apprehensions regarding the ascension of China. The US Commission on National Security/21st Century warns that "the potential for competition between the United States and China may increase as China grows stronger." Even the Global Trends 2015 prepared under the direction of the US National Intelligence Council argues that the implications of the rise of China "pose the greatest uncertainty" in the world.

The Commission on America's National Interests describes China as "America's major potential strategic adversary in East Asia," while the Council on Foreign Relations has stated that "China poses significant economic, military, and political challenges for the United States and for the nations of Southeast Asia." This theme is supported by a RAND study describing China as a potential military threat to the United States and Southeast Asia. While the United States views China as a potential threat to its national security, how do Southeast Asian countries view the rise of China? What are the implications of the growth of China for regional security, especially in the aftermath of 9/11? This chapter aims to present Southeast Asian perspectives on the rise of China and its regional security implications since 9/11.

SOUTHEAST ASIAN PERSPECTIVES

Taken individually, Southeast Asian countries have varying perspectives on the many ramifications of strategic issues in the region. Unlike some Western countries, however, Southeast Asian nations, taken as a whole, consider the rise of China as a great opportunity, with concomitant security challenges, rather than as a serious threat. From an economic standpoint, Rodolfo Severino, former Secretary General of the Association of Southeast Asian Nations (ASEAN), candidly describes China and ASEAN as "partners in competition." There is also a widespread perception in Southeast Asia that "China will be the new engine of growth for the entire region."

In a report submitted by the ASEAN-China Expert Group on Economic Cooperation in October 2001, Southeast Asia optimistically views China as an economic opportunity. The Expert Group has, in fact, proposed the forging of closer ASEAN-China economic relations in the 21st century to integrate their economies. Recognizing the economic potential that China may bring to Southeast Asia, one important recommendation of the Expert Group is the establishment of an ASEAN-China Free Trade Area (ACFTA).

The group views ACFTA as "an important move forward in terms of economic integration in East Asia," as well as "a foundation for the more ambitious vision of an East Asia Free Trade Area, encompassing ASEAN, China, Japan, and Korea." The group suggests that "the realization of a China-ASEAN free trade zone agreement indicates that historical feuds and political clashes between ASEAN member states and the PRC are no longer one of the most important factors influencing ASEAN-PRC relations." This shift in the Southeast Asian perception of China is an important landmark in China-Southeast Asian relations.

One must remember that from the 1950s to the early 1970s, Southeast Asian states regarded China as a dangerous adversary because of its perceived military expansionist scheme in Asia. During the height of the Cold War, the Chinese Communist Party was believed to have supported Southeast Asian communist insurgents, causing Southeast Asia to view China as an abhorrent ideological enemy. Because of this tragic historical experience, there was a view that "China will always be seen as posing a threat to Southeast Asia, in view of her size and past experiences in which China considered Southeast Asia as within her sphere of influence."

Chinese participation in various multilateral confidence-building activities at the end of the Cold War, however, has made Southeast Asia more optimistic about China's international behavior. Southeast Asia is pleased to see China actively involving itself in the Asia Pacific Economic Cooperation (APEC) forum, the ASEAN Regional Forum (ARF), and the Asia-Europe Meeting (ASEM) program, among others. Southeast Asia is also using these multilateral mechanisms to establish closer relations with China. Although Southeast Asian states are presently more optimistic about their relations with China, the Chinese government's passage of a law on Territorial Waters and Contiguous Areas in 1992 and the People's Liberation Army's occupation of the Mischief Reef in July 1994 caused tremendous concerns in the region at that time. Those acts were interpreted as a sign of the "creeping assertiveness" of Beijing in the contested South China Sea.

Former Philippine Defence Secretary Orlando S. Mercado even described the Chinese occupation of the Mischief Reef in 1994 and the fortification of its structures in 1999 as a strong indication of China's "creeping invasion" of the "disputed South China Sea chain." China has existing territorial disputes with a few countries in Southeast Asia, namely Brunei, Malaysia, the Philippines, and Vietnam. Although Indonesia is not actually a claimant state in the disputes, China's territorial claims overlap with Indonesia's Exclusive Economic Zones.

The South China Sea disputes continue to serve as major irritants in China-Southeast Asia relations. In fact, China has earlier fought with Vietnam over the Paracel and Spratly islands and had military skirmishes with the Philippine navy in the waters of the Kalayaan Island Group and Scarborough Shoal.

But with the signing of the Declaration on the Conduct of Parties in the South China Sea on 4 November 2002, there are high hopes that these irritants will be eventually resolved or at least be swept sufficiently under the rug to enable China and Southeast Asia to concentrate more on productive areas of cooperation. China's provocative military exercises involving missile tests in the Taiwan Strait at the time of Taiwanese elections in 1996 also caused alarm in Southeast Asia.

The tests were interpreted as an "arrogant display" of China's military might in the area and a flagrant indication of China's attempt to strengthen its influence in Asia. This incident frightened much of Southeast Asia because of the memory of Chinese military adventurism in the region at the height of communist insurgency. Indeed, the 1996 Taiwan incident continues to be an inhibiting consideration in Southeast Asia's relations with China. The most recent incident causing regional worries in connection with the rise of China was the EP3 spy plane incident with the United States in April 2001.

China decisively asserted its sovereign rights to protect its territorial airspace and strongly demanded that the United States apologize for "encroaching" on Chinese territory. Southeast Asia views China's reaction in this incident as an indication of China's growing confidence in international affairs.

During the 1980s and early 1990s, China exhibited "a passive and reactionary pattern of behavior in foreign affairs." But China's pattern of behavior has become more and more assertive recently. Since the EP3 incident increased the degree of mistrust between the United States and China, some Southeast Asian states also have been affected by it.

Encouragingly, the release of China's Defence White Paper on 9 December 2002 has created a high expectation in the region that China will be more transparent in its strategic goals and intentions. The White Paper states that China "endorses all activities conducive to maintaining the global strategic balance and stability."

To assure that China's behavior will be more benign and cooperative, Southeast Asia is engaging China in the economic sphere through various bilateral and multilateral mechanisms. Multilaterally, Southeast Asia is engaging China through the China-ASEAN Free Trade Area, ASEAN+3, the ASEAN-China Dialogue, APEC, and the ARF.

Southeast Asia understands the reality that China is dependent on the region for its own growth and prosperity. Thus, Southeast Asia adheres to the formula that engaging China in the economic sphere will create more fruitful and constructive relations. Although some Southeast Asian countries have expressed apprehensions on the growing power of China in the region, this apprehension "is normally never publicly articulated" in order to establish a constructive and productive relationship with the traditional Middle Kingdom of Asia.

THE AFTERMATH OF 9/11: IMPLICATIONS FOR REGIONAL SECURITY

The aftermath of 9/11 has greatly disturbed China's strategic scheme in Southeast Asia. The American-led war on terrorism has unleashed some "strategic losses, shocks, and reverses" in China's core strategic interests in Southeast Asia. Chinese leaders themselves admit that "the nation's geopolitical position has deteriorated since the events of September 11, 2001." Since 9/11, China has reportedly changed its security calculus and been forced to reevaluate its geopolitical position vis-a-vis its relations with the United States and with the claimant states in the South China Sea.

In response to the shifting strategic landscape in Southeast Asia, Beijing reportedly has been launching an uncharacteristically concerted diplomatic effort toward its neighbors. Although 9/11 heavily affected the security architecture of the region, the event did not alter Southeast Asian perceptions of the rise of China, however. Southeast Asia continues to view China as a serious partner for regional growth and prosperity despite the existence of some irritants in the area of territorial and border disputes.

Various confidence-building initiatives are now in place between China and Southeast Asia to enhance their relations in the aftermath of 9/11. What worries Southeast Asia is the negative reaction of major powers on the rise of China and the impact of 9/11 on major-power rivalries in the region. Moreover, 9/11 has not altered the security fundamentals in Asia affecting Southeast Asia. The security problems in the Taiwan Strait, Korean Peninsula, and the South China Sea persist. These problems continue to encumber Southeast Asia with security dilemmas, making the region highly vulnerable to major-power politics.

Yet it should be noted that Southeast Asia has always been held hostage to the power politics of major powers. Southeast Asia has been one of the principal fulcrums of major-power rivalries in Asia, and the emerging security landscape unleashed by 9/11 intensified this situation. Major powers are using the war on terrorism in Southeast Asia as an excuse for their active military engagements in the region to prepare for any military contingencies in the Taiwan Strait, Korean Peninsula, and South China Sea. In this rivalry, Southeast Asian countries are put in a strategic dilemma in managing their relations with the major powers.

THE RISE OF CHINA AND THE RETURN OF THE U.S. TO SOUTHEAST ASIA

One of the unintended consequences of 9/11 is the strategic return of the United States to the region. Before 9/11, many security analysts in the United States had lamented that Washington was neglecting Southeast Asia in its strategic agenda. Since the end of the Vietnam War, the United States has failed to formulate a clear and coherent strategy to guide its engagement with Southeast Asia at various levels. Security analysts have described relations between Southeast Asia and the United States as "a policy without a strategy," and as a "policy backwater in Washington." American officials and security analysts have even viewed Southeast Asia for the past three decades "as marginal to security in Asia," paying more attention to threats in the Taiwan Strait and on the Korean Peninsula.

Some also have bemoaned that the United States lacks expertise on Southeast Asia in both its official and unofficial sectors. It also has been observed that for most Americans, the region "remains obscure and poorly understood." Since 9/11, the United States seemingly has realized its blunder of neglecting Southeast Asia in its strategic agenda. Thus, the United States has decided to bring Southeast Asia back onto its strategic radar and declared the region as a second front in the war on terrorism. Although Southeast Asian countries welcome the US presence in the region for strategic reasons, they also express worries of American "praetorian unilateralism" triggered by the US pursuance of homeland security in the context of the global campaign against terror. The praetorian element of this new American security strategy is manifested in its penchant for a military solution to win the war on terror.

Its unilateralist policy is reflected in its latest national security strategy, which asserts that the United States "will not hesitate to act alone, if necessary, to exercise [the] right of self Defence." The return of the United States to Southeast Asia is also causing security anxieties in China because of the perception that American intentions in the war on terror in Southeast Asia aim not only to destroy terrorism in the region but also to strategically encircle China.

A recently published study of the Nixon Center, for example, states that the reinvigorated American presence in Southeast Asia not only aims to wage a war on terror, but also to hedge against a rising China. Although American Defence and security officials deny this angle, various testimonies before the US Congress and numerous reports of American think-tanks articulate a perspective of strategically encircling China to regain for America a preponderance of power in Southeast Asia. Like the United States, China also wants to maintain its presence in Southeast Asia. China regards the region as vital for its own growth and prosperity.

China regards Southeast Asia as "attractive, vulnerable, and nearby," particularly with respect to the strategic waters of the South China Sea. Indeed, China views the South China Sea as "golden lands of opportunity." Thus, it is also in the strategic and economic interests of China to assert its influence in the region. It "wants a sharp diminution" of US influence in Southeast Asia, "especially in terms of its military deployments to the region and its encircling... chain of bilateral security arrangements with many of China's neighbors."

To balance the reestablished presence of the United States in the region since 9/11, China is seeking warmer ties in Southeast Asia and is coming up with its own plan to cultivate close ties with all the ASEAN countries. China also has begun to invest "more aggressively in Southeast Asia," because economic opportunities "have opened up after 9/11." China is using its economic instrument of national power to shore up its diplomacy in Southeast Asia and to balance the preponderant military power of the United States in the region. China also has intensified its Defence and military diplomacy, as indicated in its 2002 Defence White Paper.

THE EXPANDED MILITARY ROLE OF JAPAN

As part of Japanese support to the global campaign against terrorism, Prime Minister Koizumi committed Japan's Self Defence Force ships to help the United States in collecting intelligence, shipping supplies, and providing medical services and humanitarian relief. He also pledged to strengthen protection of US bases in Japan. Using the war on terror as justification, Japanese warships are now in Asian waters. Southeast Asia has expressed concerns about the expanded military role of Japan after 9/11, remembering the experiences of the Second World War. But at the same time, Southeast Asia cautiously welcomes this development as a counterweight to China's growing influence in the region.

As opined by Robert Karniol, the Asia-Pacific editor of Jane Defence Weekly, "By Japan expanding its role, the countries in the region see it as balancing an over-dominant Chinese influence" in Southeast Asia. Carl Thayer, professor of politics at Australia's Defence Force Academy, has remarked, "Anyone adding counterweight to China is welcome." China, on the other hand, views Japan's heightened military role in Southeast Asia after 9/11 as an "unpleasant" reality. Chinese Premier Zhu Rongji has warned Japan to exercise the utmost prudence in expanding its military role. He reminded Tokyo to abide by its commitment not to be a military power and to limit its Defence power to its own territory and coastal waters. China views Japan as "a potential threat to its political influence in the region."

INDIA'S SOUTHEAST ASIAN POLICY AND THE RISE OF CHINA

India also has realized the strategic importance of Southeast Asia. During the height of the Cold War, the Indian leadership viewed ASEAN as an American "imperialist surrogate," while ASEAN dubbed India as "the surrogate of the Soviet Union." Thus, Southeast Asia was not part of the strategic sphere of Indian foreign and security policy. After the Cold War, however, India reinvented its view of Southeast Asia, adopting a "look east policy" to be actively engaged in Southeast Asian affairs. India has expressed greater interest in the region because the Straits of Malacca, which connect the South China Sea to the Indian Ocean, with Singapore, Malaysia, and Indonesia as their littoral countries, are critical to Indian maritime trade.

India also wants to be engaged in Southeast Asian security affairs to balance the growing influence of China. An Indian analyst argues:

With India's obsession towards Pakistan and with its preoccupations with China, the South East Asian region did not figure much in its foreign policy till recently. Some political analysts point out that of late, India has started taking interest in this region more with a view to balance China in the region. India in the short term cannot achieve this aim, as China has entrenched itself deeply in most of these countries over a period of time with a long term perspective.

The emerging security landscape unleashed by 9/11 has prompted India to intensify its engagement in Southeast Asia. China, however, does not want to see India enlarging its regional and international stature and profile in Southeast Asia, arguing that India's pursuit of great power status is "illegitimate, wrong, dangerous, and a sign of hegemonic imperial behavior." Thus, China maintains its strategy of "keeping India out" of Southeast Asia. Australia views itself as an integral part of Southeast Asia from a geographic standpoint. However, its strategic interests lean toward the West. Thus, the centerpiece of Australian foreign and security policy in Southeast Asia is the Australia-US alliance.

Strategically, Australia is the United States' oldest reliable ally in the Asia Pacific region and welcomes active US engagement in Southeast Asia. Australian and American interests in the Asia Pacific, in general, and in Southeast Asia, in particular, have strategically converged. This convergence of interests, especially following 9/11, is the strong tie that binds the Australia-US alliance. In its 2000 Defence White Paper, Australia describes China as "an important strategic interlocutor for Australia."

As an ally of the United States, Australia views the rise of China with apprehension and continues to be suspicious of China's strategic motives as an Asian power. Australia feels uncomfortable with the growing influence of China in international and regional security affairs. Even former Prime Minister of Australia Paul Keating once said that Beijing's "size can overwhelm" and it "can be uncomfortable to live next door to a giant." Thus, Australian strategists regard Canberra's alliance with Washington as a security blanket that will "provide a balance to any strategic uncertainty stemming from the rise of China."

Southeast Asia welcomes Australian engagement in regional security affairs as a counterweight to China. But Southeast Asia also is wary of Australian intentions because, like Tokyo, Canberra is articulating Washington's foreign and security policy in the region. While Southeast Asian countries welcome the United States, none of them wants its dominance. Southeast Asian countries are fully aware of the growing influence of China, and this growing influence has undoubtedly created some security concerns in the region. But Southeast Asian nations have officially expressed confidence that China's intentions are benign.

ASEAN, in fact, views the rise of China as more of an

opportunity with concomitant challenges, rather than a threat. What worries Southeast Asia in the midst of the rise of China is the reaction of the major powers to the idea of a "China threat" and the impact of 9/11 on major-power rivalries. Southeast Asia has always been held hostage to the power politics of major powers, and the emerging security landscape unleashed by 9/11 has intensified major-power rivalries in Southeast Asia. This rivalry is affecting the growth and prosperity of the region. Moreover, the security fundamentals in Asia have not been altered by 9/11.

The problems in the Taiwan Strait, the Korean Peninsula, and the South China Sea persist. Despite the influence of the major-power rivalry, China and Southeast Asia continue to engage in areas of cooperation to reduce their apprehensions and increase their trust. China and Southeast Asia recognize the need to deepen and widen their cooperation, because both China and Southeast Asia are becoming more and more interdependent economically and politically, particularly in the aftermath of 9/11. As Chinese Foreign Minister Tang Jiaxuan said during the China-ASEAN Ministerial Meeting in Brunei in August 2002, "We should keep developing the momentum of China-ASEAN ties and further expand and deepen our cooperation to better cope with the changed situation."

APPEASEMENT AND MUDDLING THROUGH

The appeasement and muddling through group includes Congress. By Congress, I mean the Indian National Congress Party, now a mere shadow of its former self. Congress is the party that brought India independence. It is the party of Jawarharlal Nehru, India's first prime minister and essentially the architect of modern India's foreign policy. The permanent bureaucracy of India—the Ministry of External Affairs (MEA)—in good measure also shares the perspective of Congress on China. The perspective of this group is in large part based upon fear and awe of China. This fear in turn largely stems from the traumatic experience of the 1962 border war.

This war may well be a scratch on the minds of most China-watchers, but we should not underestimate what it means to Indians. From the perspective of Indian strategists and Indian security analysts, the 1962 border war is a watershed event, perhaps *the* most significant event to take place between 1947 and the present date. They see it as more important than either the Indian nuclear tests of 1998 or the 1971 victory over Pakistan. Indian Defence strategy, foreign policy, and security planning were fundamentally altered by the war of 1961. The traumatizing impact of 1962 still pervades the thinking of much of the Indian foreign policy bureaucracy. They see China as something larger than a mere *bête noire*—or, more aptly, *bête jaune*.

They are absolutely terrified of China. As a result, they are convinced that it is vital to accommodate the Chinese. They try as far as possible to oblige China and avoid rocking the boat. They periodically beat up Tibetans in India. They do this especially—and with considerable vigor—when Li Peng is in town. They reiterate at every official function that Tibet is an autonomous part of China and do not get any commensurate statement from the Chinese on India's vexing problem in Kashmir. In short, the policy of this school involves genuflection before the Middle Kingdom. Fear of China, which drives the approach of this school, has been reinforced in the last 10 to 15 years by the phenomenal growth of the Chinese economy.

Those Indians who belong to this group envy the growth of Chinese economic power. They envy the fact that the Chinese have made significant progress towards eradicating rural poverty. Congress, their foreign policy authorities and, in particular, the permanent bureaucracy, feel besieged and threatened. They feel that India is in an acutely vulnerable state. They think that India can ill afford to do anything to provoke this extraordinarily economically and militarily powerful state that just lies beyond the

Himalayan mountains, mountains which proved, contrary to Nehru's view, unable to protect India in perpetuity.

The Ministry of External Affairs and Congress pursue a largely unimaginative set of policies. They also lack a clear sense of strategic objectives. They do not seem to know what they ultimately want from the Chinese. They have no sense of an end game, which is why I refer to this group as the "Muddling Through" group. This quality is especially visible in the Sino-Indian border talks. These have been going on since 1981. Entire careers have been built on the border talks. And yet participants do not seem to have the any idea at all of what they finally hope to achieve. Rank anti-Americanism is also a feature of this world-view. Members of the "Appeasement" school want to oppose the sole remaining superpower.

They believe that India, China, and possibly Russia can make common cause against America. They think that an alliance of this sort would enable them to challenge global regimes over a number of issues, including international climate change, human rights, sovereignty, and global trade. They also harp at great length on the importance of multipolarity. The members of this school are easily consumed by the logic (or rather illogic) of their own rhetoric. They are, for example, easily taken in by the occasional Chinese statements to the effect that India should be included in a multipolar universe. They are quick to believe this, despite the fact that important differences continue to separate India and China on all substantive issues.

STRATEGIC ENGAGEMENT

The current government is a coalition government dominated by the Bharatiya Janata Party (BJP) party. This party is rather jingoistic, and is often referred to, quite correctly in my view, as a Hindu Nationalist party. The position of this party and its coalition partners (to the extent that the coalition partners have any interest in foreign policy and, particularly, in China) is one of strategic engagement. This approach requires India to build up its own military and economic might. If they do, it does not derive from any real conviction; no one in their right mind in New Delhi really believes that such a goal is desirable or attainable.

The Nehruvian/Wilsonian vision of the world is increasingly being tossed aside. Instead it is coming to be replaced by a view that force in and of itself and forces in being both constitute very important elements of national power. The use of force, moreover, involves the use of force well beyond South Asia. The recognition of the importance of force came belatedly to India but is finally sinking in and taking very deep roots. To be sure, some analysts point to the Indian use of force to liberate Goa from Portuguese rule in 1961. They say that this shows that Indians abandoned the ideational view of the world many decades ago.

However, this is simply not true. Goa was a colonial enclave. Colonialism had been discredited, and the Portuguese had to go. India had negotiated with the Portuguese in good faith and to no avail. The Goans were utterly intransigent, and the use of force was India's only remaining option. The fact is that the invasion of Goa was only a minor episode and should be seen as a departure from the norm. Indians did not seriously consider the utility of force until recent times. Today all that is changing. A fundamental change is taking place in other areas as well, notably in economics.

Members of the current regime emphasize the need to for India to develop its economic might. They are eager to catch up with China although aware how far the Indian economy lags behind that of the Chinese, particularly in the area of attracting foreign investments. They argue that the economic liberalization program must continue because, since 1991, it has yielded rich results. India has, at long last, broken out of what the eminent Indian economist Raj Krishna used to call the "Hindu" (as opposed to the secular) rate of growth. For many years, all India could hope for was an effective growth of about 1 percent a year thanks to the fact that its 3 percent growth in gross national product (GNP) was paralleled by an annual 2 percent population growth.

Now the Indian economy is enjoying a steady growth of 6 percent. If this growth were to increase to 7 percent per annum and keep at that level for 10 years, the national income would be doubled by 2011. That is the talismanic figure that Indians are aiming for. Indian economists are now suggesting that double digit growth might be possible provided that they can find ways to deal with such exogenous shocks as hikes in oil prices. In all, the members of this party both recognize that much needs to be done, but at the same time are eager to catch up with Chinese economic might.

Strategic Engagement also calls for improved relations with Southeast Asia, a part of the world long neglected in Indian Foreign Policy. India has increased its presence in Burma (note the visit to this country by foreign minister Jaswan Singh); demonstrated a willingness to cooperate with Malaysia (upgrading its aircraft and assisting its airforce); signed a security pact in Indonesia; held naval exercises in the recent past with Vietnam; and sent naval vessels to visit Japan. All this represents, no pun intended, a sea change. At the same time, strategic engagement does not simply call for the use of force and the development of Indian military might. It also calls for a continuing dialogue with China.

The current government appreciates the need to engage in discussion with the Chinese. There are some serious areas of contention between India and China such as the border problem, the supply of ballistic weapons and nuclear weapons technology to Pakistan, and most recently the alleged dumping of cheap Chinese goods in the Indian market. Whereas previous regimes would have simply swept these things under the carpet, the BJP, for all of its flaws, is forthrightly confronting these issues. Related to this is one last component of this perspective or strategy. The current government does recognize potential areas of cooperation between India and China.

Most notable is its attempt to wean China away from Pakistan by emphasizing an issue that is of common concern, namely the rise of radical Islam. Of course, when the BJP talks about the rise of radical Islam, one has to take it with not only a few pinches of salt but also an entire saltshaker full of salt! However, the Chinese are now facing a problem from radical Muslims in Xinjiang. Consequently, this line of argument sells well.

The Indians can try to convince the powerful Chinese that the Chinese alliance (or, more accurately, their "client relationship") with Pakistan is not serving them very well any more. They can point out that the Pakistanis are in bed with the Taliban who have obvious connections with Islamic zealots in Central Asia. They can suggest to the Chinese that, under these circumstances, it might be in their best interest to recalculate their options vis-à-vis the Pakistanis. Indeed, they might be advised, to make common cause with the Indians against "Islamic terror."

THE CONFRONTATIONALISTS

Finally, we come to the lunatic fringe, namely the Confrontationalists. Fortunately, they also constitute the weakest of the three positions in the Indian political spectrum. What exactly do these Indians have in mind? It can be summed up in one word as "confrontation." They call for a policy of unremitting hostility towards the People's Republic of China. They believe that India should adopt a far more confrontational stand towards China.

They argue that India should dramatically expand the scope of its nuclear weapons program and expand the reach of its ballistic missiles. India should, moreover, adopt a far, far tougher negotiating stance on the border question. Indians should try to obtain Chinese acquiescence on the

Kashmir issue with Pakistan. If the Chinese do not prove to be tractable, Indians should exploit the Achilles heel of the Chinese: Tibet. Tibet, the confrontationalists stress, constitutes the soft underbelly of China. India should take advantage of that soft underbelly, kick the Chinese where it hurts.

If the Chinese do not prove to be tractable on the border question or on the Kashmir question, Indians should remind them that they can raise the cost in Tibet. They have done this before and are prepared to do it again. At the very least, the confrontationalists say, the Tibetans are getting restive, and this is a good time to try and milk the situation to their advantage. Interestingly enough, some members of this group are also viscerally anti-American but in spite of their viscerally anti-American position, they nevertheless feel that they can make common cause with the United States.

Certain (unnamed) senators and representatives in the United States have made remarks about how India could serve as a possible counterweight to China. Such remarks have animated this group of Indians even further, leading them to think that India might be able to make common cause with the United States and tie China down. Even though the confrontationalists are angered by American sanctions against Indian nuclear power, they see this area as one where their interests do dovetail.

THE FUTURE

The future hinges, in my estimate, on three important factors. First, it depends on who is in power. Should the BJP regime collapse and were Congress or a variant of Congress to return to power, we would once again see a policy of appeasement and muddling through. This is the only policy that the so-called foreign policy experts in Congress know how to pursue. This is because they are unimaginative, because they are absolutely terrified of China and because they do not recognize India's inherent strengths but only see its vulnerabilities.

It is above all because they are still locked in a Nehruvian prism or rather one should say "prison, " since they are certainly shackled by what William Blake would call "mind-forged manacles." I do not think, however, that there is any imminent danger of a collapse of the present regime. Second, the future hinges on how the Sino-Pakistani relationship evolves. Relations between India and China could improve significantly should China, by some miracle, be weaned away from Pakistan. The ballistic missile issue, the Kashmir issue, and the nuclear issue, are all key here. In this eventuality, in my estimation, a number of differences could be settled. However, I think that such a development is highly unlikely in the foreseeable future.

Third, and finally, nuclear developments will affect the future of Indian-Chinese relations. Much depends on how the Chinese react to the growth of Indian nuclear and ballistic missile programs and, by the same token, how the Chinese develop their nuclear and ballistic missile capabilities. This in its turn is likely to be affected by American talk of deploying missile Defence systems. If America proceeds with its Strategic Defence Initiative (SDI), will the Chinese respond by carrying through further modernization of their own nuclear forces? Will they expand the scope and capabilities of their weapons?

If they do, this will provide ammunition for those in India who want to see an expansion of the ballistic and nuclear weapons programs. It will do so regardless of whether or not these expanded forces are targeted on India or are even *capable* of being targeted on India. The lunatic fringe will point out that the Chinese are modernizing. They will remind us that, to quote American realists, it is not intentions but capabilities that matter. If it is good for the Americans, they will say, it is good for us. Nuclear weapons can be brought to bear on us and can be used to coerce us. Of course the lunatic fringe still remains fairly small and a fringe. However, that too, may change.

7

Major Concerns In China's ASEAN Policy

The end of the Cold War and the settlement of the Cambodian conflict opened a new chapter in the development of ASEAN-China relations. Four key characteristics distinguish ASEAN-China ties in the post-Cold War era from that of the preceding period. The first feature is the disappearance of the ideological barriers that eventually paved the way for the restoration or establishment of diplomatic ties between China and all ASEAN states by 1991. The second characteristic is the importance of economic links that have created both convergent and divergent interests for the two sides.

The third feature is the salience of the Spratly territorial disputes in shaping the ASEAN-China interactions. The final—equally important but less noted feature—is the gradual emergence of multilateralism as a mode of diplomatic interaction between the People's Republic of China (PRC) and the ASEAN countries. Throughout the Cold War period, China's interactions with ASEAN states were conducted solely on a bilateral basis. No institutionalized linkage was formally forged between China and the regional organization. Viewed in this light, the attendance by the then Chinese Foreign Minister Qian Qichen at the opening session of the 24th ASEAN Ministerial Meeting on July 1991 as a guest of Malaysia was an important event for Sino-ASEAN relations. This was followed by China's presence in the ASEAN meeting in its capacity as the group's consultative partner in 1992, as well as its attendance at the inaugural meeting of the ASEAN Regional Forum (ARF) in 1994.

Together, these events marked the beginning of the multilateral process between China and the ASEAN states. It must be noted that Beijing's move to involve itself in ASEAN activities since the early 1990s was part of the country's "good-neighbourliness" policy [mulin zhengce] that aimed at strengthening its ties with the neighbouring countries in the wake of the Tiananmen Incident in 1989, rather than a flesh orientation in the conduct of Chinese foreign policy.

Bilateralism remained the principal thrust of China's policy towards Southeast Asian countries. However, as a range of multi-level and multi-sector cooperation mechanisms developed one after another largely by ASEAN's initiative throughout the 1990s-notably but not exhaustively, the creations of ARF in 1994, the China-ASEAN senior official political consultation in 1995, as well as the ASEAN-China and ASEAN Plus Three (APT, i.e. ASEAN plus China, Japan and Korea) Summits in 1997 — China's increasingly active involvement in these multilateral forums has considerably shaped the dynamics of its ASEAN policy.

At the turn of the new century, multilateral diplomacy has become an important component of China's ASEAN policy in the eyes of many analysts. While China's involvement in these regional multilateral institutions has not been an overlooked phenomenon, it is nonetheless an understudied field of inquiry. To date, there is no major scholarly work that attempts to examine the dynamics of China's participation in these regional multilateral institutions in a systematic manner.

Although there are a number of important writings on China's involvement in the ARF, studies on China's participation in the APT and the ASEAN-China cooperation (also known as the ASEAN-China dialogue, hereafter ACC) remain sparse in the literature. This is surprising, considering that China's ASEAN policy is not only implemented through and affected by its participation in the ARF, but also involves other regional institutions particularly ACC and APT. Moreover, the fact that from the mid-1990s until early 2003 China's policy towards these three institutions had been managed by the same division within the Chinese Foreign Ministry's apparatus (namely the Division for Regional Cooperation of the Asian Department), strongly reflects the intertwined nature of these institutions for Chinese policymakers.

For these reasons, any efforts to examine the linkage between China's multilateral involvement and its ASEAN policy must take into consideration the interconnectedness of China's involvement in all three institutions. This selection of cases, however, does not imply that China's multilateral interactions with ASEAN states is only limited to these three institutions. There are other regional multilateral forums that involve both China and ASEAN countries, such as the Asia Pacific Economic Cooperation (APEC), the Asia-Europe Meeting (ASEM), and the Thai-initiated Asian Cooperation Dialogue (ACD).

The reason why these institutions are excluded in this study is that they are not driven by ASEAN and that their impact on China's ASEAN policy is less discernable as compared with the ARF, ACC and APT.

By focusing on China's involvement in these ASEAN-led institutions, this chapter seeks to answer three questions: First, has the PRC's multilateral involvement in these institutions led to the emergence of multilateralism in China's ASEAN policy? Second, if there is, what are key characteristics of China's strand of multilateralism? Finally, what is the key impetus driving China's multilateral involvement? In this study, multilateralism is defined as the tendency and preference of a country to use multilateral diplomacy as a means to attain its foreign policy ends. Our assumption is that, a state's multilateral involvement does not necessarily signify the rise of multilateralism in the country's foreign policy.

Rather, multilateralism is regarded as having emerged only if and when multilateral diplomacy has begun to play a complementary rather than a subsidiary role to bilateral diplomacy as a vehicle to achieve the foreign policy objective(s) at hand. Methodologically, it is difficult to measure in exact terms the relative importance of multilateral diplomacy vis-a-vis bilateral diplomacy in any country's foreign policy. Nevertheless, it is possible to ascertain if a multilateral approach constitutes an indispensable or negligible component in a country's diplomacy.

One could perform the task by looking at the degree of a country's reliance on multilateral means vis-a-vis bilateral ones in materializing its policy ends. That is, if a country's policy objectives in a particular realm can be achieved by largely or entirely relying on bilateral diplomatic approach, multilateralism does not exist. On the contrary, if a country's policy ends can only be attained by the use of multilateral diplomacy or a combination of bilateral and multilateral diplomacy, a case can be made for the emergence of multilateralism in the country's foreign policy orientation.

In short, multilateralism emerges in so far as multilateral diplomacy has become an indispensable means to attaining a country's foreign policy ends. The chapter consists of three parts. The first part traces the changing patterns of Beijing's participation in the ASEAN-led regional institutions over the past decade. It shows that China's multilateral involvement, albeit with initial reservations, has led to the rise of multilateralism in its ASEAN policy at the turn of the twenty-first century.

The second part addresses the key features of China's multilateralism, namely a preference for multilateral economic institutions, a reliance on the use of soft power, as well as an ability to capitalize on the reciprocal relationship between multilateralism and bilateralism. The final part contends that China's multilateral involvement has been motivated by an underlying aspiration to shape the "rules of the game" for regional cooperation. It demonstrates how China's calculated attempts in influencing the designs and directions of the regional institutions, have helped the country to advance a range of its foreign policy goals.

CHINA'S INVOLVEMENT IN THE ASEAN-LED MULTILATERAL INSTITUTIONS: THREE PHASES

Based on the patterns and levels of its involvement, China's participation in the ASEAN-driven institutions can be divided into three major phases:

PHASE ONE (EARLY 1990S UNTIL 1995): PASSIVE INVOLVEMENT

Throughout this period, China's perception of multilateral institutions largely remained cautious and suspicious. Due to its deep-seated concerns that multilateral security arrangements might be detrimental to its national sovereignty, China did not respond positively to the proposal of creating a multilateral security forum in the Asia-Pacific that was first put forward in the early 1990s.

Although China eventually decided to join the new security forum—named as the ASEAN Regional Forum or ARF—in 1994 and agreed to ASEAN's suggestion to embark on an annual consultation on political and security issues at the senior official level (hereafter the ASEAN-China SOC) in 1995, Beijing's involvement in these multilateral institutions was passive and apprehensive. The prime intention of Chinese officials at these meetings was to ward off any development that might jeopardize China's national interests.

China's reservations about ARF at the time had to do with its concerns in four specific issue areas. First, Beijing was worried that the proposed forum would be dominated and used by Washington to interfere in other countries' internal affairs, as has been the case in most international organizations. Second, Beijing was uneasy about the likelihood that ASEAN might use the forum to internationalize the Spratly Islands dispute and take a united stance against China. Third, Beijing was alarmed by the possibility that the Taiwan issue might be included in the ARF agenda.

Finally, Beijing was concerned about the problem of military transparency. These concerns led China to feel that the forum was created with the intention of checking its power and limiting its strategic choices. Despite this vigilance, China eventually decided to take part in the security forum. A report prepared by the influential Chinese Academy of Social Sciences (CASS)' Institute of Asia Pacific Studies (IAPS) reflects that China's decision was a product of a careful calculation over strategic benefits and political costs.

The report recognizes that the emergence of multilateral security cooperation mechanism in Asia Pacific is an unstoppable trend. It thus asserts that it is imperative for China to involve itself in the multilateral process in a pragmatic way. Specifically, it recommends that China should proactively shape the development of the mechanism from within, in order to ensure a favourable position in a fluid and complex security environment. Non-participation is not considered an option, as it would only result in self-isolation.

Non-participation might also run the risk of arousing ASEAN's suspicious about China's intentions in the region. For Beijing, the latter scenario must be avoided at a time when it was determined to cultivate a closer relationship with its southern neighbours. As noted by Alice Ba, ASEAN gained importance in China's foreign policy reevaluation after Tiananmen, offering attractive investment and trading partners, as well as potential political allies that shared many of Beijing's developmental priorities and sensitivities about external interference.

Beijing's involvement in the newly established forum, however, was not immediately translated into enthusiastic participation. Driven principally by the aforementioned concerns, China cautiously guarded against any institutional development of ARF that might challenge its sovereignty. This can be seen by China's response at the second ARF meeting in Brunei in 1995. At the meeting, participants discussed the ARF Concept Paper that outlined the forum's future development and institutional structure.

The paper proposed that the development of the forum in three stages, namely (i) promotion of confidence-building measures (CBMs); (ii) preventive diplomacy (PD) mechanisms; and (iii) conflict-resolution mechanisms. China had no problem with the first two stages, but voiced its objections to the third. The Chinese representative insisted that the ARF is only a dialogue forum and hence should not be designed as a formal institution that aimed to resolve conflicts. As a result, the third stage was modified as "the elaboration of approaches to conflict". This clearly reflects Beijing's reluctance in seeing ARF to develop into a CSCE-style, highly institutionalized security mechanism.

PHASE-II (1996-99): ACTIVE PARTICIPATION

After a period of participating and observing for several years, China gradually changed its perception of multilateral cooperation. It increasingly realized that multilateral forums like ARF and the ASEAN-China SOC might not necessarily be harmful to its national security. Instead, multilateral cooperation could be used as a diplomatic platform to promote its own foreign policy agenda. During this period, although bilateral diplomacy still remained the main thrust of China's ASEAN policy, multilateral diplomacy had slowly begun to play a supplementary role. This was indicated by China's increasingly active participation in ARF activities and other forums for multilateral cooperation in the region.

The shift in China's perceptions of the multilateral forum was due to two important factors that Beijing came to realize in the process of participating. The first is the institutional features of the ARF. The forum, being an extended model of ASEAN, has been operationalized on the basis of the "ASEAN Way" which is featured in the forms of informal, wide consultative, consensus and incremental approach.

According to Foot, such features enable China to participate in a comfortable manner. There is less need for Beijing to form coalitions of supporters to vote against any agenda that may harm its national interest. The second factor that assuages China's suspicion of multilateral institution is ASEAN's unique role in maintaining equal relationships with major powers. For China, the fact that ARF is led by ASEAN and not other big powers such as the United States and Japan is politically acceptable and in fact preferable. These two factors, together, convinced Beijing that the ARF would not develop into an anti-China alliance.

Perceptual change logically led to a shift in China's actual involvement. In April 1996, Beijing offered to co-chair with Manila the next ARF intersessional support group (ISG) meeting on CBMs. In 1997, in addition to hosting the ISG meeting China also sent representatives to take part in the first meeting of defence college chiefs held in Manila. The following years witnessed China's further widening of involvement in the forum. Through its participation in various CBM activities, China hoped to reassure its neighbours and to dampen the "China threat" theory.

In addition, by repeatedly stressing the "New Security Concept" [Xin Anquan Guan] through ARF and other multilateral meetings, China also hoped to promote what they regard as the most appropriate means for organizing the post-Cold War security relations in the Asia Pacific. Beyond the ARF framework, China had also been actively involved in the expanded ACC and the newly created APT process.

In July 1996, China became a full dialogue partner of ASEAN. The following year witnessed the creation of the ASEAN-China Joint Cooperation Committee (ACJCC) in February, as well as China's attendance at the first informal APT Summit and the first informal ASEAN-China summit in July. By 1997, the ACC had evolved into a full-fledged diplomatic arrangement that involves mechanisms at the summit, ministerial, as well as senior officials working levels. The changing atmosphere in the ASEAN-China SOC during this period was particularly noteworthy. Established in 1995, the annual SOC was created by the two sides to prepare for the ministerial meeting, and to review the ASEAN-China relations in a "friendly and relaxed atmosphere".

As it turned out, the ambience of the first few meetings was hardly a relaxed one. Owing to the fact that the meetings were overshadowed by conflicting concerns over the South China Sea disputes, the mood was tense and the tone stiff. Regular interactions between the two sides in the subsequent years, however, have gradually transformed the atmosphere into a much more relaxed and constructive mood. Issues that were previously deemed sensitive are now brought up freely and discussed in a comfortable manner. China's involvement in the APT process has mostly been enthusiastic. At the second APT Summit, China proposed to organize a meeting involving the deputy governors of central banks of the APT countries.

This proposal materialized the next year, when thirteen central bank deputy governors from the region met for the first time to discuss financial cooperation between them. China then further proposed that the meeting be held regularly. Four factors explain China's enthusiasm towards the APT process. First, China's earlier involvements in the

ARF, ACC, APEC and ASEM have substantially enhanced Beijing's level of confidence over regional cooperation. Second, Beijing learned from the 1997-98 Asian financial crisis that, given the high level of interdependency among the East Asian economies, financial problems of one country would inevitably produce contagious effects for other countries in the region.

Like other East Asian countries, China realizes that financial cooperation is imperative to prevent a recurrence. China thus takes part actively in regional cooperation like the Chiang Mai Initiative. Third, China recognizes that the wave of globalization has become irreversible. Regionalism is seen as a means to protect national interest against the onslaught of globalization. Finally, based on geopolitical calculations, China views APT as an ideal platform to push for East Asian cooperation that is likely to expand its political influence and to reshape regional security order in the long run.

The same period also witnessed China's growing involvement in other multilateral institutions outside the ambit of China-ASEAN interaction. For instance, in 1996 China, together with Russia and three Central Asian countries, gathered in Shanghai to initiate what was known as the "Shanghai Five" cooperation process. In addition, China also took part in the first ASEM meeting in 1996. Taken together, these developments reflect China's rising level of comfort and confidence with multilateral diplomacy.

PHASE-III (2000-PRESENT): PROACTIVE PROPOSITION

China's embrace of multilateral diplomacy reached new heights in 2000, when it proposed the idea of establishing the ASEAN-China Free Trade Area (ACFTA) at the APT and the ASEAN-China Summits. In November 2001, leaders from the two sides reached the agreement to establish the proposed FTA within the next ten years. The development signified that, unlike the two earlier stages in which Beijing merely responded to ideas put forward by ASEAN, Beijing has now entered a new phase in which it begins to proactively initiate bold regional proposals. Multilateral forums have since been used as valuable diplomatic platforms that are aimed at transforming its foreign policy propositions into long-term strategic reality.

The ACFTA plan, in particular, is instrumental to achieving many of China's foreign policy goals, in both economic and political realms. In the former case, Beijing anticipates that ACFTA will serve to expand Sino-ASEAN trade and investment links. ASEAN has long been China's fifth largest trading partner. With an average growth rate of 20 per cent since 1990, ASEAN-China trade totalled US$39.5 billion in 2000. ACFTA is expected to further enhance the Sino-ASEAN trade. According to the ASEAN-China Economic Expert Group, the FTA will increase China's exports to ASEAN by 55.1 per cent, and will increase Southeast Asian exports to China by 48 per cent. By creating a liberal and facilitative investment regime, the FTA is also likely to enhance Sino-ASEAN investment cooperation.

In addition, ACFTA is hoped to help China's efforts to acquire much needed energy and raw resources. As the Chinese economy continues to grow, supply of raw materials and energy resources has become increasingly critical. As a resource-endowed region, Southeast Asia is an important source for China's present and future needs. Although the supply from the region will not meet China's overall demand, it would nonetheless help Beijing to diversify its sources of raw imports, similar to Japan in Southeast Asia during the 1990s. China has recently stepped up its efforts to secure resources from the region. For instance, it is acquiring liquid natural gas and pulp from Indonesia, and rubber and palm oil from Malaysia.

This factor, combined with the enhanced Sino-ASEAN trade and investment links, is creating favourable conditions for China's future economic development. More importantly for China, the ACFTA is expected to create considerable political advantages. As rightly observed by Sheng Lijun, this is the first time China has found common interest to engage all ASEAN states constructively and exclusively to talk about cooperation, rather than quarrelling over issues like the Spratly dispute.

The FTA negotiations would mean that Beijing could engage ASEAN capitals constructively for at least ten years under one friendly framework. The ACFTA thus can be viewed as "political confidence-building" for both sides. Over time, this is likely to expand Chinese influence in the region. The political benefits of the ACFTA will be explored further below. Here, it is suffice to say that these goals would help Beijing to transform its political ties with the ASEAN states, and to reshape the regional order in Asia-Pacific. Clearly, it will be difficult for China to effectively pursue these economic and political goals if it relies merely on bilateral diplomacy.

It seems clear that multilateral diplomacy now plays a complementary rather than supplementary role in China's ASEAN policy. The ACFTA plan is the first of a series of Beijing's carefully calculated moves to use multilateral forums to attain its foreign policy ends. At the 7th China-ASEAN Summit in 2003, Beijing joined the grouping's Treaty of Amity and Cooperation (TAC), making itself the first major power to join the non-aggressive pact. More significantly, upon Beijing's initiative, China and ASEAN also signed the "Joint Declaration on Strategic Partnership" at the same meeting.

This partnership, despite its "non-aligned, non-military, and non-exclusive" nature, is likely to make the two sides move closer to each other. In the APT, China recommended that the institution should function as the main channel of cooperation among East Asian countries. It also proposed the APT countries to expand their collaboration from purely economic cooperation to political and security dialogue. Beijing specifically stressed the need for non-traditional security cooperation. It made a parallel attempt in ARF. At the 2003 meeting, China proposed to create the "ARF Security Policy Conference" (ASPC), attended by military personnel of the Asian Pacific countries.

The latter move is a great leap forward for a country that had reservations about multilateral security cooperation just a decade ago. Beyond the auspices of the Sino-ASEAN framework, this period has also witnessed the inauguration of the Boao Forum for Asia (BFA), the expansion of the Shanghai Five into the Shanghai Cooperative Organization (SCO), China's accession to the Bangkok Agreement, as well as China's hosting of APEC Summit, the Third Foreign Ministers Meeting of the ACD, and three rounds of the Six-Party Talks. The timing of these developments is by no means coincidental. Rather, it unequivocally marks the emergence of China's multilateralism at the regional level.

MAJOR CHARACTERISTICS OF CHINA'S MULTILATERALISM

The preceding section has discussed the trend of China's multilateral involvement. What does the trend tell us about the traits of China's multilateralism? This section elaborates on three major features that constitute China's strand of multilateralism. China's enthusiasm about ACFTA is in sharp contrast to its cautious attitude towards the implementation of preventive diplomacy in the ARF. China stresses that, in view of the complexity of security issues and the cultural heterogeneity of the region, ARF should progress gradually and step-by-step.

Specifically, China contends that confidence building should remain the main thrust of the ARF, and that the forum should continue to deepen the discussion and practice on CBMs before moving towards the implementation of the PD stage. The divergent postures reflect Beijing's tendency of accentuating multilateral economic cooperation over security institutions. The fact that China shows different patterns of participation in different types of multilateral institutions may well be explained by the notion that different institutions bear different degrees of what Keohane and Ruggie term as expectations of "diffuse reciprocity".

For multilateral institutions that China regards as bearing a high degree of diffuse reciprocity—that is, short-term concession may bring about larger long-term benefit, or today's sacrifice in one area may bring about larger benefits in other areas in the future—China appears to have participated in a more proactive and enthusiastic manner. The ACC and the APT fall into this category. On the ACFTA arrangement, Beijing has not only agreed to the "early harvest package" that will give ASEAN states earlier access to Chinese markets than other WTO members, it has also granted special treatment to Vietnam, Cambodia, Laos, and Myanmar.

China obviously hopes that the short-term generosity in economic cooperation will lead to long-term political and economic gains. Similarly, China's active involvement in APT is based on an anticipation that its diplomatic efforts will bring about favourable geopolitical and economic outcomes. However, the reciprocity in multilateral security institutions is much more problematic. According to Guo Longlong, a senior researcher at the Shanghai Institute for International Studies, participation in multilateral institutions always involves a certain degree of concession of sovereignty. In the case of economic institutions, this concession can be exchanged or compensated with market benefits.

However, in the case of security institutions, a more intrusive arrangement may result in the erosion of national sovereignty and territorial integrity. Such a concern explains China's cautious stance towards PD implementation, which will inevitably involve particular types of intrusive practices. China's cautious stance over the PD issue reveals that in spite of Beijing's growing comfort towards the multilateral security forum, China is still concerned about developments that might directly challenge its sovereignty. It dichotomizes security agreements into "less restrictive" and "highly restrictive"; and apparently prefers the former to the latter. For this reason, while China continues to be actively involved in ARF, its bottom line is to ensure that the forum will retain its diplomatic and political nature, and not evolve into an intrusive security mechanism that could undermine its strategic interests.

A RELIANCE ON THE USE OF SOFT POWER

The second feature is China's readiness to use its growing soft power—notably economic leverage and national image—as a persuasive means to translate its influence into concrete policy interests. Within the economic sphere, ACFTA clearly is Beijing's prioritized tool that is hoped to bring about a number of political benefits. To begin with, China's ASEAN watchers view that improvement of Sino-ASEAN economic relations is likely to alleviate the China threat theory both in the security and economic senses. In the security realm, close economic links between the two sides is seen as a boon to the management of the Spratly dispute. For instance, CASS researcher Tang Shiping writes:

If the economic gap between ASEAN and China widens, these countries will be more concerned about the outcome of the Spratly problem. On the contrary, if these countries can benefit from China's growth, they will be more inclined to emphasize on consultation (in managing the Spratly issue).

In the economic domain, China has adopted a number of approaches to assuage ASEAN concerns. These include granting ASEAN access to its market earlier than other WTO members, encouraging Chinese firms to invest in Southeast Asia, as well as providing financial aid for ASEAN's infrastructure development. Through such "co-prosperity" approaches, China hopes to convince ASEAN that "a prosperous China is an opportunity, rather than a challenge, to ASEAN". ACFTA is also expected to bring Beijing other political mileages. Most notable is the closer collaboration between China and ASEAN over international issues.

At the moment, the two sides have already seen eye-to-eye on issues such as human rights, multipolarity, and developing countries' position in the global economic order. China hopes that once Sino-ASEAN economic interests became even more intertwined as a result of ACFTA, the two sides will work together even closer on regional and international issues. No less significant for Beijing is that better Sino-ASEAN economic ties also means that Taipei will be left with little room to carry out economic diplomacy with ASEAN. China's soft power does not only derive from its growing economic clout, but also stems from its emerging image as a responsible power.

During the Asian financial crisis in 1997-98, China responded by contributing to the IMF-led rescue package for Thailand and Indonesia, and pledging not to devalue the renminbi. Beijing's moves, whether or not carried out entirely altruistically, helped avoid another round of regional economic downturn, thus projecting China as a positive factor in managing the regional crisis. Along with its increasingly cooperative pattern of involvement in regional institutions, China's actions have helped to project it as a responsible and cooperative big power.

For China, this newly emerged image is not just an end in itself. Rather, it is an effective means for Beijing to materialize its foreign policy goals. Cultivating a responsible image is a sine qua non for China's efforts to alleviate the China threat theory, to expand its influence, as well as to construct a favourable regional order. As noted by two Chinese analysts, since political influence can only be effective "when other states not only respect your power but also your opinion, China reasons that the best way for regional political influence is through cultivating an image of 'a responsible (regional) great power'".

Largely driven by this consciousness, China has made numerous efforts to further deepen its cooperative image. Examples are: acceding to TAC, expressing its willingness to accede the Protocol to the Treaty on the Southeast Asia Nuclear Weapon-Free Zone (SEANWFZ), as well as highlighting the peaceful nature of its rise.

THE RECIPROCAL RELATIONSHIP BETWEEN MULTILATERALISM AND BILATERALISM

Having emphasized the role of multilateralism in China's ASEAN policy, I do not mean to imply that bilateralism has lost its traditional significance. To be sure, close bilateral ties between China and individual ASEAN members have always been an essential foundation for Beijing's multilateral diplomacy. On the other hand, China's increasing involvement in regional multilateral institutions has in turn enhanced ASEAN's political trust in Beijing, thus strengthening the bilateral ties between China and individual ASEAN members.

Between 1999 and 2000, China has succeeded in signing bilateral political agreements with all ASEAN countries that are aimed at boosting bilateral long-term cooperation in the new century. Moreover, Chinese leaders have made full use of their attendance at almost all multilateral forums to conduct bilateral meetings with their ASEAN counterparts. For China, the relationship between multilateralism and bilateralism, thus, is a reciprocal one. Interestingly, the dynamics of this reciprocal relationship are not only found in the Sino-ASEAN relations; it can also be observed in China's relations with other big powers particularly the United States and Japan. The annual ARF ministerial meeting, for instance, has provided opportunities for Beijing and Washington to talk on the sidelines.

These opportunities are especially important for both sides at times when direct bilateral diplomacy is difficult to conduct, as illustrated by Tang Jiaxuan and Colin Powell's meeting in July 2001 in the aftermath of the EP-3 incident. The same can be said for Beijing-Tokyo interaction. In addition to the ARF meeting, the two countries also have opportunities to meet at the annual APT Summit since 1997, as well as the "China-Japan-Korea Leaders' Meeting" since 1999. As observed by Susan Shirk, in recent years Beijing has attempted to use the APT as a platform to improve the Sino-Japanese relations.

THE "RULES OF THE GAME" FOR REGIONAL COOPERATION

In this section, it is argued that China's rising multilateralism has been driven by its underlying aspiration to shape the "rules of the game" for regional institutions, for the ultimate ends of fulfilling the needs of a range of foreign policy concerns. Unlike other global multilateral institutions at whose organizational designs and rules had largely been determined prior to Beijing's participation, the embryonic regional multilateral institutions — most notably the ASEAN-led institutions and the SCO but also the ASEM and ACD — provide PRC an opportunity to shape their design, dynamic, and direction, which in combination is bound to have a far-reaching impact on the evolving regional order in the twenty-first century.

China's determination in influencing the institutional design of the regional forums is clearly illustrated by Beijing's attempts to avoid the ARF turning into a highly intrusive and institutionalized security mechanism as discussed earlier. It is also reflected in Beijing's preference in retaining the diplomatic and political nature of the 24-member forum. In the APT, Beijing has urged the East Asian countries to move beyond economic cooperation and to strengthen their security dialogue and consultation. In a similar vein, Beijing has also shown its readiness to stimulate the dynamic of regional cooperation.

An example is China's enthusiasm for developing the ASEAN-China dialogue into a vibrant web of multilevel and multi-sector cooperation. As noted above, by 1997 the ACC has developed as a full-fledged diplomatic mechanism spanning the summit, ministerial, and senior official levels. Over the past few years, the mechanism has stretched into various semi- and non-governmental sectors that include research institutes, the media, youth, and the business community. Its scope has also expanded beyond the realms of political dialogue and trade cooperation, to include agricultural cooperation, transport infrastructure development, as well as energy cooperation. While it is important not to attribute this entirely to China's deliberate acts, it is safe to say that the PRC has played a crucial role in pushing for the expansions.

Over time, these expansions have interwoven into a web of interdependence between China and ASEAN. Such a web has served as an essential institutional foundation for China to advance its policy ends, as illustrated in the initiation and negotiation processes of ACFTA. Without these institutionalized and regularized consultative mechanisms, it would have been difficult for China to advance its various propositions toward ASEAN. More critically, the PRC has demonstrated its desire to influence the direction of the regional institutions to its strategic advantage. In ACC, Chinese initiative for the Sino-ASEAN strategic partnership was proposed with an original idea of calling for "coordination" in foreign and security policy between the two sides.

In ARF, China's ASPC proposal is seen as its attempt to prevent the Western-sponsored Shangri-La Dialogue from emerging as the key regional security mechanism, and to "start a separate track". Beijing's assertions in the APT reflect an even more important long-term calculation. China has persistently stressed the need to make the APT the main channel to boost the overall East Asian cooperation. It has been supportive of the goal of establishing an East Asian Community, and took the initiative to push for the creation of the Network of East Asia Think-Tanks (NEAT).

More recently, Beijing offered to host the second East Asian Summit in 2007. China's enthusiasm about East Asian cooperation, clearly, is driven by its aspiration to shape the direction of the extant regional institutions. As noted by Tang,

If the East Asia community can gradually emerge from the basis of the APT process, the function of the existing multilateral institutions is likely to undergo a fundamental qualitative change [emphasis added]. For instance, the ARF is likely to transform itself from being a platform for ASEAN to engage in security dialogues with other [non-ASEAN] states, into a platform for East Asian countries to forge security dialogues with other [non-East Asian] states. This will lead to a situation in which the East Asian countries would first seek to reach their consensus within the forum [before they proceed to talk to other non-East Asian countries].

For Beijing, regional cooperation with favourable rules of the game—that take the forms of advantageous institutional design, dynamics, and directions—is central to achieving its foreign policy goals towards the region. These policy objectives are myriad and interrelated, covering political, economic, and ideational interests, as we have discussed elsewhere. Three are of crucial importance, and deserve careful scrutiny here. They are: (a) maintaining a stable regional environment; (b) cultivating a multipolar international order; and (c) expanding its political influence.

What follows is an illustration on how multilateral institutions with favourable designs have enabled Beijing to advance these policy interests. The role of the regional institutions in helping China to preserve a stable external environment can be seen from the management of the South China Sea disputes. Realizing that it is unlikely to resolve the dispute in near future, China has proposed the idea of "shelving the dispute and developing together". Such proposition enables China to insist on its sovereign claim, while avoiding direct confrontation with ASEAN states.

ASEAN states, on their part, have persisted in exploring more concrete ways to manage the dispute, In this regard, the two sides have held different preferences.

While ASEAN has always sought to negotiate the problem on a multilateral basis, China insists to approach it bilaterally. The ASEAN-China SOC — an exclusive dialogue mechanism that involves senior officials from the 11 countries — has provided the two sides an acceptable platform to discuss the issue since 1995. In 2000, the SOC established a working group to explore the possibility of creating a code of conduct in the disputed area. After three years of discussion, China and ASEAN signed the Declaration on Conduct in the South China Sea in November 2002. For China, this declaration is the best it could hope for.

In addition to protecting its sovereignty, the declaration helps to preserve regional stability and a stable Sino-ASEAN relationship. More importantly, it also reduces the possibility for external powers to interfere in the disputes. Regional institutions are also central to China's aim to promote a multipolar international order. This goal is closely related to the post-Cold War U.S.-China relations. For Beijing, pushing for multipolarity appears to be its only viable option to balance Washington's preponderant power. Partly due to the nature of Sino-American relations that features both cooperative and competitive impulses, and partly due to China's limited comprehensive national strength, Beijing knows that it could only push for this end via diplomatic means, and at the regional level.

The ASEAN-led regional institutions thus are critical for this larger goal. China's multipolarity policy goes hand-in-hand with its move to push for regionalism. Through its efforts to promote regional cooperation and integration, Beijing aims to accelerate the emergence of a tripartite world between NAFTA, EU and East Asian groups. Chinese scholars envisage that a successful East Asian integration will substantially enhance the possibility of a multipolar world. In their view, as regional integration deepens and widens, common interests among the East Asian countries will be increased, and their common identity strengthened. As these countries are increasingly forming a collectivity, their interests will become more and more different from those of the United States.

Over time, their relationships with the United States are expected to adjust drastically. Finally, China sees multilateral forums as instrumental to expanding its international influence, especially towards Southeast Asia. Due to geographical, historical and cultural reasons, the region has always been seen as a periphery to which Beijing could exert its influence more effectively. Moreover, considering that other major powers—namely the United States, Japan, and increasingly, India—have also been eyeing the region to wield their influence, Beijing has found it imperative to maintain, and whenever possible, to expand its clout in this adjacent region. The advent of regional institutions seems to have offered Beijing a valuable platform to advance these ends.

Specifically, China has adopted a three-prong strategy to increase its influence via regional cooperation:

a) Trade and economic cooperation. At the core of this strategy are free trade arrangements and regional financial cooperation among East Asian countries.

b) Political cooperation. Beijing's focus is twofold: deepening ASEAN-China political trust and cultivating East Asian consciousness.

c) Security cooperation.

These three components are mutually reinforcing. Each requires a multilateral setting. Thus far, China has made progress in all three areas. ASEAN and China began to execute the early harvest plan in January 2004, and signed the Agreement on Trade in Goods in November 2004. Total ASEAN-China trade reached US$105.8 billion by the end of 2004, reaching a target set by Chinese Premier Wen Jiabao one year earlier than anticipated. In comparison, ASEAN-U.S. trade was US$120 billion in 2003.

Politically, a more benign view of China has emerged in the region. Political trust between the two sides has developed tremendously. In the security sphere, the strategic partnership action plan calls for increased dialogues in defence and military fields. Simultaneously, the two sides have forged cooperation on non-traditional security issues, ranging from SARS and avian flu to a tsunami warning system. All in all, the net effect is a steady growth of Chinese influence in the region. As observed by an American security analyst, China's present strategic position within the region has never been stronger.

The preceding discussion reveals that multilateralism has emerged as an essential component in China's ASEAN policy at the turn of the twenty-first century. While the creation of the multilateral institutions was not initiated nor preferred by China in the beginning, the PRC has in the course of participation gradually shifted its perceptions and policies toward multilateralism. Over the past decade, China's views of these institutions have undergone drastic change, from caution and suspicion to optimism and enthusiasm. Instead of perceiving multilateral forums as malign arrangements that could undermine its sovereignty and strategic interests, Beijing now sees multilateral institutions as useful vehicles for advancing its own policy objectives.

Such perceptual changes have slowly but significantly led to a greater emphasis on multilateral diplomacy in China's Southeast Asia policy. Two main arguments can be posited. First, multilateralism now plays a complementary rather than a supplementary role to bilateralism in China's ASEAN policy. Second, China's multilateral involvement has been driven by an aspiration to shape the rules of the game for regional cooperation.

This trend is likely to endure in the decades to come. In the long run, China's mounting multilateralism will bring profound implications for its overall foreign policy orientation. As Beijing continues to push for a host of multilateral initiatives in shaping the future direction of regional forums, it will inevitably depart from the long-held stance of "never aspire to lead" in international affairs. How the development will impact on the emerging regional order is an issue of crucial importance, because the way China exercises its newly acquired power at the regional level today will provide some clue as to how the fast rising power will act on the global stage tomorrow.

8
China's Efforts As A Responsible Power

There are certainly some doubts about the accuracy of such statistics. In particular, in a country, which still at times of inflationary stress relies on price controls for certain key commodities and raw materials, inflation may be underestimated and output overestimated. Output growth may also tend to be overestimated in the transition from a traditional to a market economy. Nevertheless the evidence of rapid expansion is clearly visible, especially in the coastal regions. Moreover, the increasing openness of the Chinese economy means that domestic growth is being accompanied by a similar, indeed even faster, expansion of exports and imports. These latter data can be checked, roughly, against the counterpart data of other countries; data, for example, of trade flows between China and other countries passing through Hong Kong, which have been growing at around 20 per cent per annum in real terms, are consistent.

The aggregate growth data can also be checked more or less, by looking at personal consumption statistics from nation-wide household sample surveys, of which some are shown overleaf. While few aggregate economic data for any country are fully reliable, and inter-country comparisons particularly suspect, (owing to differences of taste and the unreliability of exchange rates as measuring rods), there is no good basis for dismissing China's recent growth as representing, to any serious extent, a statistical illusion. It may nonetheless be helpful both to place China's real income in an international context, and to illustrate how different such comparisons can look when measured by the official exchange rate or on an estimated purchasing power parity (PPP) basis.

Moreover, neither the exchange rate nor the PPP comparisons suggest as fast a growth rate between 1985 and 1992/93. While this underscores the unreliability of all growth rate and comparative income data, one cannot pinpoint which, if any, of these various data might be incorrect. They all suffer from various weaknesses. In their Human Development Report the UN ranked countries on an HDI index, which is a weighted combination of life expectancy, adult literacy, years of schooling and income (PPP$). China had an HDI value of 0.644, just below South Africa, 0.650 and above Peru, 0.642; Canada, 0.932 was top and Guinea, 0.191 bottom.

In Eastern Europe and the Former Soviet Union (EEFSU), age specific mortality rates have increased since the collapse of communism, sharply so for middle-aged men,; by contrast in China a reduction in infant mortality has raised life expectancy at birth from 67.9 years in 1981 to 68.5 in 1990; while age specific mortality and life expectancy beyond childhood have remained static. Given the huge size of China, whose population at about 1.2 billion represents almost 25 per cent of the world's estimated population, the acceleration of growth there represents a massive uplift for mankind as a whole.

Together with the recent sharp improvement in India's growth (by 2030, India is expected to have a population of more than 1.53 billion), the last decade has, almost certainly, seen the greatest improvement in global living standards ever recorded, despite transitional problems in Eastern Europe and the former Soviet Union (EEFSU), continuing African stagnation, Eurosclerosis, etc. Moreover, Chinese growth rates have been, and are predicted to remain, at a level consistent with a take-off into self-sustaining growth.

They are, and may remain, comparable with the earlier experience of rapidly expanding economies both in East Asia and in the USA. If so, according to World Bank estimates, the Chinese economic area [China, Hong Kong and Taiwan] might, in purchasing power parity terms, become the world's largest economy, in absolute, but not of course in per capita terms, within one decade.

This development raises a whole host of questions: why, and how, China's progress from a Communist commands economy towards a decentralised market economy has been, in terms of real economic growth, so different from, and so much better (so far) than those countries engaged in the same transition in EEFSU. Such differential growth has occurred despite China running into some seemingly similar problems as in EEF-SU, for example problems in controlling and improving loss-making State Owned Enterprises (SOEs), relatively declining fiscal revenues accruing to the Central Government, endemic and occasionally severe inflationary pressures, and a lack of the underlying institutional infrastructure (e.g. laws on bankruptcy and property rights, standardised and transparent accountancy, etc.) that supports a market economy.

We shall also ask whether these deficiencies or political problems more broadly, might yet reverse recent economic success in China. One issue, however, which we shall not explore, is what continuing growth in China (and India) might mean for us in Europe. Growth in developing Asian countries has already been blamed for widening income inequalities between unskilled male workers and skilled workers, and for the continuing shift out of manufacturing into (information-based) services in the West, but for reasons of both space and comparative expertise we shall leave such analysis to others and concentrate on economic developments within China. The Chinese ruling elite has appreciated that a command economy, based on state owned industrial enterprises and collective communes, was incapable of providing satisfactory growth, e.g. to become a leading international power.

Deng's justification for pushing reforms in the late 1970s was to enable China to catch up with the other major powers. The problem was perceived as how to move towards a more vibrant and decentralised (market) economy without weakening the political supremacy of the Party. This has not been an easy exercise. This dilemma has led the Chinese authorities to look for a middle way towards a decentralized market-based system without losing their political Party control. There has been no blueprint for this, and it has been likened to trying cautiously to feel for stepping stones across a river. It is these experiments in a variety of forms of corporate governance and economic control that are so fascinating.

Note, however, that the accompanying decline in the share of industrial output of SOEs does not imply that the balance has been taken up by Western-style standard capitalist organizations. The growth of private sector output, especially in joint ventures between domestic and non-resident businesses, including those from Hong Kong and Taiwan, started from a very low base, but has grown extremely rapidly in recent years, and now produces a considerable share of total industrial output. Although there has been much publicity of joint ventures involving major Western multi-nationals, these represent only a tiny fraction of output, and they are dwarfed in importance by those involving ethnic Chinese outside the PRC, e.g. from Hong Kong and Taiwan.

Given the relatively untried and somewhat experimental nature of China's emerging systems of corporate governance it is, perhaps, intriguing that real growth there has been so strong. Sachs and Woo argued that, compared with Russia, China had some initial advantages, in part paradoxically because of China's initial comparative backwardness. They noted that the industrial base in China, initially dominated by the SOEs, was comparatively small at the start of the transition, only taking about 18 per cent of the employed population, as compared with about 90 per cent in Russia.

So, when a large proportion of the SOEs began to make losses during the transition, in China as in the EEFSU, the comparative burden on the rest of the economy, in terms of forced reallocation of resources to the SOEs, often via an inflation tax, was less severe. Although in terms of employment the share of the state sector was then small, in terms of its contribution to GNP its share was above 60 per cent in 1978, when the reform started. If their share of output had remained constant, the influence of a badly performing state sector on the Chinese economy could also have been disastrous.

What saved it has been the fast growth of the non-state sector. The surge of the Chinese economy since 1978 mainly came from the new entry and excellent performance of non-state-owned firms, particularly TVEs. The rise of this sector has caused the share of the state sector in GNP to shrink steadily. It is this which differentiates Chinese reform from the transitions in the EEFSU, and thus should be analysed carefully. The Chinese planning system has been organized differently from those of the EEFSU; this provided suitable conditions for the growth of TVEs. Indeed, a strong expansion in TVEs began before the reform started. Another, and a vital, part of the non-state sector is agriculture. Since 1979, the 'Household Responsibility System' gradually became the main structure in Chinese rural areas.

The essence of this reform is to lease out land to rural households, who pay rent and taxes and enjoy the residual income and partial residual rights to the land. Thus rural households have both the incentive and responsibility to take risks and make efforts to improve the land 'allocated' to them, and are held responsible for the outcome. This reform greatly improved agriculture productivity. The average annual growth rate of agriculture increased from about 2 per cent in the 30 years or so before the late 1970s to about 7 per cent in the next five years, 1979-84. So successful was this reformed system, that in 1984 the People's Commune system was officially abolished. Agricultural output accounted for less than one third of Chinese GNP in the late 1970s. Moreover, the growth rate of agriculture has remained lower than that of aggregate GNP.

So, the direct influence of agriculture's improved growth rate should not be exaggerated. By comparison, the growth rate of TVEs' output has been higher than that of agriculture, and the share of TVEs' output in rural material output soon superseded that of agriculture. The importance of the agricultural reform partly lies in its interaction with the TVE sector. First, by abolishing collective farms, rural households were given greater freedom to re-allocate their resources, both labour and investment, optimally between agriculture and TVEs. Second, improved productivity in agriculture further released labour and increased savings/investment for the development of TVEs. Finally, TVEs were developed under the commune system (called commune-brigade enterprises in that system).

The abolition of the commune system shifted the focus of community governments from agriculture to TVEs, and had considerable influence in changing the governance of TVEs. One of the main differences between the reform process in China and in the former Soviet Union (FSU) has been the reaction to agricultural privatisation, enthusiastic in the former, grudging in FSU. Moreover, EEFSU, especially FSU, faced political turmoil, the economic effect of which has been magnified by their central planning system.

Under their previous centrally planned system much industrial production was concentrated in a few vast production units, both from a misplaced belief in economies of scale and to make centralised control easier. This was done both nationally and internationally, with all the Eastern Bloc countries linked by COMECON. It was, therefore, vital that trade within the system, especially between these huge units, flowed freely, because there were no potential substitutes. This made comprehensive planning and administrative coordination at the highest levels in the hierarchy (a nation or COMECON) crucial for continuing normal operation. Such an organisation is more susceptible to exogenous economic or political shocks.

When such a shock occurred with the break-up of the communist empire, COMECON broke apart and that tore the prior trading structure in EEFSU apart. In contrast the regions of China had gained more power vis-a-vis the centre in Beijing within the regionally based planned economy. This happened for a variety of politico/economic reasons long before the reform officially started. By then, the centre already had abandoned much direct control over trading, or material allocation, and there was no similar extent of dislocation to trading patterns.

So, as will be discussed subsequently, political disturbances at the centre, even such extreme manifestations as the Cultural Revolution, had less impact on the relatively self-sufficient regions. While the object lesson to the Chinese elite of what not to do is given by the collapse of the USSR, the pattern that they would like to emulate is, probably, provided by Singapore, with its combination of continuing tight political control with a free market, competitive, successful economy. Whether it is possible to translate the experience of a small city state to a vast continental power is uncertain.

The demise of Deng Xiaoping, which has probably for all practical purposes already taken place, is not expected to divert the Party leadership from pursuing this path, however improbable, and to liberals undesirable, its viability in the longer term. The Chinese government's comparative economic success so far has been largely based on their way of organizing the economy, with the development of new forms of corporate entities, e.g. cooperatives, especially TVEs, alongside the SOEs.

THE INSTITUTIONAL FOUNDATIONS OF CHINESE REFORM

Many economists argue that the success of China's economic reforms is due to the practice of gradualism, to competition across regions, to the growth of the non-state sector, and to the experimental and the bottom-up approach. These are fair summaries of major features of the reform. But why China followed such routes still needs to be explored. As noted earlier, China began its reform period with a relatively small, undeveloped state sector, a fact emphasized by Sachs and Woo.

Nevertheless, (i) all the most successful regions in this process have been relatively developed with more regionally controlled state-owned (SOE) firms. Such locally controlled firms are representative of the specifically Chinese-type institutions, to be discussed further in this Section; (ii) growth rates in all the developing regions with more centrally controlled SOE firms, an organisational structure closer to the Soviet model, are below average; and (iii) growth rates in all the less developed (rural) regions are below average. These data suggest that, as will be discussed further, the institutional and organisational factors have been predominant in determining relative growth.

Although both PRC and EEFSU were centrally planned economies, the Chinese economy was organised differently. The centrally planned economies in EEFSU were organised according to the principle of functional specialisation. Every state-owned firm there was under the control of one ministry which specialised in administering one type of product or service produced by such SOEs. For example, the automobile ministry controlled all the firms in the automobile industry. In contrast, the Chinese economy is organised into a multi-layer-multi-regional form (M-form).

The Ministries of the Central Government controlled only a small proportion of SOEs.

Most Chinese SOEs are under the control of regional governments. Each regional government's functions are further divided along geographic lines and functional specialisation lines. For example, provincial governments control county governments and provincial level SOEs in different industries; county governments control township governments and some county level SOEs. This structure is duplicated from the centre to the bottom level of the hierarchy of the Chinese economy.

The transformation of the organisational structure of the Chinese economy into an M-form started from the late 1950s. In the mid-1960s regional governments were already much more powerful and important than ministries (as contrasted with their counterparts in the EEFSU). In the 'Cultural Revolution' (1966-76) the transformation of the organisational structure was pushed further. In the early 1970s, more than 98 per cent of centrally controlled SOEs were transferred to local governments, including large and very large scale firms.

The number of SOEs under direct control of ministries decreased from 10,533 in 1965 to 142 in 1970. Most ministries lost their power to control state firms altogether. For example, all SOEs directly controlled by the ministries of metallurgy, coal, the first machinery industry (all non-defence production of automobile, machine tools, electrical machinery), and commerce were transferred to local governments. As a result, all government revenues came under the local governments' control except import duties, tariffs and profits from a small number of centrally controlled SOEs.

Correspondingly, local governments became responsible for most government expenditures, including investment. In the mid-1970s about 60 per cent of fixed asset investment in the state sector nationwide was made by local government. The product planning/allocation system was also transformed onto a region-based system under which the central government took care only of the residual balance of the supply and demand in each region, including raw materials and heavy machinery, such as cement, coal, timber, iron and steel, automobiles, tyres.

ECONOMIES OF SCALE AND DUPLICATION

In the Chinese M-form economy regions are relatively self-contained and self-sufficient in terms of functions and production. Accordingly, the size of enterprises generally is small, and industries are less concentrated. By the same token, there have been many duplications of similar types of firms. Such duplication assists the Chinese reform process for the following reasons. First, duplication is necessary for creating a competitive environment within the state sector. Second, it facilitates technology diffusion across firms and regions. Third, it increases the reliability of supply in the uncertain conditions created by the reform process itself and thus reduces vulnerability.

Obviously, there are also costs associated with this, notably the loss of scale economies. The best example is the Chinese automobile industry; there were more than 100 independent firms producing automobiles in the 1980s. Most produced only several thousand or even fewer automobiles per year, which is much too low from an efficiency point of view. But, compared with EEFSU, the Chinese economy has gained more than it has lost from such duplication.

EXPANSION OF SMALL STATE-OWNED INDUSTRIAL FIRMS IN THE EARLY 1970S

The best example of government policies encouraging duplication among regional industrial firms is the so-called 'five small industry' policy. The five small industries are small steel and iron, machinery, fertilizer, coal mining and cement. It was the central government's policy in the early 1970s to develop these in each region to make each region relatively self-sufficient. Moreover, the five were regarded as the basis for agricultural mechanisation in each region. In the first five years of the 1970s, 8 bn yuan was allocated to regional governments for setting up county-run small industrial firms.

These small firms also obtained preferential treatment in taxation and bank loans. Most of the profits of these small SOEs were reinvested in these firms. In 1970, almost all the counties in China established SOEs in producing agricultural machinery; 300 counties established steel plants, more than 20 provinces established tractor plants and motor plants. In 1975, these small regional SOEs produced 58.8 per cent of China's total cement output, 69 per cent of fertilizer, 37.1 per cent of coal and 6.8 per cent of steel.

COORDINATION

The second feature associated with the Chinese M-form structure is its mechanism for coordination. Unlike the EEFSU, where the centre played the critical role in coordinating the economy, regional governments in China have had considerable responsibility for regional economic coordination. Such decentralisation has had important benefits. First, local information is better, since local governments are closer to sites. Second, communication and information processing between the centre and the regions is greatly facilitated.

So, in China a small task force can cope with the exercise of making central plans and collecting aggregate statistics; in comparison, in the FSU, a large body of officials is needed. Third, regionally based coordination makes economy-wide coordination failure less likely when there are external shocks. In contrast to the U-form, which is fragile to shocks, the M-Form structure localizes the effects of such shocks. This also makes it easier to introduce institutional changes on an experimental scale, without causing disruption to the rest of the economy. Such benefits are particularly crucial when the centre's functions are disrupted.

A good example is the sustainability of the Chinese economy during the 'Cultural Revolution'. During that period, the Chinese central government almost completely lost its ability to coordinate the economy, and economies in some regions collapsed due to factional conflicts. However, the national economy did not. Chinese national income merely declined for two years - by 7.2 per cent in 1967 and 6.5 per cent in 1968. The economy recovered quickly thereafter even though the central government did not recover its coordination function. In sharp contrast, during their transition, the EEFSU economies apparently suffered dramatic and persistent declines in measured output by 30 per cent or more, over a period of four, or more, years.

INCENTIVES

Chinese local governments were given greater incentives (together with autonomous power) to introduce reforms than their counterparts in EEFSU, prior to the transition in the latter. Regional competition in getting rich quicker was a slogan set by central government. When a region has a higher growth rate than others, the head of the region will enjoy greater power and be more likely to get promotion. Moreover, the central government encouraged regional governments to try their own approaches to speed up growth. The combination of these policies implies a 'tournament' competition among regional governments.

An example is land reform. The famous 'household responsibility system' in agricultural reform was developed through the initiative of local governments. It was local government officers in Fengyang County, Anhui province, who took initiatives and risks in distributing land to rural households. This practice and its achievement were discovered later by the central government. Only then was similar nationwide reform measures approved.

Chinese local governments have now been enjoying their semi-autonomous power, and the incentives this provides for self-advancement, for more than twenty years. In contrast, where central coordination is critical for the operation of the economy, the implementation of the centre's instructions will have the highest priority. In this case the incentives of subordinates are primarily designed for implementing commands from above, and autonomous initiatives may well conflict with that priority.

THE ROLE OF THE TVE SECTOR IN THE SUCCESS OF THE CHINESE REFORM

The township-village enterprise (TVE) has been the most important engine driving the unprecedented growth of the Chinese economy during the last 15 years. Moreover, the development of the TVE is the most important feature distinguishing the Chinese transition path from those of the EEFSU. A TVE is a collectively-owned communal enterprise located in a township or a village. Since most TVEs are in the industrial sector, they are often treated as synonymous with rural industrial firms.

All the residents of the township or village that has established the TVE own the firm; the property rights of the TVE can only be exercised collectively through community representatives. If we have to make an analogy to a counterpart in the West, then the closest equivalent might perhaps be a combination of a municipally-owned enterprise and producer cooperatives. In their comparative studies of TVEs and other institutions throughout the world, Gelb and Svejnar also conclude that the institutions most similar to the Chinese TVE are producer cooperatives, including cooperatives in Eastern Europe, Mondragon enterprises in Spain, and labour managed firms in the former Yugoslavia. With some exceptions, such cooperatives have been comparatively unsuccessful in Western countries; we discuss subsequently some reasons why TVEs in contrast have succeeded so well in China.

The community is deeply involved in governing the TVE's operations (neither private; nor state owned). Regardless of the seemingly diffuse and unclear ownership structure, TVEs have been enormously successful. Their growth and performance are outstanding. This largely accounts for the difference between the growth rate for industry as a whole and that of the SOEs.

The share of the TVE sector became second largest after the state sector from the mid-1980s, and the remaining gap shrank rapidly. It has also been much more efficient than the state sector, e.g. as measured by total factor productivity. Their impact on the economy extends far beyond the TVE sector itself. Their activities generate much demand for intermediate products and capital goods predominantly produced in the state sector (e.g. steel, machine tools, automobiles, etc.).

At the same time, TVEs greatly intensify competition with SOEs in those industries where the state sector does not dominate, e.g. textiles, most light industries, conventional mechanical and electrical machinery, etc. Such competition has improved many SOEs' efficiency, but has also driven many others into large losses or even to the verge of bankruptcy. Institutional Features of TVEs The phenomenal growth of TVEs was neither planned nor expected by the Chinese central government, as publicly acknowledged by Deng Xiaoping. Before 1984, TVEs were known as collectively-owned commune-brigade enterprises (CBEs); and these were initiated in 1958 when the people's communes were established.

During the 1970s, CBEs developed alongside the increasing power of local governments; their share in GNP increased by about 1 per cent annually. In 1976, at the end of the Cultural Revolution, employment in this sector had risen to 17.9 million, with about 5 per cent of gross social product (GSP), or 11.2 per cent of the national income (NI). In 1984, after the dissolution of the people's commune system, the CBEs were renamed township-village enterprises (TVEs). As products of often spontaneous initiatives by local people over vast areas, institutional arrangements in TVEs vary a lot.

Here we outline some of the major variations. First, there are important differences between township enterprises (TEs) and village enterprises (VEs). A typical village will have a population of hundreds (no more than a couple of thousand at most). Most residents in a village have lived there for decades, and know each other well. Kinships are prevalent in village politics. Typical townships, on the other hand, have a population numbered in tens of thousands. Given this difference in community size, there are differences in closeness among the residents, who are the nominal owners of the firms, in methods of monitoring them, in ways of managing them. In a typical case, these collective owners do not have clearly defined shares as the term is normally understood.

Participation in the TVE is not a decision made by the residents voluntarily and independently. Instead, their participation is determined by their residency and mandated by the community government. That is, the ownership is linked with the residency of the community (township or village). Leaving and joining a community means giving up and gaining ownership of the assets of the community's firms. Residency is defined either by family ties, such as parental/marital relationship or other kinship, or by authorized migration. Official residency is enforced by the household registration system (similar to the propiska - the Russian internal passport system).

Unlike the pre-reform era, unauthorized migration now is not counted as illegal. But immigrants do not enjoy nominal ownership as official (or recognized) residents of the community. In this aspect, the TVEs are different from a typical producer co-operative, where all the workers enjoy ownership equally. Immigrant labourers are becoming an underclass group in all developed regions. This may become a serious social problem, since in all the developed regions with great concentrations of TVEs, immigrant workers play important roles. On the other hand such migrant labour allows for greater wage and labour force flexibility, thereby enabling better adjustment to shocks. Second, TVEs are organized differently in different regions. Amongst the most successful, there are three well-recognized models: from Sunan (southern Jiangsu province, the Yangtse delta); Guangdong; and Wenzhou (in southern Zhejiang province).

These three regions cover a vast area with a population of about 200 million, where most workers are in non-agriculture sectors and include a large number of immigrants from other regions in China. In Sunan community governments maintain a strong influence over the TVEs. TVEs started to be developed in Sunan on a large scale from the 1970s and since the early 1980s have employed most of the labour force. About half of the richest townships and villages in China are concentrated in this region. Close to Shanghai, its TVEs produce all types of products, including automobile parts, machine tools, radios, printing, textile products, plastic products, and even jewellery.

The superiority of the Sunan model went unchallenged until the late 1980s when the Wenzhou model and Guangdong model appeared. A key feature of the Wenzhou model is the important role of private ownership. Although privately-owned firms are not typical TVEs, the Wenzhou model is nonetheless frequently mentioned as a special type of TVE. Greater Wenzhou, a region with a population of some 300,000, did not really develop TVEs until the mid-1980s when private firms started to grow rapidly. Now Wenzhou's economy is dominated by the private sector and the per capita GDP is among the highest in China.

The Guangdong model, which refers to the TVEs in the Zhujiang delta area (southern Guangdong) is closer to the Sunan model, but with more joint ventures with foreign capital, more direct trade with Hong Kong and more private firms. Its enterprises are prominent in high technology sectors, such as the pharmaceutical and electronics industries. The largest Chinese air conditioner, refrigerator, automatic rice cooker, electric fan producers are TVEs in this region. One of the authors visited some TVEs there and was very impressed by their scale (with eight thousand employees in one firm) and modern production technologies and management.

A considerable fraction of the richest townships and villages in China are here. It is always dangerous to predict the future, especially of a process still in transition. Nevertheless TVEs have operated successfully for a quarter of a century already, and we expect them to continue to play a major role in the PRC economy. But the scale of the (more successful) TVEs is likely to expand, and their ownership structure may become more akin to capitalist firms as an increasing proportion of migrant workers become employed. Some successful TVEs will transmute into nation-wide large corporations. Not only did TVEs outperform the state sector, but their record in PRC has also been much better than that of Western cooperatives. This was in part due to weaker competition in PRC, than from Western private firms, but it was also due to such factors as more flexible labour arrangements, a stronger urge to save, invest and grow, and the informal institutional arrangements.

What Has Helped the Development of the TVE:

(a) The M-form structure

Under the Chinese M-form structure, local firms, including SOEs, constitute a relatively self-contained regional economic network. This regional network fosters development of the TVEs for the following reasons. First, non-specialized regional economies and the decentralized planning system gave TVEs the opportunity to grow without much disturbance to the existing system. There are broad ranges of products which the TVEs can produce to meet local demand, and often sufficient local products to supply to TVEs as inputs.

Close links between TVEs (or their predecessors, the CBEs) and local SOEs were started in the 1970s (before the reform) when the central government promoted the small industrial SOEs at the county level, and implemented the plan of mechanization of agriculture through regional initiatives. This often facilitated technology transfer from SOEs to TVEs. The philosophy was to modernize without destroying the country's (rural) base, thereby avoiding the extreme urbanisation of many LDCs.

Second, the M-form structure provides strong incentives to regional governments to support the development of TVEs, e.g. for fiscal reasons. Third, the banking system in the M-form structure gives regional branches autonomous power to lend to TVEs, as long as they keep an overall balance between deposits and lending within their region.

(b) Informal Institutions in TVEs

Another factor greatly helping TVEs is the existence of informal institutions. These include implicit contracts, both in inter-firm transactions and in internal relationships, as well as other informal financial, employment and trading arrangements. These institutions are popular as substitutes for formal rules, contracts and ownerships. Their function is particularly important when market imperfections are severe. Some examples of the areas in which informal institutions have helped TVEs are as follows.

First, fund raising: TVEs which are in the same community, or several TVEs which have good long-term relationships, provide mutual guarantees among themselves to assist each other with getting bank loans. In Wenzhou, a popular informal financial institution among private business is 'zuohui (forming an informal credit union)'.

Members of a 'hui (credit union)' know each other well and there are no written contracts among them. They put funds together periodically and draw funds out among members based on a revolving principle and mutually agreed priority projects (rather like the earlier 19th century British building societies).

Second, TVEs are often integrated within industry groups. Member firms of each group are related in producing one type of final product, such as automobiles, diesel engines, computers, etc. These groups coordinate and stabilize long term relationships between member firms in sales and purchases, promote the reputation of the group, and help member firms in raising funds.

Typically member firms of an industry group are regional firms with different ownership structures (this is related to the M-form structure). The relationship within such a group is often informal with no binding legal contracts. Long term reputation is what matters.

Third, TVEs often operate without formal employment contracts, which can help to provide flexibility. For example, when a TVE is hit by a temporary adverse shock to supply or demand, a common practice is to shut the firm down temporarily to reduce cost.

At such times, the TVE pays only a subsistence wage to its employees, usually about one eighth of normal. This practice is usually not specified in written employment contracts.

The effectiveness and scope of informal institutions varies with circumstances. For example, informal relationships are more important and more widespread in village than in township enterprises, because of the closer relationships involved.

The transition from a centralized system to a market system ultimately involves the creation of formal institutions, such as legal and contractual systems and property rights, etc., that are both complex and complementary. When informal institutions emerge, as substitutes for such previously non-existent formal institutions, the transition can subsequently be made easier and smoother.

MAJOR DIFFERENCES BETWEEN TVES AND SOES

Compared with SOEs, the crucial feature of TVEs is that government, whether central or regional, has no financial responsibility for them. TVEs have to finance themselves, a hard budget constraint. Major sources of financing of TVEs include funds derived from the collective assets of the community, funds raised from individuals and borrowing from the state bank(s). Such community collective assets are different from state assets being subject neither to state intervention nor protection, e.g. by direct subsidy or cheap bank loan.

In the TVE sector there are no guaranteed positions for either managers, or workers (though local resident workers have the priority for keeping their jobs when there are lay-offs). Persistently loss-making TVEs must either go bankrupt or be taken over, (in the latter case typically within the same community). In 1989 and 1990, the 'recession period' of the Chinese economy, hundreds of thousands of TVEs went bankrupt.

MAJOR PROBLEMS IN THE CHINESE ECONOMIC SYSTEM

In spite of the success of the Chinese economy, serious problems remain. If these are not resolved, growth may be checked or even reversed. Here we list some of the most serious problems.

ENFORCING THE BANKRUPTCY LAW

Facing tough competition, e.g. after price reforms, an increasing number of SOEs are making losses. According to official data, in the first nine months of 1995 the SOEs lost Yn 41.7 bn, up 18.8 per cent on the same period of 1994. Moreover, triangular debt, (long chains of unpaid and overdue debts between enterprises), swelled to Yn 750 bn at the end of August, up from Yn 630 bn at the start of the year. A conservative estimate is that if the bankruptcy law was vigorously enforced, then about 10 percent of SOEs, i.e. about 11,000 SOEs would go bankrupt.

Meanwhile the government has met much of the cost of such losses by direct subsidies, which has used up a sizeable proportion of its total revenues. However, most potentially bankrupt SOEs continue to operate and to accumulate losses. The Chinese government has identified the enforcement of bankruptcy, particularly in the state sector, as a central issue in the current reform. Although a bankruptcy law was passed by the People's Congress in 1986, its implementation has never gone beyond the experimental stage.

An official investigation in 1993 in five provinces, which account for more than one quarter of the total number of SOEs, (and more than one third of the losses in the state sector), found that since the Bankruptcy Law was officially implemented, 948 bankruptcy cases had come before the courts, of which about 80 percent occurred between 1991 and 1993. Most of those bankrupt SOEs had more than 1,000 employees; the largest had 3,000. There are many obstacles preventing full implementation of the bankruptcy law.

First there are financial problems. Creditors prefer not to let SOEs go bankrupt, since if they let the firm keep running, the state may help and the loss may not materialize. According to an estimate made by four Chinese specialized banks, nearly Yn 400 bn, or about 16.7 percent of China's Yn 2,400 bn loans to the state sector were non-performing (Joint Enterprises Bankruptcy Investigation Group, 1993).

Such losses have been handled through the postponement of repayment of debts (47 per cent), government subsidies (7 per cent), renegotiation of contracts with the government (5 per cent), use of previously accumulated profits (36 per cent), others (5 per cent). Once a SOE goes bankrupt, the creditors will face a crystallised loss.

Indeed, according to this study, in almost all the bankruptcy cases it was the debtors, not the creditors, who applied for bankruptcy. A second problem is that many profitable SOEs served as guarantors for other SOEs to get bank loans, or else government agencies served as guarantors for enterprises under their control. As a result, the bankruptcy of loss making SOEs may trigger a chain reaction. Finally, a formidable barrier against enforcing bankruptcy law is the lack, in China as in Russia, of a social safety net for redundant workers.

Consequently, at present, before an enterprise declares bankruptcy, the government tries to arrange a take-over by another SOE. Until this is tried, no bankruptcy application can be handled by a court. If no willing SOE is found, the proceedings may simply drag on. Political concern over unemployment caused by bankruptcy is paramount among Chinese government officials. Zhu Rongji, Deputy Prime Minister responsible for economic reform (the tsar of the Chinese economy, according to the Western media), admitted this to visiting Western economists and joked that 'If any of you are able, to solve our bankruptcy problem without causing workers to go on the street, I would apply for a Nobel Prize for you.'

POLITICAL STABILITY

Amongst all the problems facing Chinese reform, the most serious concerns uncertainty about the future political stability of the regime. There are many factors making the future of the system uncertain. The most immediate is the hand-over of power after Deng, which may take many years to accomplish. Second, corruption among government officials generates great popular resentment, threatens the legitimacy of the government and could even trigger upheaval. The 1989 Tian-an-men pro-democracy demonstrations were partly caused by popular detestation of such wide-spread corruption. Third, as discussed above, the worsening performance of the state sector could lead to massive unemployment in future. Finally, the possibility of loss of control of the centre over the regions remains a threat. This tends to restrict the central government's capacity to improve monetary and fiscal policies, and to coordinate inter-regional activities. This, in turn, has limited central government's ability to prevent worsening inequality, both across regions and across households, accompanying the transitional process, Hussain, Lanjouw and Stern and Putterman.

FISCAL AND MONETARY PROBLEMS

One of the (relatively few) merits of the previous central planning system was that it made the control of nominal magnitudes - the government's borrowing requirement, the money supply and inflation - relatively easy. In aggregate, the controlled price level of outputs could be adjusted relative to the controlled level of payments to factor inputs, so as to generate sufficient surpluses (savings) in the SOEs to meet both the expenditures of central, regional and local governments and the planned investments of the SOEs.

The banking system, usually comprising a single combined central/'commercial' monobank, acted simply as an accounting 'score-keeper' to record whether the SOE's actual surpluses and investments met their targets. Individual workers, farmers and bureaucrats were paid in cash and usually had only a strictly limited outlet for savings in the shape of savings deposits. Hoarding or dishoarding of such assets could cause disturbances to nominal magnitudes, but this could be observed and fairly readily offset. In this context government expenditures, albeit a large proportion of GDP, could be fully matched by revenues, and the growth of the money supply held roughly in line with the planned growth of real output - although the shortage of quality goods that people wanted to buy often resulted in a monetary overhang and repressed inflation.

This mechanism for controlling nominal magnitudes eroded once prices were freed from the late 1970s onwards and competition encouraged. With economic inefficiency and/or the low quality of their products exposed by competition from the non-state sector and from imports, the surpluses of the SOEs melted away, and to an increasing extent were replaced by losses. This happened in China, as in the other economies in transition. Since the central government had relied on such surpluses as its revenue base, this led to a swift erosion of revenue as a per cent of GDP, as severe in China as elsewhere in EEFSU.

Another problem relates to the regional decentralization of the fiscal system. This is based not on types of taxes and expenditures, but on the level of administrative control. The central government collects taxes only from centrally controlled entities. Each regional government is responsible for collecting tax revenues within its region. Then the regional government turns over a proportion of that revenue to the central government. Every year the central government has to negotiate with regional governments for the division of regional tax revenues. This system has greatly weakened the central government's control over fiscal policy and revenue.

In the last decade, both in terms of the ratio to GDP and in terms of its share of total fiscal revenue, the central government's fiscal position has deteriorated. Given both this deterioration, and the perceived need to continue subsidising the loss-making SOEs, expenditures on education, scientific research, inter-provincial highways, railways, etc., have been held back, in order to keep the overall fiscal deficit within reasonable limits. Both the expenditures and revenue of the Central Government have fallen, as a per cent of GDP, by about a third in the last decade.

A further serious consequence of the decline of the central government's fiscal position has been a great increase in inequality across regions. By the early 1990s, regional inequality in China was claimed by some scholars to be among the worst in the world. This trend could be politically threatening. Recent government statements have announced measures, e.g. reallocations of funds and tax privileges, to try to reverse it. In order to counter the shortcomings of the central government's fiscal position, a programme of measures was introduced in January 1994. This created a national tax administration; introduced a value-added tax; unified the taxation of enterprises and of personal incomes; and established a transparent division of revenue between central and local government, which was expected to raise the central government's share to about 60 percent.

However, the ratio of total fiscal revenue to GDP reportedly fell further in 1994, though now stabilising in the first three quarters of 1995. Many problems remain, e.g. of evasion and fraud, and of administration. The greater part (58 per cent) of all revenue now comes from VAT, but tax increases here would have an adverse effect on inflation. Only a tiny proportion comes from personal income tax, with fewer than 2 per cent of individuals liable. As China's prosperity increases, higher personal taxes are surely necessary; but as other governments have discovered, they are not popular.

This shortage of tax revenue makes it more difficult for the central government to establish a nation-wide social safety net, without which it will be much harder for the authorities to reform and remove the soft budget constraint from SOEs, who currently provide such services as health care, education and housing to their employees. Regional governments may have to play a larger role. These issues are broadly similar to those encountered elsewhere in the FSU.

Despite holding back desirable expenditures, e.g. on education, the weakness of fiscal revenues has led the government to run overall deficits in recent years, albeit nothing like as large as in many other countries in EEFSU.

The central government's deficit stood at 1.28 per cent of GDP at end 1994. The central government has recently attempted to finance its continuing deficit in a non-monetary fashion by encouraging the development of a government bond market. This started in 1981 when 4.87 Yuan bn were issued.

By the end of 1993, 166 Yuan bn were outstanding, 4.8 per cent of GDP. In 1994, the authorities expanded their use of this market, issuing about 100 Yuan bn. They are likely to make even further use of the bond market in future, in order to avoid recourse to monetary financing from the central bank, the People's Bank of China. The government's deficits are calculated exclusive of the losses of loss-making SOEs. Since the authorities have not been willing, for the most part, to close them, such SOEs are on a soft budget constraint. They meet both their operating losses and their new investment expenditures by borrowing from the banking system.

Meanwhile the banking system has also been adjusting in this transition period. The first stage, around the mid-1980s, was to give the four huge 'commercial' banks, the Industrial and Commercial Bank of China (ICBC), The Agricultural Bank of China (ABC), the People's Construction Bank of China (PCBC), and the Bank of China (the export/import bank) more independence from the People's Bank of China, and some greater latitude for competition. But they too remained SOEs with a soft budget, which they needed for survival. As central elements in the central planning system, their asset portfolio had consisted largely of loans to SOEs. With a large proportion of such SOEs becoming loss-making, the related loans became non-performing.

As noted earlier, many SOEs, without a credible bankruptcy threat, have tried to invest and grow their way out of their current problems. Moreover, that same lack of a hard budget constraint meant that the SOE's behaviour was relatively impervious to increases in interest rates. So the capitalist technique of varying interest rates to (bank) borrowers to control credit expansion, investment booms, monetary increases and inflation was not seen as practicable in China. Instead, the control method was quantitative credit restriction. Such methods, however, provide room for political pressure, favouritism and corruption.

In general the massive SOEs had much more political pull than the nascent cooperatives and TVEs, so that such quantitative methods reinforced a misallocation of capital and perpetuated a system in which the least efficient sector of the economy, the SOEs, did most of the investment. In part, the problems for borrowers other than SOEs of obtaining credit, especially during periods of restriction, have been mitigated by the development of a dual track system in banking, with a very rapid growth of rural and urban credit cooperatives, as well as other non-bank financial institutions (insurance companies, investment and trust institutions, etc.), which have been able, to some extent, to avoid or evade the centrally-imposed quantitative credit controls. So, the efficacy of such quantitative controls is being eroded.

Moreover, in so far as the credit controls are redirected to bite at the SOEs, this has typically just led to a countervailing expansion of inter-company debt (unpaid bills), the notorious triangular debt, again as in EEFSU. The continuing problems of fiscal deficit at the centre, and loss-making SOEs financed by bank loans, in a system where direct credit controls are becoming less effective raise dangers of loss of monetary/financial control and worsening inflation. The authorities are fully aware of this.

They are beginning very tentatively to harden SOEs budgets. '156 enterprises in 18 major cities were earmarked for bankruptcy in the course.... However the number of redundancies involved has been quite small, with only 11,000 workers losing their jobs but nearly all of them finding alternative employment. Since 1988, after a bankruptcy law was enacted, 1,400 enterprises have been liquidated but only 300 of these belonged to the state.' But the political punch of the SOEs and concern over unemployment and social cohesion has made progress on this front glacially slow.

Meanwhile the authorities have been pressing on with reforms to the laws and constitution of both the central bank and the commercial banks. The latter is intended to provide a basis for the (four main) commercial banks to become competitive, profit-maximising entities. But they cannot become so while they are stuck with so many bad loans. At one stage in 1994 it was mooted that a new group of banks, called state policy banks, would be established, which would not only extend longer-term 'policy loans', but might also take over the deadweight of existing bad or non-performing loans from the state commercial banks.

While these development banks have been set up, their executives, not surprisingly, have refused to become a dumping ground for existing bad loans. In any case removing existing bad loans from the commercial banks will not solve their problems unless they can prevent a build-up of further bad loans in future, which cannot be assured under the present system. Although there has not been significant monetary financing of central government in recent years, the erosion of its tax base, and the need for the central government to take over and extend the social safety net from its current (limited) provision by SOEs, makes the fiscal position fragile.

Meanwhile a combination of good prospects for growth, soft budgets for SOEs, and a hope that enterprises can grow out of their problems has led to enormously high investment ratios and an insatiable desire for bank credit, much of which is largely impervious to interest rate adjustments. This is aided and abetted by local government, which encourages its SOEs to invest as a way of expanding its overall tax base, income and power. China must be one of the few countries which regards its investment ratio as too large, and looks for policy measures to reduce it. 'Secondly, more and stronger efforts are needed to continue to control the total size of fixed asset investment.

Currently, the size of the social fixed asset investment is still too large.... it is hard to bring down investment rate to the appropriate level around 30 percent', China Financial Outlook. This puts enormous upwards pressure on domestic credit expansion, which has been reinforced in the last year or so by a huge expansion in foreign exchange reserves, which was not sterilized by extra bond sales. This has led to continuing extremely fast growth in the monetary aggregates. With monetary growth (M2) averaging about 25 per cent per annum recently, and real growth approaching 10 per cent per annum, one might have expected inflation to have been around 15 per cent per annum.

During this period price controls have been progressively removed, though with occasional backsliding when the authorities try to counter inflationary peaks (sometimes reflecting adverse agricultural supply shocks) with temporary controls on certain staple products. This will no doubt have affected the time path of the index. Nevertheless prices have grown more slowly on average during these years than might have been expected, given the rapid rate of monetary expansion. This outcome is, as an identity, due to a fall in velocity, as the Chinese have been prepared to raise their ratio of money holdings to income, a major component of an impressively high savings ratio.

This fall in velocity in China is in sharp contrast to its rapid rise in most of EEFSU, where a flight from money has exacerbated inflationary problems. To some significant extent this fall in velocity has been aided by the authorities' willingness to raise interest rates on bank deposits as inflation increases, so that they have normally offered a positive real return. With interest rates on deposits being varied more flexibly than those on bank loans, in some part out of concern for the loss-making SOEs, the spread between bank loan and deposit rates in China has at times been negative in recent years, a measure of how far the Chinese 'commercial' banks and monetary control system are from the capitalist norm.

Many countries in transition in EEFSU have found their economic and political problems greatly exacerbated by massive inflation. Although China's inflation has been high, the PRC has managed, more or less, to avoid levels that cause really severe problems. This, however, has been assisted by a fall in velocity which can hardly be expected to go much further, since the money/income ratio has reached levels normal in more developed countries. Unless China can solve the problem of controlling excess credit demand (especially from the inefficient SOEs), and/or generate a countervailing central government budget surplus, there will be a continuing threat of monetary indiscipline and high inflation.

EXTERNAL RELATIONSHIPS

Shortly after the end of the Cultural Revolution and the death of Mao Zedong in 1976, the new leadership took the strategic decision that they would gradually open the Chinese economy towards integration with the world economy. At that time, in 1978, exports were small both absolutely (less than $100 mn) and as a proportion of GDP (4.67 per cent). Thereafter exports increased rapidly (measured in constant US 1990 $ prices), and largely shifted from primary products to manufactures. After an initial burst of export expansion in 1978-81, when growth averaged about 22.2 per cent annually, there was a hiatus in 1982-1985, followed by a resumption of rapid expansion from 1986 to date, with growth averaging about 20.7 per cent annually.

On average, imports grew at much the same rate, so that there has been no trend in the balance of trade. The path of imports has, however, been even more variable than that of exports, shooting up during the more expansionary years, twice rising by over 50 per cent in a year (1978 and 1985), but, per contra, twice falling during years of credit restrictions and cutbacks in 1982 and 1990. By the end of September 2008, the reserves topped USD 1.9 trillion, equal to nearly USD1,500 per head for the entire population of China. It remained around this level until the end of 2008 as trade growth slowed and foreign investment inflows declined. Then, as 2009 progressed, the upward march resumed, with reserves rising above USD2 trillion in April and reaching a record USD2.447 trillion billion at the end of March 2010.

With other external flows - invisibles, and the capital account - being quite small, though usually positive, until the 1990s, the authorities were forced to ensure that imports remained in line with exports. In any case foreign trade was closely managed through a limited number of foreign trade corporations (FTCs), whose plans were submitted to and agreed by the government, and whose profits and losses were passed through to the central authorities. The FTCs had to surrender all foreign exchange earnings to, and purchase all foreign exchange requirements from, the government at the official renminbi exchange rate.

So, at this time, the exchange rate served little economic function; it was only a price for budgetary allocations under the centralised plan for foreign trade. Following the decision to open the economy, and to increase the role of market forces and reduce the burden of state subsidies on foreign trade losses (since the RMB was artificially overvalued), China began to decentralize its foreign trade and foreign exchange systems in 1979. Subsidies for the FTCs were reduced, and by the mid 1980s anybody, or any enterprise, was allowed to export. Exporters were allowed to retain a (variable) proportion of foreign exchange proceeds while surrendering the remainder to central government.

This system led to the development in 1986 of foreign exchange adjustment centres, (FEACs, or swap centres as they were called). Within FEACs, enterprises whose foreign exchange retentions were greater than they needed were able to sell any excess to other enterprises allowed to enter the market. The official RMB rate still governed transactions under the foreign trade plan and most capital transactions. But an increasing proportion of current account transactions (80 per cent according to Huang and Wong) were diverted into the swap market. The swap market exchange rate was determined by demand and supply, but neither was totally free.

Supply was affected by the retention quota, whereas demand was even more administratively determined, since no one was officially allowed to obtain foreign exchange without the permission of the State Foreign Exchange Administration Bureau, a subsidiary of the People's Bank. Even so, movements of the exchange rate in the swap market did appear to be influenced by fundamental factors, such as inflationary expectations, trade flows and financial conditions. So, between 1986 and 1994, China had a dual exchange rate system, with a fixed, and artificially high, official value for the RMB, and a lower, time varying rate in the still heavily administered swap market, though this latter remained inefficiently segmented between separate regional centres. As noted by Huang and Wong, pages 4 and 5:-

'On January 1, 1994, China unified its official and swap market exchange rates. The official exchange rate was depreciated from RMB 5.8 to US$1 at end of 1993 to RMB 8.7 to US$1 which was the swap rate in Shanghai at that time. The system of FEACs was replaced by a national interbank foreign exchange market. The market is a network of designated foreign exchange banks (DFEB) in 26 major cities, with its headquarters in Shanghai. The retention system was abolished and Chinese enterprises are required to sell all their foreign exchange earnings to and purchase foreign exchange from the DFEBs at the exchange rate quoted by the banks. The exchange rate now is determined in the following way. At the beginning of each trading day, the PBoC publishes the middle rate of the previous trading day. The DFEBs quote their own rates within a range of this rate set by the PBoC. To ensure competitive operation of the market, the foreign exchange balances of the DFEBs must fall within a certain percentage of their foreign exchange assets. Any surplus or shortfall must be eliminated by trading with other DFEBs or the PBoC.

The new system has certainly improved the efficiency of foreign exchange allocation since foreign exchange is traded at the unified rate. The elimination of the retention system has made hoarding of foreign exchange by FTCs for speculative purposes no longer possible. On the other hand, the central government's control over foreign exchange resources is strengthened. Chinese enterprises no longer have the proprietary right to their foreign exchange earnings. Meanwhile, despite the 'abolishment' of the priority list, purchases of foreign exchange from the DFEBs are still subject to approval and presentation of valid documents.

The new system has essentially reduced the availability of foreign exchange outside the control of the central government.' The unification not only encouraged exports, by removing the effective tax implied by the surrender of a portion of earnings at an artificially high rate, but also removed an impediment to capital inflows. The official rate was perceived as artificially high, and likely to be devalued. This deterred capital inflows despite the other attractions of PRC as a potentially enormous emerging market. So the change in the exchange rate regime at the start of 1994 contributed to the recent massive upsurge in capital inflows, largely foreign direct investment.

So long as such enormous, but volatile, capital flows continue, the People's Bank will have a difficult job of managing the RMB, while simultaneously seeking to curb domestic inflationary pressures, which are threatening to make Chinese exports increasingly less competitive, again a common problem among countries in transition. Most reports in the Western Press on such capital inflows refer to huge prospective deals between major multi-nationals and their prospective domestic partners in China.

These projects are driven, it is said, largely by the desire of the multi-nationals to gain a foothold in what shortly may become the world's largest single market. Rumours suggest that few projects have yet proven very profitable for the Western partner. Such Western investment in China has hitherto been dwarfed by the inflows from the ethnic Chinese outside China itself, especially from Hong Kong and Taiwan, but also elsewhere in South East Asia, e.g. Singapore. Much of the previously sizeable manufacturing sector of Hong Kong has been relocated in Guangdong province, and Taiwanese entrepreneurs have played a large role in the expansion in the coastal provinces of Jiangsu, Shanghai, Zhejiang, Fujian, and Guangdong.

The volume of such capital flows has been artificially exaggerated, since certain internal regulations, e.g. on luxury imports such as cars, make it attractive for domestic entrepreneurs to establish joint ventures with nonresidents. So, some Chinese capital is routed via Hong Kong and Taiwan, e.g. via under invoicing of exports, to return to the mainland in the guise of foreign capital participation. Even so, the involvement of non-resident Chinese in China's growth has become very large, though geographically patchy.

Besides capital flows, this has involved large transfers of technological know-how, and, just as important, of entrepreneurial and market skills of various kinds. It is impossible to quantify the contribution of the non-resident Chinese in general, and of Hong Kong in particular, to China's successful growth record, but it has been substantial. There is no parallel in the EEFSU - East Germany's re-absorption being a different process.

The scale of capital inflow into China recently has been such that the People's Bank has been forced to face strong upward pressure on the RMB, despite an inflation rate well in excess of that among Western countries. It has met this pressure in part by allowing some appreciation in the nominal rate, from 8.7 yuan per 1 US\$ on January 1, 1994 to 8.32 yuan in December 1995; and in part by accumulating a large foreign exchange reserve. Indeed so comfortable has their external position become that the authorities have been able in 1995 to contemplate large imports of food and raw materials, e.g. cotton and wool, as a way of containing inflationary pressures.

In the longer term, China might become a large net importer of primary products and services and an increasingly large net exporter of manufactures. The comfortable external position also has allowed China to announce at the APEC forum in Osaka sweeping liberalizations of trade and foreign investment regulations in 1996, including a 30 per cent cut in tariffs, steps towards currency convertibility, elimination of many import quotas and controls, and an easing of restrictions on operations by joint ventures with foreign shareholders. This package was viewed as an important step towards China's membership of the World Trade Organization (WTO).

The Cultural Revolution was brutal and destructive. But it did have one entirely unintentional effect that was indirectly beneficial to China's long term growth. This was by further weakening the powers of the central bureaucracy, thereby limiting the development of a centralised and functionally specialised (U form) EEFSU style economic planning system. Power and control remained with the Party and the State, but was diffused and dispersed much more widely, regionally and locally. This enabled initiatives to be taken at lower (political) levels to establish institutions, both in agriculture and industry (TVEs), which were too small and too local to get (much) state protection.

Moreover, even in the case of regionally controlled SOEs, 'tournament rivalry' between regions, provinces, etc., and between SOEs and TVEs injected considerable competition into the system. Thus what China has had over the last few decades, in considerable contrast to EEFSU, was competition, increased scope for individual initiative, notably in agriculture, and for an increasing share of the economy, in particular the TVE sector, a hard budget constraint. It is only in the last few years, however, that joint ventures, and other forms of (private) ownership, have come to play a significant role in industrial output.

The PRC still lacks the infrastructure of legal, accounting and information systems necessary for the support of private ownership, and remains without a proper hard budget constraint in the state sector. Does the success of China's economic development in recent decades imply that the key factors for growth are incentives, competition and a hard budget constraint? Does the fuzziness of the ownership arrangements, especially in the TVE sector, and the lack of a legal infrastructure, not then matter so much? Or is China's path unique and sui generis? In any case, will the continuing growth of TVEs, and the now rising involvement of joint ventures (especially with firms from Hong Kong and Taiwan) and even of purely privately owned firms, create an irreversible dynamic towards the adoption of the institutional infrastructure of a market economy?

Probably the latter will occur. But in the meantime China still faces severe problems. In common with EEFSU countries, China has not managed to rid itself of the albatross of loss-making SOEs, and the associated problems that this has caused for monetary and fiscal policies, and hence inflation. While China has suffered less, because the rest of the economy has managed to grow around the SOEs, a successful transition to a full market economy can hardly be managed until a solution to this problem is found. One crucial aspect of the SOE nexus is that they provide a social safety net for their work force.

If that safety net was otherwise provided, in part surely by government, it would both reduce the cost burden of the SOEs, and make it easier to impose a hard budget constraint on them. In the longer term, of course, some form of social safety net should be made available to everyone, but in the short run the major practical problems, both political and economic, relate to the SOEs. It may seem paradoxical that the transition to a market economy requires a shift of functions, in the form of the social safety net, from firms back to governments! But if such social expenditures are to revert to government, that will require a stronger fiscal basis.

That, in turn, leads on to the question of whether the balance of power between regional and central government is now optimal. Because the central planning regime, as practised in EEFSU, was so inherently flawed, the comparatively greater strength of regional government in China has been beneficial. It limited the full-scale adoption of central planning, and even introduced some much-needed competition and local initiative, via the M-form structure.

But now that China has embarked on the path towards a market economy, is the comparative weakness of the central government, vis-a-vis the regions, still optimal? In all other developed industrial economies the central government is much the more powerful. Of course, one is not comparing like with like, since the other industrial countries are democracies and China remains a single Party state. Undoubtedly the greatest question mark over the future of China relates to its political evolution and stability. But that all-embracing issue is outside both our remit and our competence.

9

China In Postcold War Asia

On the southernmost tip of the Maldives lies the island of Gan, a tiny patch of coconut palms and powdery white beaches. It was here that Britain set up a secret naval base in 1941, building airstrips and vast fuel tanks to support its fleet in the Indian Ocean during the Second World War. The RAF then used it as a Cold War outpost until 1976, when the British withdrew and the officers' quarters were converted into a resort called Equator Village. Now, 33 years later, India is preparing to reopen the base to station surveillance aircraft, helicopters, and possibly ships, to monitor Chinese vessels in the Indian Ocean.

Under a deal signed in August, India is also installing radar across the Maldives, linked to its coastal command. Both countries publicly deny that the move is aimed at Beijing, but privately admit that it is a direct response to China's construction of a giant port at Hambantota in nearby Sri Lanka. The plan is also being seen as the latest move in a low-level, but escalating struggle for economic and military supremacy between Asia's two emerging giants.

This week the flashpoint is their disputed Himalayan border, as China protests over the Dalai Lama's visit to a northeastern Indian state that it claims. But they are also competing over naval control of the Indian Ocean, resources and markets in Africa, strategic footholds in Asia — and are even in a race for the Moon. "It doesn't have the same proportions as the Cold War," said Alexander Neill, head of the Asia programme at the Royal United Services Institute, a research centre. "But there is potential for this to spiral out of control. Allies of both countries need to think carefully about the consequences of this rivalry."

Relations were cordial for the first decade after India's independence in 1947, and the founding of communist China in 1949. They quickly deteriorated, however, when the Dalai Lama escaped from Tibet in 1959 and was granted refuge in India. China then humiliated India in 1962 when its troops briefly occupied the northeastern state of Arunachal Pradesh and seized the region of Aksai Chin. Beijing also began to provide aid and weapons to Pakistan — India's rival. In the past decade, the frost had been thawing as bilateral trade expanded from $3 billion in 2000 to $51 billion last year — the two even began joint military exercises.

Yet this year, things have taken a sudden turn for the worse as China seeks to project its economic and military clout, and a more assertive India tries to respond. Militarily, India frets over China's recent efforts to improve infrastructure around its frontiers and force a compromise on the disputed border. It also worries about China's plans to develop a "blue water" navy capable of protecting trade routes through distant waters, including the Indian Ocean. India feels particularly threatened by China's "string of pearls" strategy, building ports in Burma, Sri Lanka and Pakistan that could be used by its navy.

Beijing is concerned that a nuclear deal finalised last year between India and the US, was designed as a counterbalance to China. The deal not only lifted a ban on India buying US nuclear supplies, it also opened the door for India to take part in joint military exercises and buy billions of dollars of US weaponry.

"Since 1962, I think Chinese strategists have basically decided that they can deal with India on their own terms," said Evan Feigenbaum of the Council on Foreign Relations, an American research centre. "But when you introduce the United States into that equation, it introduces all kinds of uncertainties. I think we're in for a period of India-China tension."

Economically, the competition is most intense in Africa, where India and China are vying for resources and markets in a rerun of the "Scramble for Africa" by colonial powers. China began courting African nations a decade ago, offering investment and trade in exchange for soft loans and development aid with no political conditions attached.

But India is catching up fast, pledging $5 billion in credit and hundreds of millions of dollars in financial help at an inaugural India-Africa summit, 2008. At stake is not just access to industrial raw materials, but support for India's bid for a permanent seat on the UN Security Council, which China opposes. India is also trying to make up lost ground in South, South-East and Central Asia.

China has been trying to negotiate a friendship treaty with Nepal to replace the one that has tied the country to India since 1950. Beijing's growing clout in Bangladesh was highlighted on Nov. 2009 when armed police closed a photo exhibition organised by Tibetan activists.

India has poured $1 billion in aid into Afghanistan, while a Chinese company has invested $3 billion in a giant copper mine in the country. Technologically, the contest is playing out in a 21st-century Asian version of the Cold War space race. India launched its first unmanned lunar mission, Chandrayaan-1, 2009 and plans to land a man on the Moon by 2020.

China sent its first *taikonaut* into space in 2003, and plans its first manned lunar mission by 2024. Yet the most fundamental source of rivalry is also the most abstract: the relative merits of Indian-style democracy and Chinese-style autocracy. Although neither promotes its political system, they are seen as rival models for the developing world. And if this is the "Asian Century", as many agree, then it will be defined to a large extent by that ideological contest.

CHINA'S POSITION IN THE COLD WAR

The Cold War was characterized by the tension between the two contending superpowers — the United States and the Soviet Union. Yet the position of Mao's China in the Cold War, in many key respects, was not peripheral but central. The observation made by political scientists Andrew J. Nathan and Robert S. Ross certainly makes good sense: "During the Cold War, China was the only major country that stood at the intersection of the two superpower camps, a target of influence and enmity for both." China's leverage in the Cold War was primarily determined by its enormous size. With the largest population and occupying the third largest territory in the world, China was a factor that neither superpower could ignore.

In the late 1940s and early 1950s, when Mao's China entered a strategic alliance with the Soviet Union, the United States immediately felt seriously threatened. Facing offensives by Communist states and revolutionary/radical nationalist forces in East Asia, Washington, with the creation and implementation of the NSC-68, responded with the most extensive peacetime mobilization of national resources in American history. In its efforts to "roll back" the Soviet/Communist threat, the United States became involved in the Korean War and the Vietnam War, overextending itself in a global confrontation with the Soviet/Communist camp.

In the late 1960s and early 1970s, the situation reversed completely following China's split with the Soviet Union and rapprochement with the United States. As a result of having to confront the West and China simultaneously, the Soviet Union overextended its strength, which contributed significantly to the final collapse of the Soviet empire in the late 1980s and early 1990s.

China's leverage in the Cold War, though, went far beyond changing the balance of power between the two superpowers. The emergence of Mao's China as a unique revolutionary country in the late 1940s (discussed more extensively below) also altered the orientation of the Cold

War by shifting its actual focal point from Europe to East Asia.

This shift, as it turned out, would make East Asia *the* main battlefield of the Cold War, while, at the same time, would help the Cold War to remain "cold." When the Chinese Communist revolution achieved nationwide victory in 1949, the global Cold War was at a crucial juncture. Two important events — the 1948-49 Berlin blockade and the Soviet Union's first successful test of an atomic bomb in August 1949 — combined to pose a serious challenge to the two superpowers.

If either tried to gain a strategic upper hand against the other — and if a showdown were to occur in Europe, where the dividing line between the two contending camps already had been drawn in a definitive manner — the Cold War could have evolved into a global catastrophe, one that might have involved the use of nuclear weapons. Against this backdrop, Moscow's vision turned to East Asia. In June-August 1949, on the eve of the victory of the Chinese Communist revolution, the number two leader of the Chinese Communist Party (CCP), Liu Shaoqi, secretly visited Moscow to meet with Joseph Stalin.

The two leaders concluded that a "revolutionary situation" now existed in East Asia. In an agreement on "division of labor" between the Chinese and Soviet Communists for waging the world revolution, they decided that while the Soviet Union would remain the center of international proletarian revolution, China's primary duty would be the promotion of the "Eastern revolution." The implementation of this agreement resulted in China's support for Ho Chi Minh's Viet Minh and, in October 1950, massive intervention in the Korean War, making Mao's China a "front-line soldier" fighting against the U.S. imperialists.

Throughout the 1950s and 1960s, East Asia continued to be a main focus of the Cold War. While China was playing a central role in the two Taiwan Strait crises and the Vietnam War — the longest "hot" war during the Cold War period — the strategic attention of the United States, following the assumption that China was a more daring enemy than the Soviet Union, became increasingly fixed on East Asia. Ironically, though, the active role China played in East Asia turned this main Cold War battlefield into a strange "buffer" between Washington and Moscow: with China and East Asia in the middle, it was less likely that the United States and the Soviet Union would become involved in a direct military confrontation.

The situation would remain like this until the early 1970s, when d,tente began to redefine the rules of the U.S.-Soviet confrontation, decisively reducing the possibility of a nuclear showdown between the two superpowers. In terms of its impact on the essence of the Cold War, China's emergence as a revolutionary country dramatically enhanced the perception of the Cold War as a battle between "good" and "evil" on both sides, making the conflict more explicitly and extensively framed by ideological perceptions. This was particularly true because, as shall be made clear by a brief comparison of the two Communist countries, Mao's China was more revolutionary in its behavior than the Soviet Union by the late 1940s.

Taking Marxism-Leninism as the guideline for its state policies, Soviet Russia/the Soviet Union had been a revolutionary country from the time of its establishment. While persistently working to establish a socialist society in Russia, the leaders in Moscow made promoting the proletarian world revolution and overthrowing capitalism's global reign the Soviet Union's sacred state mission. However, the situation had changed subtly by the late 1940s. If the dissolution of the Comintern in 1943 symbolized Moscow's retreat from pursuing world proletarian revolution as a state-policy goal, the Soviet-American agreement at Yalta in February 1945 represented the completion of a crucial step in the Soviet Union's "socialization" process.

Although Moscow continued to profess its belief in the Marxist-Leninist theory of international class struggle, the Soviet Union was no longer the same kind of revolutionary country it used to be — isolated and excluded from the existing international system; rather, as a main patron of the postwar world order created at Yalta, Stalin's Soviet Union was changing into an insider of the big-power club, assuming the identity of a quasi-revolutionary country and a status quo power at the same time. Consequently, as Vojtech Mastny points out, "despite Stalin's ideological dedication, revolution was for him a means to power rather than a goal in itself." Mao's China was different.

The Chinese Communist regime was established by breaking up the Yalta system. When the "new China" was born, Mao and the CCP leadership were determined to break with the legacies of the "old" China, to "make a fresh start" in China's foreign affairs, and to lean to the side of the Soviet-led socialist camp. From its birth date, Mao's China challenged the Western powers in general and the United States in particular by questioning and, consequently, negating the legitimacy of the "norms of international relations," which, as Mao and his comrades viewed them, were of Western origins and inimical to revolutionary China. Thus Mao's China had its own language and theories, its own values and codes of behavior in regard to external policies.

The revolutionary features of Chinese foreign policy, combined with the reality that the Cold War's actual emphasis was then shifting from Europe to East Asia, inevitably caused the global Cold War to entail a more ideological form of warfare as a whole. China's emergence as a revolutionary country also created an important connection between the global Cold War and the decolonization process in non-Western countries, linking the two historical phenomena in ways that would not have been possible without China's input. Different from the Soviet Union, which was established on the ruins of the czarist Russia, China was a country whose modern history was said to have suffered from the aggression and incursion of Western imperialism/colonialism.

Throughout the course of the Chinese revolution, the CCP always viewed China's national independence and national liberation as the revolution's key mission. In the late 1940s, Mao introduced his "intermediate zone" theory, claiming that between the United States and the Soviet Union existed a vast "intermediate zone" mainly composed of "oppressed" non-Western countries, including China. Before U.S. imperialists could attack the Soviet Union, according to Mao, they first had to control the intermediate zone, thus making Asia the central arena of the Cold War.

When Mao and the CCP seized political power in China, they immediately proclaimed that revolutionary China, as a natural ally of the "oppressed peoples" in the intermediate zone, would hold high the banner of anti-imperialism and anticolonialism, challenging the United States and other Western imperialist/colonial powers. Mao and his comrades regarded this stance as important both for defending the socialist camp and for promoting Communist/radical nationalist revolutions in non-Western countries. Thus Mao's China dramatically enhanced the theme of decolonization in the Communist Cold War discourse that had been overwhelmingly dominated by class-struggle-centered language.

As a result, the emerging anti-imperialist/anticolonialist movements in non-Western countries became more tightly connected with the "proletarian world revolution." By emphasizing the importance of the role played by Mao's China in the Cold War, I do not mean to argue that China's overall position was more important than that of the Soviet Union or the United States. Although China was a major Cold War actor, its capacity and will to influence global issues and international affairs were inevitably compromised by the fact that it was backward in technology and economic development.

In addition, its foreign behavior was profoundly restricted by a Chinese ethnocentrism, which was deeply rooted in its history and culture. Therefore, in the Cold War's global framework, China played an important role only in certain dimensions (especially those with close connections to East Asia or in China itself), and it was the Soviet Union and the United States that occupied the indisputable central position. Yet, as John Gaddis points out, "The diversification of power did more to shape the course of the Cold War than did the balancing of power." Indeed, the complexity and singularity of the Cold War were determined by its multipolarity and multidimensionality, which came into being with each and every actor leaving its stamp on them. In this sense, China's position in the Cold War is clearly important.

IDEOLOGY MATTERS

The Cold War was from the beginning a confrontation between two contending ideologies — communism and liberal capitalism. The compositions of the two Cold War camps were defined along ideological lines, and the conflict between them, at its core, represented not only a contest to determine which side was stronger but also, and more importantly, a competition to demonstrate which side was superior. The Cold War did not end as the result of the Soviet empire suffering economic collapse or military defeat at the hands of Western countries; rather, it happened in the wake of the "inner surrender" by the people in the Soviet Union and East European Communist countries to the superiority of liberal capitalism and Western democracy.

However, throughout the Cold War period, a majority of political scientists and diplomatic historians played down ideology as an essential agent in determining the basic orientation of a nation's foreign policy. From "traditionalists/realists" to "postrevisionists," theorists and diplomatic historians differed on many issues, but they had one thing in common: by defining "power" basically in material terms, they did not take the power of ideas seriously. A prevailing assumption among scholars was that although the two contending camps used strong ideological language to attack each other and defend themselves, they did so more to justify already existing policies than to shape decisions yet to be made.

Scholars also believe that what mattered were state leaders' concerns over, as well as calculations about, their nation's "vital security interests," rather than their "superficial" ideological commitments. Within this context, a "China under threat" approach dominated the study of China's Cold War history, until recently. Many scholars assumed that the key to understanding China's external policy lay in a comprehension of Beijing's "security concerns," which, as in any other country, could be defined in terms of its physical safety, its economic development, and its political and societal stability, as well as its perception of external threats.

All of these assumptions are now being challenged. Indeed, one of the most important revelations of the "new" Cold War history is that ideology mattered. To make this assertion more accurate, I will further argue that ideology not only played a decisive role in bringing Communist countries together but also contributed to driving them apart. During the early phase of the Cold War, a shared belief in Marxist-Leninist ideology served as a central force to unite Communist states and parties in the world.

After World War II, when national identity consciousness was stronger than ever before, this force did not produce a monolithic international Communist movement with Moscow as its supreme headquarters; but it did create, and in turn was enhanced by, a profound conviction among Communists all over the world that "history is on our side," thus allowing them to pose a serious challenge to international capitalism, while, at the same time, constructing the moral foundation on which the "socialist camp" was established.

It should also be pointed out that, forty years later, the final collapse of this conviction led to the dismantling of the socialist camp and, in the wake of that, the end of the Cold War. As far as the external policies of Mao's China are concerned, the role played by ideology is evident. The CCP leadership adopted the "lean-to-one-side" approach when it established the People's Republic of China (PRC), which, in a practical political sense, meant allying China with the Soviet Union as well as other socialist countries and confronting the Western "imperialist powers." In October 1950, only one year after the Communists seized power in China, the CCP leadership decided to enter the Korean War.

In a series of internal discussions and correspondence, Mao used highly ideological language to argue that if China failed to intervene, the "Eastern revolution" and the world revolution would suffer. Throughout the 1950s and 1960s, Beijing's foreign policy consistently demonstrated a strong ideological color. For example, in October 1956, the CCP leadership urged Moscow to suppress the "reactionary rebellion" in Hungary for the sake of the international Communist movement. In the mid-1960s, Beijing, under the banner of fulfilling China's duties of "proletarian internationalism," provided Vietnamese Communists with substantial support, including the dispatch of 320,000 Chinese engineering and antiaircraft troops to North Vietnam in 1965-69.

All of these developments clearly suggest that the role of ideology in Beijing's external policies cannot be overlooked. In a deeper sense, ideology's impact upon China's Cold War experience is reflected in Mao's "continuous revolution" as his central theme in shaping Chinese foreign policy and security strategy. Mao's revolution never took as its ultimate goal the Communist seizure of power in China; rather, as the chairman repeatedly made clear, his revolution aimed at transforming China's state, population, and society, and simultaneously reasserting China's central position in the world.

The domestic and international goals of the revolution were deeply connected. On the one hand, it was precisely by virtue of the revolution's domestic mission that the revolution's international aim became justified; on the other hand, the international aspect of the revolution served as a constant source of domestic mobilization, helping to legitimate the revolution at home and to maintain its momentum. Mao's and his comrades' belief in Marxist-Leninist ideology was always interwoven with their devotion to using ideology as a means to transform China's state, its society, and its international outlook. This belief stood at the core of their conceptual realm, providing legitimacy to the Chinese *Communist* revolution.

It is here we see the complicated interplay between the Mao generation's conversion to Communist ideology and its continuous exposure to the influence of China's age-old history and culture. At a glance, the two experiences are contradictory. As twentieth-century revolutionaries, Mao and his comrades were highly critical of the Chinese past, declaring that their revolution would render a thorough transformation of China's "old" state, society, and culture. But when Mao and his comrades were posing challenges to the Chinese past, the ideology on which they depended as the lodestar and guiding philosophy for the transformation had to be articulated through the discourse, symbols, norms, and identities that had been a part of the Chinese past.

Consequently, a profound continuity existed between the Mao generation's revolutionary behavior and the "old" China they meant to destroy. In this regard, a conspicuous example is the impact that the age-old "Central Kingdom" mentality had on Mao and his comrades. Their aspiration for promoting a world proletarian revolution by following the model of China revealed unmistakably how deeply their conceptual realm had been penetrated by that mentality. The message delivered here is of broad theoretical significance: in a cross-cultural environment, the creation, transmission, and representation of an ideological belief must be subjected to the definition and interpretation of the discourse, symbols, norms, and values that formed a particular actor's historically/culturally bound conceptual lens.

The outcome of the process could lead either to convergence of or to divergence between actors with the same ideological belief. Consequently, ideology, like religious faith, could either bring people together or split them apart, and, in certain circumstances, even cause them to engage in deadly confrontations with one another. Indeed, have we not witnessed enough examples of conflicts and wars between different sects within the same religion in world history? A fundamental flaw of the "old" Cold War history lay in scholars' inability to comprehend this complicated dual function of ideology.

As a result of an oversimplified "ideology versus national security interest" dichotomy, a prevailing assumption was that if countries with shared ideological beliefs (such as China and the Soviet Union) were to disagree, then that shared faith must have been overwhelmed by a conflict of national interests. In the study of China's Cold War history, scholars have often used Beijing's split with Moscow and rapprochement with Washington to prove this assumption. Careful study of the history of Sino-Soviet relations demonstrates that the split was not caused by uncompromising conflicts in national interests but rather by different understandings and interpretations of the same ideology.

When serious disagreements began to emerge between Beijing and Moscow in the mid- and late 1950s, China and the Soviet Union had more shared "national interests" than ever: given the hostility of the United States and other Western countries toward the PRC, Beijing's strategic alliance with Moscow served China's national security needs well; the Western economic embargo against China made Sino-Soviet trade relations ever more valuable for Beijing; and China's economic reconstruction benefited greatly from

Soviet aid. In turn, China's support significantly enhanced the Soviet Union's position in a global confrontation with the United States.

The national interests of China and the Soviet Union were highly compatible at that time, or at least should have greatly outweighed any explicit or implicit conflict that might have existed between them. But it was exactly at such a moment that conflicts between Beijing and Moscow surfaced. The key to the conflicts lay in Mao's changing perceptions of China's relations with the Soviet Union.

After Stalin's death, Mao increasingly perceived the CCP, and himself in particular, as qualified to claim centrality in the international Communist movement. In its criticism of Moscow's "big-power chauvinism" and the Soviet leader Nikita Khrushchev's de-Stalinization effort, Maoist discourse was dominated by metaphors, myths, and symbols crucial to the promotion of Mao's continuous revolution, which also caused Beijing's deepening discord with Moscow. All of these developments served as the prelude to the great Sino-Soviet polemic debate in the 1960s, eventually leading to each of the Communist giants to regard the other as a "traitor" to true Marxism-Leninism.

Following the intensifying ideological warfare, the state-to-state relations between China and the Russia deteriorated substantially, causing sharp conflict in their "national security interests." It was the deepening discrepancy over how to define/interpret the same ideology, rather than conflict over national security interests, that should be identified as the primary cause for the Sino-Soviet split. Ideology matters, yet not without fundamental limits.

As indicated by China's Cold War experience, while ideology was central in legitimizing important foreign policy decisions, ideological terms alone could not guarantee "legitimacy." Thus Mao and his comrades *always* tried to present important foreign policy decisions in terms of both ideological *and* other concerns. For example, when Beijing's leaders decided to enter the Korean War, they announced to the Chinese people and the whole world that if they did not participate China's security interests would be seriously jeopardized.

In the Taiwan Strait crisis of 1958, Mao argued that shelling Jinmen was necessary to prevent the U.S. imperialists from permanently separating Taiwan from the socialist motherland. In these cases, security concerns were real, but they also helped justify decisions made primarily based on the leadership's ideological commitments.

Ideology's role also withers along with the ideology's declining "inner" support from the people — this was particularly true in the case of communism. As a utopian vision, communism was most beautiful when it was not a political philosophy *in action*. When Communist ideology was put into practice in a favorable historical/social environment — such as in twentieth-century China, where radical revolutions had accumulated tremendous momentum and strength — it ignited popular enthusiasm and support.

But when communism repeatedly failed the test of people's lived experience with its inability to turn the utopian vision into reality, popular enthusiasm and support eventually died. In Mao's China, Maoist continuous-revolution programs such as the "Great Leap Forward" and the "Great Proletarian Cultural Revolution" suffered this fate. Consequently, ideology would no longer be able to legitimate Chinese Communist policies — which were in itself a sign that the Chinese Communist regime was losing its legitimacy.

MAO AND FOREIGN POLICY PATTERNS OF MAO'S CHINA

In any historical study, scholars must pay special attention to the role of personalities, and it is imperative in a study about Mao's China. Mao was CCP/PRC's single most important policymaker. Behind every crucial decision — such as China's intervention in Korea, its alliance and split with the Russia, its shelling of Jinmen, its support to the Vietnamese Communists, and its rapprochement with the United States — Mao always was the central figure. In order to understand the dynamics and logic of the PRC's revolutionary foreign policy, one must comprehend Mao's concept of continuous revolution.

Underlying the concept was Mao's "post-revolution anxiety," a psychological/conceptual force constantly pushing him to persist in a revolutionary agenda for China's domestic and external policies. As discussed earlier, Mao's revolution aimed to transform China's "old" state and society as well as to destroy the "old" world. Mao never concealed his ambition that his revolution would finally turn China into a land of universal justice and equality and that the Chinese revolution would serve as a model and revive China's central position in the world. China's domestic and external policies thus were deeply interrelated.

When the CCP seized power in 1949, Mao claimed that this event was only "the completion of the first step in the long march of the Chinese revolution," and that carrying out the "revolution after the revolution" was for the CCP a task more complicated and challenging. How to prevent the continuous revolution from losing momentum emerged as one of Mao's major concerns. Around 1956, as the nationwide "socialist transformation" (e.g., nationalizing industry and commerce and collectivizing agriculture) was nearly completed, Mao's concerns changed into worries because he sensed that many of the party's cadres and ordinary members were becoming less interested in deepening the continuous revolution.

After the failure of the Great Leap Forward in 1958-60, Mao realized that even among the Communist elite, his revolution was losing crucial "inner support." As Mao approached the last decade of his life, he found that in pursuing the ideals he cherished he had become a "lone monk with a leaky umbrella," and a majority of the

Communist elite were unable — or unwilling — to follow the development of his thinking. A pivotal challenge obsessed Mao constantly: through what means could he transform China and the world? Even with his seemingly unrestricted political power, he often found himself powerless. What he encountered was a paradox sitting deeply in the challenge itself: he had to find the means needed for transforming the "old" world from the very "old" world that was yet to be transformed.

Throughout Mao's twenty-seven-year reign in China, he was never able to overcome this profound anxiety. In order to maintain the momentum of his continuous revolution, Mao needed to find the means to mobilize the masses. It was in the process of searching for such means that he realized that the adoption of a revolutionary foreign policy had great relevance. On Beijing's management of the Korean War, the Taiwan Strait crisis, and the Vietnam War, during the early years of the PRC, a revolutionary foreign policy helped to make Mao's various state and societal transformation programs powerful *unifying* and *national* themes supplanting many local, regional, or factional concerns.

When tension between Mao and other members of the Communist elite, as well as between the Communist regime and China's ordinary people, intensified following the failure of the Great Leap Forward, a revolutionary foreign policy further served as an effective — and probably the only available — way through which Mao could enhance both his authority and the legitimacy of his continuous revolution. The role of revolutionary foreign policy in Mao's continuous revolution must be understood in the context of the Chinese people's "victim mentality" and its connections to the age-old Central Kingdom concept so important in China's history and culture.

During modern times, the Chinese people's perception of their nation's position in the world was continuously informed by a conviction that political incursion, economic exploitation, and military aggression by foreign imperialist countries had undermined the historical glory of the Chinese civilization and humiliated the Chinese nation. Consequently, a victim mentality gradually dominated the Chinese conceptualization of its relations with the outside world. Indeed, this mentality is extraordinary. While it is common for non-Western countries to identify themselves as victims of the Western-dominated worldwide course of modernization, the Chinese perception of their nation being a victimized member of the international community is unique, because it formed such a sharp contrast with the long-lived Central Kingdom concept.

The Chinese felt that their nation's modern experience was more humiliating and less tolerable than that of any other victimized non-Western country in the world, and they firmly believed that China's victim status would not end until its weaknesses had been turned into strength. So they willingly embrace Mao's revolutionary programs aimed at reviving China's central position in the world. The central role China's foreign policy played in Mao's revolution drove the CCP leadership to adopt a highly centralized decision-making structure in external affairs. The political institutions of Mao's China were characterized by tight central control; but the control over foreign policymaking certainly was the tightest.

As early as August 1944, when the CCP Central Committee issued the first comprehensive inner-party directive on diplomatic affairs, Mao made it clear that party organs and cadres must not take action in diplomatic affairs without Central Committee authorization. On the eve of Communist seizure of power, Mao stressed that "there existed no insignificant matter in diplomatic affairs, and everything should be reported to and decided by the Central Committee." After the PRC's establishment, Mao further confirmed that the politburo, the Central Secretariat, and, indeed, Mao himself, controlled the decision-making power. The missions of the Foreign

Ministry, headed by Premier Zhou Enlai from 1949 to 1958, were defined as keeping the central leadership well informed of China's external situation and carrying out the central leadership's decisions.

Under these circumstances, even Zhou Enlai became more a policy carrier than a policymaker. During the Cultural Revolution years, this highly centralized foreign policy structure became more rigid when Foreign Minister Chen Yi lost virtually all power. For a time even the politburo did not matter, since the real power fell into the hands of the "Cultural Revolution Group," the institutional instrument Mao created to implement the Cultural Revolution. Because of Mao's perception of the Chinese revolution's sacred mission, which was reinforced by the Chinese victim mentality, he and his comrades were filled with an exceptional sense of insecurity throughout the twenty-seven years he ruled China.

In general, it is understandable that, in the divided Cold War world in which peace and stability had been severely threatened by factors such as the emergence of nuclear weapons and the intensifying confrontation between the two superpowers, any country would feel less secure than ever before. Mao's sense of insecurity, however, was special in several respects. First, the ambitious hope on the part of Mao and the CCP leadership to change China into a central international actor conflicted with China's power status, which was still weak during the Maoist era.

As long as Mao and his comrades were determined to chart their own course in the world and to make China a prominent world power, they would continue to feel insecure until China's weakness had been turned into strength. Second, since Mao and the CCP leadership emphasized the central role the Chinese revolution was to play in promoting the worldwide proletarian revolution, thus making China the primary enemy of world reactionary forces, they logically felt that they faced a very threatening world.

The more Mao and his comrades stressed the significance of the Chinese revolution, the less secure they would feel in face of perceived threats from the outside world. Third, re Mao made this insecurity more serious when he highlighted international tension and treated it as a useful tool for domestic mobilization. Through anti-foreign-imperialist propaganda, Mao and his comrades used foreign threats to mobilize the Chinese masses. This propaganda, in turn, would inevitably cause a deepening sense of insecurity on the part of Mao and his comrades.

Hence, in the practical process of policymaking, Beijing broadly defined the threats to China's national security interests. Compared with policymakers in other countries, Beijing's leaders in the Maoist era were under great pressure to take extraordinary steps to defend and promote revolutionary China's security interests. This explains to a large extent why the PRC frequently resorted to violence in dealing with foreign policy crises. Because of the domestic mobilization function Mao attached to China's external policies, Beijing's use of force during the Maoist period was characterized by three distinctive and consistent patterns.

First, Beijing's leaders resorted to force only when the confrontation was in one way or another related to China's territorial integrity and physical security. Even when China's purpose in entering a military confrontation was broader than the simple Defence of its border (such as during the Korean War), Beijing's leaders always emphasized that they had exercised the military option because China's physical security was in jeopardy.

When China's involvement in a military confrontation resulted in its occupation of foreign territory, such as during the Chinese-Indian border war of 1962, Beijing's leaders ordered a retreat in order to prove that China's war aims were no more than the Defence of China's borders. Second, Beijing's leaders used force *always* for the purpose of domestic mobilization. Mao and his comrades fully understood that the tension created by an international crisis provided them with the best means to call the whole nation to act in accordance with the will and terms of the CCP.

This was particularly true when Mao met with difficulty in pushing the party and the nation to carry out his continuous-revolution programs. Mao's decision to shell Jinmen in the summer of 1958 was closely related to a nationwide wave of mass mobilization, which made it possible for the Great Leap Forward to reach a high point.

On the eve of the Cultural Revolution, China's involvement in the Vietnam War and the extensive mass mobilization that accompanied it created an atmosphere conducive to the rapid radicalization of China's political and social life. Third, Beijing's leaders used force only when they believed that they were in a position to justify it in a "moral" sense. If they did not morally justify their actions, the mobilization effect they hoped to achieve would be compromised. During the Korean War, the Beijing leadership's public war aims, "Defend our nation! Defend our home!" and "Defeat American arrogance!"were established as central mobilization slogans. During China's involvement in the Vietnam War, Mao compared the relationship between Vietnam and China to that between "lips and teeth," emphasizing that China had an obligation to proletarian internationalism to support the just struggle of the Vietnamese people.

"Justice," indeed, became the talisman of China's international military involvement during the Cold War. China's external behavior during the Maoist era was a contradictory phenomenon. Despite its tendency toward using force, Mao's China was not an expansionist power. It is essential to make a distinction between the pursuit of *centrality* and the pursuit of *dominance* in international affairs in terms of the fundamental goal of Chinese foreign policy.

While Mao and his comrades were never shy about using force in pursuing China's foreign policy goals, what they hoped to achieve was not the expansion of China's political and military control of foreign territory or resources

— which was, for Mao and his comrades, too inferior an aim — but, rather, the spread of their influence to other "hearts and minds" around the world. Mao fully understood that only when China's superior moral position in the world had been recognized by other peoples would the consolidation of his continuous revolution's momentum at home be assured.

10

China's New Security Concept And Asia

The Report to the 16th National Congress of the Communist Party of China pointed out, "……foster a new security concept featuring mutual trust, mutual benefit, equality and coordination". This is the important new thinking in the international security, which conforms to the historical trend of the times. The new security concept is against the Cold War mentality and will show its strong vitality in its overcoming Cold War mentalities. The new security concept is the important part of "Three Presents", and will be the security assurance of China's peaceful rise. During the Cold War Period, the two superpowers, namely the United States and the Russia, had had long-term severe military confrontation and armed races, competing for world hegemony.

As one of the serious consequences, both sides had developed the enormous arsenals of nuclear weapons, which can destroy the whole human beings for several times and became the sword of Damocles over the peoples in the world, threatening the security and survival of the human beings. Being compatible to this situation, in the international security field, the two superpowers had formed a complete series of the Cold War mentality, which was based on geo-politics, balance-of-power strategy, "Zero Sum" games theory and anti-communism. Since the end of the Cold War, the international situation has been greatly changed. Peace and development have become the main theme of the current times.

To maintain world peace and promote common development is the common willingness of the peoples of all countries and the irresistible historical trends. The development of the trend of multi-polarization in the world and economic globalization has brought opportunities and beneficial conditions to world peace and development. Under the situation, the international society should abandon out-date Cold War mentality and accept the new concepts in international fields. During recent years, to counter the existence of the Cold War mentality and power politics thinking, China has hold, with the spirit of keeping pace with the times, that we need new concepts to maintain peace.

China has advocated setting up the new security concept with "mutual trust, mutual benefit, equality, and coordination" as the core. It has promoted that mutual trust should be improved through dialogue and common security should be realized through cooperation. The new concept is the development of the Five Principles of peaceful co-existence, and should become the foundation of the theory to establish the framework of international security in the new century. In the first, mutual trust is with honest as its roots and with trust as the first. Every country should abandon the Cold War mentality and power politics and be beyond the difference of idealism and social systems, not harboring suspicions with each other and not adopting a hostile attitude towards each other.

Countries should often make dialogue about their security and Defence policy, and should circulate to each other about their significant actions. They should actively establish mechanisms of regional security cooperation and dialogue through all kinds of confidence and security-building measures to increase mutual trust. In the second, mutual benefit indicates that in order to conform to the trends of globalization, all the countries should respect the security interests of other sides when maintaining its own national interests, and should create conditions for security of other sides realizing its own security interests, setting up global security on the common interests and realize common security.

In the third, equality refers to the maintaining of the principle that every country, whether it is big or small, strong or weak, is an equal member in the international society. All the countries should respect with each other and treat each other equally, not to interfere in other country's internal affairs. They should push forward the trend of democratization of international relations together. In the fourth, coordination indicates that all the countries should carry out broad and in-depth cooperation to deal with security problems of all concerns, so as to cope effectively with challenges in global security.

They should remove hidden dangers and resolve disputes through peaceful means, to prevent war and armed conflicts and realize universal and persistent security. The purpose of the new concept of security is to surmount differences, to increase mutual trust through dialogue, to resolve disputes through negotiations, and to promote cooperation through security. Since the end of the Cold War, with the development of the trends of world multi-polarization and economic globalization, some countries have made efforts in carrying out the new concept of security in their mutual relationship and international relationship.

For example, China and Russia have regarded each other as friends and help each other in many issues. They have committed that "they will not use or threaten use of force in their mutual relations", "if one party consider that there are threats to peace, threats to its security interests or threats of invasion, both sides will contact and consult with each other immediately in order to remove the threats." Furthermore, the fields of common interests between China and Russia have been greatly broadened, including anti-terror, economic cooperation, arms transfer, maintaining of stability in Central Asia.

If the two countries can resolve the some existing problems between them and do their best to develop their strategic partnership of coordination, which on equal footing and mutual trust, they will be able to realize their thought of peace "friendship of all generations and never being enemy to each other". China-Russian relationship on the basis of this thought is not a relationship, which is not mainly based on the concept of balance of power to balance of the United State. Although the considering of balance of power is not totally be ruled out, the relationship is in general guided by the new security concept.

In the international multilateral relations, we also can find some new changes, which is beneficial for the new concept of security. For example, the foundation of theory of China-US-Soviet strategic triangle during the Cold War period was the theory of balance of power. The history of China-US-Soviet strategic triangle was in fact one in which China, the US and the Russia interacted, so as to maintain international strategic balance. Because the former Russia had been rising, and had been pursuing the policy of expansion and the offensive posture, China and the US cooperated to balance the former Russia.

During the periods, the thinking of balance of power in US foreign policy was most evident. Mr. Richard Nixon realized even during his campaign for President: "because the relations between China and the Russia is very intense, the US can regard Beijing as its important weapon in diplomatic struggle and make use of the intense relationship to press the Kremlin to make concession." In 1969 Kissinger predicted, "there will be a new world, in which there are five power centers—the United States, West Europe, Russia, China and Japan. In the enlarged world, to have close relations with China will make benefit. It can make Russia take the position of relative flexibility, so as to relax the stalemate between Moscow and Washington, which had dominated the post-the Second World War period."

As to the question of the establishment of China-US diplomacy, Dr. Zbigniew Brzezinski pointed out, "China has been playing central role in maintaining the global balance of power. In our world of pluralism, a strong and independent China is of the powers maintaining peace." Under the guide of the thought, China and the US realized the normalization of their relations. In China-US-Soviet strategic triangle, US policy towards China was mainly influenced by US-Soviet relations. When China and the US relations made important breakthrough or made big progress was usually the time that the US wanted to press Russia to make important concession or to rely on for support from China to check the expansion of the Russia.

When US-Soviet relationship was in relaxation, China-US relations was usually at a standstill and even unstable to some extent. Since the end of the Cold War, According to the changed situation, China and Russia have initiated a new relationship between countries with partnership instead of alliance as the core, which has gradually developed into the new concept of security with the contents of mutual trust, disarmament and cooperative security. The new concept of security is embodied in the "Shanghai Spirit", characterized with mutual trust, mutual benefit, equality and consultation, respecting the diversity of civilization and seeking for common development.

The "Shanghai Spirit" has become the guiding principle of Shanghai Cooperation Organization (SCO), a regional multiple organization. Furthermore, China holds that security should be mutual and security based on other countries' insecurity will not permanent and stable. However, since it become the only superpower in the world, the United States has been pursuing the strategy of hegemonism plus balance of power or the strategy of "world empire", which purpose is realize and maintain the international peace under US hegemony for a long time.

Some American scholars hold, "under the situation of only one hegemony, it is much more possible that the international environment is in peace."

At present, there are two different concepts between China-Russia and the US on how to see and deal with the international relations during the post-Cold War period:

Firstly, both China and Russia hold that pushing forward the process of the world multi-polarization "beneficial for establishing a new international order of stability, democracy, no confrontation, justice and equitability. The trend accords objectively with the fundamental interests of all the countries." However, the US has done its best to maintain its position as "uni-polar and only superpower" for a long time.

Secondly, both China and Russia see and cope with their mutual relations, and their relations with the US and other countries according to the new concept of security, which goes beyond the theory of balance of power. They hold that their friendly relationship is based on non-alliance, non-confrontation, and non-aiming at the third country. However, the US continues to use the policy of balance of power as one of the main measures to maintain its position as world hegemony. It has still strengthened it military alliances with its allies, which is based on aiming at the third country.

Thirdly, both China and Russia see the national security from broad angle, thinking that national security is comprehensive, including political, economic, military, scientific, financial and IT factors, in which some untraditional security factors, such as economics, science, finance and IT (information technology), have been more and more important.

However, the mainstream of US government still sees the national security interests from narrow angle, stressing the role of traditional security factor—military and regarding military superiority as the main pillar to maintain the US as the only superpower. It is unavoidable for the two different concepts to collide and interact with each other, the results of which will have significant impacts on international strategic situation. The new concept of security reflects the grand trend of the world development of closer and closer economic interdependence.

The theory of balance of power reflects the international mechanism of balance of power under the situation of anarchism, which is being gradually replaced by the new international mechanism of integration.

THE STRUGGLE WITH THE COLD WAR MENTALITY

The New Security Concept is one of the important parts of the new thinking of international strategy with Chinese characteristics. It is the products of breaking with the Cold War mentality and will further develop in colliding with the Cold War mentality and power politics. Because the US is the only superpower in the current world and the international strategic strength is very unbalanced, the Cold War mentality has been still existing and some new theories of power politics has appeared. The global strategy of Clinton Administration can be summarized as the strategy of hegemony plus balance of power.

However, the global strategy of Junior Bush Administration is in fact the strategy of the world empire, which has been most influenced by the new conservatism and offensive realism. The founding father of the new conservatism was Dr. Leo Straus, professor of University of Chicago, who held, "if we want Western democracy will not threatened by the world, we must make the whole world—every country and every nation—realize democracy." Some of his students and worshipers have become the leading people of American new conservatism and played the central role in it.

The representative of American offensive realism is Professor John J. Mearshheimer, who has advocated the off-shore balancing strategy, which stresses that the US should become the off-shore balancer, making use of the contradictions between major powers in a region, so as to prevent any major power from becoming regional hegemony to compete with the US. The traditional realism has also had some impacts on the global strategy of Bush Administration and become the important factor to balance the new conservatism.

One of the important current representative of the traditional realism is Dr. Richard Harsh, who has advocated the Theory of Integration, holding that the US should use diplomatic means to "make other countries and international organizations to be integrated into the world arrangements, which are identical with US interests and values", so as to promote the world peace and help the US cope with traditional and untraditional security threats, including regional conflicts, terrorism, proliferation of weapon s of mass destruction, and so on. According to the theory of new conservatism and offensive realism, Bush Administration has pursued its foreign policy, which is characterized with two factors, unilateralism and balance of power policy.

The unilateralism is that Bush Administration is seeking for the freedom of the US in international affairs and refuses some binding multilateral commitments, disregarding some international mechanisms and treaties. For example, Bush Administration declared that the US withdrew from the Kyoto Protocol, which places the restrictions on discharging of global greenhouse gas. Another example is that Bush Administration declared that the US withdrew from the Treaty of Anti-Ballistic Missile (ABM). The unilateralism also is a kind of hegemolism. During the late Cold War period, the US sought for using China to balance the Russia.

Different from that, current US policy of balance of power is that in order to prevent the emerging of a major power in Euro-Asian Mainland to challenge US leading position, the US should play "unique and final balancing role" in some important regions. Some new con even advocated the establishment of "the Americana" or "benign hegemolism". However, it is impossible for the international mechanism under US hegemolism to have real peace, because the US as hegemony without balancing strength may often launch attacks against some middle or small countries, which are regarded by the US as running count to its will or being harmful to its interests.

If the Cold War mentality and new theory of power politics prevail, the zero-sum games are still the basic model of interaction in the international relations, indicating that one side gets benefit means other side suffers, or that two sides have closer relations means the third side suffers. However, under the new situation of peace and development becoming the theme of the current times, the zero-sum games will come to the end, although it will take very long time. Under the current situation, major powers share many common interests, although they still have many contradictions at the same time. So they will establish their relations of both cooperation and competition.

For example, because of the development of economic interdependence and existence of many transnational problems, China and the US have to seek for cooperation and are facing "win-win" model or "loss-loss" model. Even as to some traditional security problems, like Korean nuclear issue, China and the US have many common interests and need to cooperate. Because China and the US are major powers and nuclear powers, if there is war between them, both of them will suffer a lot, although China may suffer much more than the US. So the two countries should make their great efforts to maintain the stability of their relations and to prevent their armed conflicts.

If both China and the US can deal with their mutual relationship with the new concept of security, they can establish constructive cooperative relations. If all the countries in the world can deal with their mutual relationship with the new concept of security, they can create a world with peace and development as the mainstream. Even in Europe where geo-politics had prevailed before the end of the Cold War, although the model of geo-politics has still existed, some new models of interactions between major powers have appeared during the recent years, including:

a) Model of international mechanisms

The basic feature of this model is "to require the actions of members of the international community to be under the control of universal indorsed norms, rules and conventions". A main example is the eastward expansion of the NATO and its interaction with Russia. After the end of the Cold War, the disintegration of the Russia and disbanding of the Warsaw Treaty Organization, the NATO did not disappear and even has expanded eastward. In December 2002, the NATO Summit Meeting held in Prague decided that the NATO would permit seven nations to join the NATO in 2004.

After the seven nations complete the procedure to join the NATO, members of the NATO will increase to 26 nations, and will expand to North Europe, East Europe and Southeast Europe. At the same time, the role of the NATO has also been expanding. November 2002, the NATO Summit Meeting decided to set up quick reaction forces, so as to interfere in crisis outside the NATO Territory. The NATO eastward expansion extruded the strategic space of Russia. From the angel, to some extent, the model of geo-politics has been playing some role. However, because Russia has been focused on internal economic development, and the military functions of the NATO have been decreased, Russia and the NATO have not had the confronting contradictions now.

The relations between Russia and the NATO have been greatly changed. In May 1997, Russia and the NATO singed the Basic Document on Mutual Relationship, Cooperation and Security, declaring that both sides were partners, which lead to the Mechanism of 19+1. In May 2002, 19 heads of NATO member nations and Russian President Putin signed the Rome Statement, declaring the formal establishment of the NATO-Russia Council, which is also called as the Mechanism of 20, replacing the Mechanism of 19+1.

The new Council has become the framework of discussing and establishing the common security mechanism in Europe, indicating that the depth and broadness of security cooperation between the two sides have been greatly increased. Since the establishment of the Mechanism of 20, NATO and Russia have strengthen their consultation and cooperation in anti-terror, preventing nuclear proliferation, arms control, coping with regional crisis and participating in international peace-keeping. In those fields, Russia has got the responsibilities and obligations equal to member nations of the NATO. In this way, the Mechanism of 20 has gone beyond geo-politics and model of international mechanisms have played the most important role in it.

b) Model of geo-economics

One of the key viewpoints of Geo-economics is that with the development of economic globalization and regional economic integration, three major regional economic groups, namely European Union (EU), North American Free Trade Agreement (NAFTA) and East Asian economic group, have been gradually formed and will compete with each other. One example is the economic interaction of NAFTA and the EU. Another example is the Eastward expansion of the EU and its interaction with Russia. Because another ten nations of Central Europe and East Europe jointed the EU, member nations of the EU have been increased from 15 to 25. Its population has reached 450 million and its economic scale is nearly as same as the US.

The Eastward expansion of the EU has also increased 100 million consumers and extended the potential cheap manufacturing capabilities, so as to spur the competition and dynamics in the EU, bringing evident economic interests to member nations of the EU. At the same time, the expansion of the EU will enhance its international position and influence. Russia has paid great attention on the Eastward expansion of the EU, but not opposed it. Since the 1990s, Russia has strengthened its contacts with the EU, hoping to join the economic mechanism of the Europe and get economic aid from Europe. Geo-economics has played the major role in the interaction of Russia and the EU.

c) Model of win-win

The basic feature of this model is that all the nations have to seek for win-win model in their relations or face loss-loss model, because they share many common interests. For example, the US, the EU and Russia cooperate to deal with untraditional security threats. Since the end of the Cold War, especially September 11 Incident, untraditional security threats have been rising, including terrorism, proliferation of weapons of mass destruction, drug trafficking, transnational crimes, environmental pollution, AIDS/HIV and so on. The US, the EU and Russia share common interests in coping with those threats and have made some important progress in their cooperation.

The appearance of those new models of interaction of security relations indicates that the Cold War mentality has been declining and the new security concept has been playing more important role. This is the historical trend, although it will take a long time.

THE NEW SECURITY CONCEPT

The new security concept is the new thinking, which keeps abreast of the times, and has new form and contents. At present, the mechanism of international relations has been transforming from the balance-of-power and anarchism to the interdependence, which will encourage every nations to adapt its foreign strategy to the change. During recent years, a series of important incidents have happened in the world. They have critical impacts on the current international order and are changing the international structure. The connotation and extension of security are getting larger.

Uncertain factors have increased, influencing world peace and development. The traditional and nontraditional security threats have been interweaving. The traditional security problems, like armed conflicts caused by territory, resources and ethnic contradictions, have still existed. Furthermore, the untraditional security problems, like terrorism, drug trafficking, transnational crimes, environmental pollution, SARS, are getting more projecting.

All the countries have shared more and more common interests, and have to push forward multilateral cooperation. New concepts and means to safeguard security should be adopted. In the current world, power politics and the Cold War mentality have still existed. We should further substantiate and develop the new security concept, and then promote it as one of new basic norms of international relations. We should also find the way by using the new security concept to fight power politics and the Cold War mentality. In 1996, China first advocated the establishment of a new security concept according to the trend of the times and the features of the Asia-Pacific region.

Afterwards, China put clearly forward that the core of the new concept of security should be mutual trust, mutual benefit, equality and coordination. According to the new concept of security, China has actively push forward the establishment and development of Shanghai Cooperation Organization, and China joined the World Trade Organization (WTO). All these show that China has been taking the leading role in adapting itself to the change of the times. China has pursued the guideline of building good-neighborly relationships and partnerships with its neighboring countries, and has regarded peace, security, cooperation and prosperity as the goal of its Asian policy, actively pushing forward the good-neighborly relationships and the regional cooperation.

The purpose of security of China in the Asia-Pacific region is to defend state sovereignty and territory integrity, to maintain regional peace and stability, and push forward the regional security dialogue and cooperation. At present, China's security concepts are more open and policy more transparent. China has participated more broadly in multilateral security cooperation. China holds that comprehensive is one of the basic features of current security issues, cooperative security is the effective way to maintain international security, and common security is the final goal of maintaining East Asian security.

At present, Asia-Pacific countries are working for economic development and social stability, deepening their cooperation of mutual benefit. Their consciousness of seeking for common security and development has been increasing. The major powers have more common interests than differences between them, promoting consultation and cooperation. To maintain stability and to accelerate cooperation has become the mainstream of the situation In the Asia-Pacific region. This depends on China and other Asia-Pacific countries' common efforts, based on the new concept of security.

For example, with the development for more than ten years, ASEAN Regional Forum (ARF) has gradually become the largest multilateral official channel of security dialogue and cooperation, defining the new effective model of reaching unanimity through consultations, following in order and advancing step by step, noninterference in each other's internal affairs, and showing full consideration for comfortableness of all parties. During the past more than ten years, China and ASEAN have developed their relationship from the establishment of comprehensive dialogue relations to good-neighboring, mutual-trust partnership. Both sides have more strengthened their politically mutual trust, have developed their much closer economic interdependence, and have made their cooperation more effective.

In 2002, both, China and ASEAN signed the Treaty on Framework of Comprehensive Economic Cooperation, formally beginning the process of negotiating China-ASEAN free trade area. Both sides declared the Joint Statement on Cooperation in Untraditional Security Fields, exploring the new space of cooperation between them. China and ASEAN also signed the Declaration on the Condact of Parties in the South China Sea, reaching the consensus on resolving the disputes through peaceful means, commonly maintaining the regional stability, and cooperation in South China Sea. In June 2003, at the ARF Foreign Ministers' Meeting held in Phnom Penh, Chinese Foreign Minister put forward the initiative that the conferences on security conference should be held at a suitable time.

In October 2003, China formally joined the Treaty of Amity and Cooperation in Southeast Asia, and jointly declared to establish the "strategic partnership for peace and prosperity". Shanghai Cooperation Organization (SCO) has gradually improved its organic structure, beginning its new stage with pragmatic cooperation as the core. The practices proved that making use of the new security concept is beneficial for peace, stability and development of the Asia-Pacific region as well as in the world. China has made significant progress with its neighboring countries in their bilateral relationship.

In 2003, China and India relations have entered the new phase of comprehensive development, declaring the China-India Statement on Principles of Relationship and Comprehensive Cooperation. In its relations with Japan, China has stuck to the guidelines of reviewing the history and facing the future, pushing forward the stable development of cooperation of the two countries in many fields. China and South Korea have established the cooperative partnership. Friendship between China, and Pakistan and other countries in South Asia has been continuing to develop.

China can not develop without peace and stability in the Asia-Pacific region, and China's development is one of the important parts of prosperity and progress in the Asia-Pacific region. It is necessary for China to pursue the guideline of building good-neighborly relationships and partnerships with its neighboring countries, cooperating with Asia-Pacific countries to set up the healthy and stable regional security environment, and making more contributions to the peace and stability of the Asia-Pacific region. With the advent of the new century, the world is undergoing tremendous changes and adjustments.

Peace and development remain the principal themes of the times, and the pursuit of peace, development and cooperation has become an irresistible trend of the times. However, global challenges are on the increase, and new security threats keep emerging. Economic globalization and world multi-polarization are gaining momentum. The progress toward industrialization and informationization throughout the globe is accelerating and economic cooperation is in full swing, leading to increasing economic interdependence, inter-connectivity and interactivity among countries.

The rise and decline of international strategic forces is quickening, major powers are stepping up their efforts to cooperate with each other and draw on each other's strengths. They continue to compete with and hold each other in check, and groups of new emerging developing powers are arising. Therefore, a profound readjustment is brewing in the international system. In addition, factors conducive to maintaining peace and containing war are on the rise, and the common interests of countries in the security field have increased, and their willingness to cooperate is enhanced, thereby keeping low the risk of worldwide, all-out and large-scale wars for a relatively long period of time.

World peace and development are faced with multiple difficulties and challenges. Struggles for strategic resources, strategic locations and strategic dominance have intensified. Meanwhile, hegemonism and power politics still exist, regional turmoil keeps spilling over, hot-spot issues are increasing, and local conflicts and wars keep emerging. The impact of the financial crisis triggered by the U.S. subprime mortgage crisis is snowballing. In the aspect of world economic development, issues such as energy and food are becoming more serious, highlighting deep-seated contradictions.

Economic risks are manifesting a more interconnected, systematic and global nature. Issues such as terrorism, environmental disasters, climate change, serious epidemics, transnational crime and pirates are becoming increasingly prominent. The influence of military security factors on international relations is mounting. Driven by competition in overall national strength and the development of science and technology, international military competition is becoming increasingly intense, and the worldwide revolution in military affairs (RMA) is reaching a new stage of development.

Some major powers are realigning their security and military strategies, increasing their Defence investment, speeding up the transformation of armed forces, and developing advanced military technology, weapons and equipment. Strategic nuclear forces, military astronautics, missile Defence systems, and global and battlefield reconnaissance and surveillance have become top priorities in their efforts to strengthen armed forces. Some developing countries are also actively seeking to acquire advanced weapons and equipment to increase their military power. All countries are attaching more importance to supporting diplomatic struggles with military means. As a result, arms races in some regions are heating up, posing grave challenges to the international arms control and nonproliferation regime.

The Asia-Pacific security situation is stable on the whole. The regional economy is brimming with vigor, mechanisms for regional and sub-regional economic and security cooperation maintain their development momentum, and it has become the policy orientation of all countries to settle differences and hotspot issues peacefully through dialogue. The member states of the Shanghai Cooperation Organization (SCO) have signed the Treaty on Long-Term Good-Neighborly Relations, Friendship and Cooperation, and practical cooperation has made progress in such fields as security and economy. The conclusion of the ASEAN Charter has enabled a new step to be taken toward ASEAN integration.

Remarkable achievements have been made in cooperation between China and ASEAN, as well as between ASEAN and China, Japan and the Republic of Korea. Cooperation within the framework of the East Asia Summit (EAS) and the South Asian Association for Regional Cooperation (SAARC) continues to make progress. The Six-Party Talks on the Korean nuclear issue have scored successive achievements, and the tension in Northeast Asia is much released. However, there still exist many factors of uncertainty in Asia-Pacific security. The drastic fluctuations in the world economy impact heavily on regional economic development, and political turbulence persists in some countries undergoing economic and social transition. Ethnic and religious discords, and conflicting claims over territorial and maritime rights and interests remain serious, regional hotspots are complex.

At the same time, the U.S. has increased its strategic attention to and input in the Asia-Pacific region, further consolidating its military alliances, adjusting its military deployment and enhancing its military capabilities. In addition, terrorist, separatist and extremist forces are running rampant, and non-traditional security issues such as serious natural disasters crop up frequently. The mechanisms for security cooperation between countries and regions are yet to be enhanced, and the capability for coping with regional security threats in a coordinated way has to be improved. China's security situation has improved steadily. The achievements made in China's modernization drive have drawn worldwide attention.

China's overall national strength has increased substantially, its people's living standards have kept improving, the society remains stable and unified, and the capability for upholding national security has been further enhanced. The attempts of the separatist forces for "Taiwan independence" to seek "de jure Taiwan independence" have been thwarted, and the situation across the Taiwan Straits has taken a significantly positive turn.

The two sides have resumed and made progress in consultations on the common political basis of the "1992 Consensus," and consequently cross-Straits relations have improved. Meanwhile, China has made steady progress in its relations with the developed countries, strengthened in all respects the good-neighborly friendship with its neighboring countries, and kept deepening its traditional friendship with the developing countries. China is playing an active and constructive role in multilateral affairs, thus notably elevating its international position and influence. China is still confronted with long-term, complicated, and diverse security threats and challenges. Issues of existence security and development security, traditional security threats and non-traditional security threats, and domestic security and international security are interwoven and interactive.

China is faced with the superiority of the developed countries in economy, science and technology, as well as military affairs. It also faces strategic maneuvers and containment from the outside while having to face disruption and sabotage by separatist and hostile forces from the inside. Being in a stage of economic and social transition, China is encountering many new circumstances and new issues in maintaining social stability. Separatist forces working for "Taiwan independence," "East Turkistan independence" and "Tibet independence" pose threats to

China's unity and security. Damages caused by non-traditional security threats like terrorism, natural disasters, economic insecurity, and information insecurity are on the rise.

Impact of uncertainties and destabilizing factors in China's outside security environment on national security and development is growing. In particular, the United States continues to sell arms to Taiwan in violation of the principles established in the three Sino-U.S. joint communiques, causing serious harm to Sino-U.S. relations as well as peace and stability across the Taiwan Straits.

In the face of unprecedented opportunities and challenges, China will hold high the banner of peace, development and cooperation, persist in taking the road of peaceful development, pursue the opening-up strategy of mutual benefit, and promote the building of a harmonious world with enduring peace and common prosperity; and it will persist in implementing the Scientific Outlook on Development in a bid to achieve integration of development with security, persist in giving due consideration to both traditional and non-traditional security issues, enhancing national strategic capabilities, and perfecting the national emergency management system. At the same time, it will persist in pursuing the new security concept featuring mutual trust, mutual benefit, equality and coordination, and advocating the settlement of international disputes and hotspot issues by peaceful means.

It will encourage the advancement of security dialogues and cooperation with other countries, oppose the enlargement of military alliances, and acts of aggression and expansion. China will never seek hegemony or engage in military expansion now or in the future, no matter how developed it becomes. China pursues a national Defence policy which is purely defensive in nature. China places the protection of national sovereignty, security, territorial integrity, safeguarding of the interests of national development, and the interests of the Chinese people above all else. China endeavors to build a fortified national Defence and strong military forces compatible with national security and development interests, and enrich the country and strengthen the military while building a moderately prosperous society in all aspects.

China's national Defence policy for the new stage in the new century basically includes: upholding national security and unity, and ensuring the interests of national development; achieving the all-round, coordinated and sustainable development of China's national Defence and armed forces; enhancing the performance of the armed forces with informationization as the major measuring criterion; implementing the military strategy of active Defence; pursuing a self-defensive nuclear strategy; and fostering a security environment conducive to China's peaceful development.

According to the requirements of national security and the level of economic and social development, China pursues a three-step development strategy to modernize its national Defence and armed forces step by step in a well-planned way. This strategic framework is defined as follows:

Promoting the informationization of China's national Defence and armed forces. Taking informationization as the goal of modernization of its national Defence and armed forces and in light of its national and military conditions, China actively pushes forward the RMA with Chinese characteristics. It has formulated in a scientific way strategic plans for national Defence and armed forces building and strategies for the development of the services and arms, according to which it will lay a solid foundation by 2010, basically accomplish mechanization and make major progress in informationization by 2020, and by and large reach the goal of modernization of national Defence and armed forces by the mid-21st century.

Overall planning of economic development and national Defence building. Sticking to the principle of coordinated development of economy and national Defence, China makes overall plans for the use of its national resources and strikes a balance between enriching the country and strengthening the military, so as to ensure that its strategy for national Defence and armed forces building is compatible with its strategy for national development. It makes national Defence building an organic part of its social and economic development, endeavors to establish scientific mechanisms for the coordinated development of economy and national Defence, and thus provides rich resources and sustainable driving force for the modernization of its national Defence and armed forces.

In national Defence building, China makes it a point to take into consideration the needs of economic and social development and insists on having military and civilian purposes compatible with and beneficial to each other, so as to achieve more social benefits in the use of national Defence resources in peacetime.

a) Deepening the reform of national Defence and armed forces

China is working to adjust and reform the organization, structure and policies of the armed forces, and will advance step by step the modernization of the organizational form and pattern of the armed forces in order to develop by 2020 a complete set of scientific modes of organization, institutions and ways of operation both with Chinese characteristics and in conformity with the laws governing the building of modern armed forces. China strives to adjust and reform the systems of Defence-related industry of science and technology and the procurement of weapons and equipment, and enhance its capacity for independent innovation in R&D of weapons and equipment with better quality and cost-effectiveness.

China endeavors to establish and improve the systems of weaponry and equipment research and manufacturing, military personnel training and logistical support that integrate military with civilian purposes and combine military efforts with civilian support. In addition, China makes an effort to establish and improve a national Defence mobilization system that is centralized and unified, well structured, rapid in reaction, and authoritative and efficient.

b) Taking the road of leapfrog development

Persisting in taking mechanization as the foundation and informationization as focus, China is stepping up the composite development of mechanization and informationization. Persisting in strengthening the military by means of science and technology, China is working to develop new and high-tech weaponry and equipment, carry out the strategic project of training talented people, conduct military training in conditions of informationization, and build a modern logistics system in an all-round way, so as to change the mode of formation of war-fighting capabilities. Persisting in laying stress on priorities, China distinguishes between the primary and the secondary, and refrains from doing certain things, striving to achieve leapfrog development in key areas. China persists in building the armed forces through diligence and thrift, attaching importance to scientific management, in order to make the fullest use of its limited Defence resources.

China implements a military strategy of active Defence. Strategically, it adheres to the principle of featuring defensive operations, self-Defence and striking and getting the better of the enemy only after the enemy has started an attack. In response to the new trends in world military developments and the requirements of the national security and development strategy, China has formulated a military strategic guideline of active Defence for the new period. This guideline aims at winning local wars in conditions of informationization. It takes into overall consideration the evolution of modern warfare and the major security threats facing China, and prepares for defensive operations under the most difficult and complex circum-stances.

Meeting the requirements of confrontation between war systems in modern warfare and taking integrated joint operations as the basic approach, it is designed to bring the operational strengths of different services and arms into full play, combine offensive operations with defensive operations, give priority to the flexible application of strategies and tactics, seek advantages and avoid disadvantages, and make the best use of our strong points to attack the enemy's weak points. It endeavors to refine the command system for joint operations, the joint training system and the joint support system, optimize the structure and composition of forces, and speed up the building of a combat force structure suitable for winning local wars in conditions of informationization.

This guideline lays stress on deterring crises and wars. It works for close coordination between military struggle and political, diplomatic, economic, cultural and legal endeavors, strives to foster a favorable security environment, and takes the initiative to prevent and defuse crises, and deter conflicts and wars. It strictly adheres to a position of self-Defence, exercises prudence in the use of force, seeks to effectively control war situations, and strives to reduce the risks and costs of war. It calls for the building of a lean and effective deterrent force and the flexible use of different means of deterrence. China remains committed to the policy of no first use of nuclear weapons, pursues a self-defensive nuclear strategy, and will never enter into a nuclear arms race with any other country.

This guideline focuses on enhancing the capabilities of the armed forces in countering various security threats and accomplishing diversified military tasks. With the focus of attention on performing the historical missions of the armed forces for the new stage in the new century and with raising the capability to win local wars in conditions of informationization at the core, it works to increase the country's capabilities to maintain maritime, space and electromagnetic space security and to carry out the tasks of counter-terrorism, stability maintenance, emergency rescue and international peacekeeping. It takes military operations other than war (MOOTW) as an important form of applying national military forces, and scientifically makes and executes plans for the development of MOOTW capabilities.

China participates in international security cooperation, conducts various forms of military exchanges and promotes the establishment of military confidence-building mechanisms in accordance with this guideline. This guideline adheres to and carries forward the strategic concept of people's war. In accordance with this guideline, China always relies on the people to build national Defence and the armed forces, combines a lean standing force with a powerful reserve force, and endeavors to reinforce its national war potential and Defence strength. China is working to set up a mechanism for unified and efficient national Defence mobilization, stepping up the mobilization of economy, science and technology, information and transportation, and making improvements in the building of the reserve force.

China is striving to make innovations in the content and forms of people's war, exploring new approaches of the people in participating in warfare and support for the front, and developing new strategies and tactics for people's war in conditions of informationization. Moreover, the People's Liberation Army (PLA) subordinates its development to the overall national construction, supports local economic and social development, and consolidates the unity between the PLA and the government, and between the PLA and the people.

In the great historical course of China's reform and opening-up over the past three decades, the PLA has invariably taken modernization as its central task, continuously engaged in reform and innovation, comprehensively advanced revolutionization, modernization and regularization, and made important contributions to safeguarding national sovereignty and security, and maintaining world peace. In recent years, the PLA has accelerated RMA with Chinese characteristics, and pushed forward its military, political, logistical and equipment work in a coordinated way, in an effort to achieve sound and rapid development.

THIRTY YEARS OF REFORM AND DEVELOPMENT

From the late 1970s and into the 1980s, the PLA set out on the road of building a streamlined military with Chinese characteristics. According to the scientific judgment that peace and development had become the principal themes of the times, it made a strategic shift in its guiding principle for military building from preparations for "an early, large-scale and nuclear war" to peacetime construction, and advanced its modernization step by step in a well-planned way under the precondition that such efforts should be both subordinated to and in the service of the country's overall development. It set the general goal of building a powerful military, revolutionary in nature, modernized and regularized, and blazed a trail for building a lean military with Chinese characteristics.

It underwent significant adjustment and reform, and streamlined the size of its armed forces by a million troops, thereby taking an important step forward in making itself streamlined, combined and efficient. Entering the 1990s, the PLA began to vigorously promote RMA with Chinese characteristics. It established the military strategic guideline of active Defence for the new era, based on winning local wars in conditions of modern technology, particularly high technology. It began to adopt a strategy of strengthening the military by means of science and technology, and a three-step development strategy in modernizing national Defence and the armed forces, and promoted the coordinated development of national Defence and economy.

Regarding RMA with Chinese characteristics as the only way to modernize the military, it put forward the strategic goal of building informationized military and winning informationized wars. Driven by preparations for military struggle, it accelerated the development of weaponry and equipment, stepped up the development of the arms and services of the armed forces, as well as forces for emergency mobile operations, optimized its system and structure, and reduced the number of personnel by 700,000. As a result, its capability of defensive operations increased remarkably.

At the new stage in the new century, the PLA has been striving to create a new situation in its modernization drive at a new historical starting point. With the Scientific Outlook on Development as an important guiding principle for national Defence and armed forces building, it has acted in accordance with the strategic thought of balancing economic and national Defence development and integrating efforts to enrich the country and strengthen the military. It has been dedicated to performing its new historical missions and improving its capabilities to counter various security threats and accomplish diversified military tasks.

It has accelerated the composite development of mechanization and informationization, vigorously conducts military training in conditions of informationization, and boosts innovation in military theory, technology, organization and management, to continuously increase the core military capability of winning local wars in conditions of informationization and the capability of conducting MOOTW.

PROMOTING THE IMPROVEMENT OF MILITARY TRAINING

Regarding military training as the basic approach to furthering the comprehensive development of the military and raising combat effectiveness, the PLA is working to reform training programs, methods, management and support, and create a scientific system for military training in conditions of informationization.

Increasing training tasks. The PLA is intensifying strategic- and operational-level command post training and troop training in conditions of informationization, holding trans-regional evaluation exercises with opposing players, conducting whole-unit night training and carrying out integrated exercises for logistical and equipment support.

Moreover, it is attaching more importance to MOOTW training in counter-terrorism, stability maintenance, emergency response, peacekeeping, emergency rescue and disaster relief. Deepening training reform. The PLA is creating a task list for military training in conditions of informationization, developing a new edition of the Outline for Military Training and Evaluation, and promoting the application of innovations made in training reform. It is also reinforcing the joint training of the services and arms, strengthening functional training, giving prominence to command and coordinate training and the studies of ways of fighting, and improving training in regional cooperation. It is improving on-base training and simulated training, promoting web-based training, and conducting training with opposing players. It is also reforming training evaluation mechanisms, making training standards stricter, and enforcing meticulous management of the whole process and all aspects of military training.

Conducting training in complex electromagnetic environments. The PLA is spreading basic knowledge of electromagnetic-spectrum and battlefield-electromagnetic environments, learning and mastering basic theories of information warfare, particularly electronic warfare. It is enhancing training on how to operate and use informationized weaponry and equipment, and command information systems. It is working on the informationizing of combined tactical training bases, and holding exercises in complex electromagnetic environments.

STRENGTHENING IDEOLOGICAL AND POLITICAL WORK

The PLA insists on putting ideological and political work first, and pushing forward the innovative development of ideological and political work, to ensure the Party's absolute leadership over the armed forces, the scientific development of the military, the all-round development of the officers and men, the increase of combat capabilities and the effective fulfillment of historical missions. In January 2007 the General Political Department of the PLA issued the Guideline for the Ideological and Political Education of the Chinese People's Liberation Army (Trial).

This guideline spells out clearly that such education refers to the work by the Communist Party of China (CPC) to arm the military with political theories and provide it with ideological guidance; scientifically regulates such education for all kinds of PLA forces and personnel; and further strengthens the development of rules and regulations for such education.

Pursuant to the guideline, units whose ratios of political education to military training are 3 to 7 and 2 to 8 should devote 54 and 42 workdays, respectively, to political education each year. The PLA persists in arming its officers and men with the theory of socialism with Chinese characteristics, educates them in its historical missions, ideals, beliefs, fighting spirit and the socialist concept of honor and disgrace, and carries forward the fine traditions of obeying the Party's orders, serving the people, and fighting bravely and skillfully.

The PLA's ideological and political education adheres to six principles: to be guided by scientific theories, to put the people first, to focus on the central task and serve the overall interests, to aim at concrete results, to educate through practical activities, and to encourage innovation and development. Following these principles, the PLA has flexibly applied and innovatively developed educational forms and means, improved radio, television and network educational facilities, and built military history museums, cultural centers, "homes of political instructors," study rooms, and company clubs and honors exhibitions.

In April 2008 the Central Military Commission (CMC) approved the Regulations of the Chinese People's Liberation Army on the Work of Servicemen's Committees, which was jointly issued by the Headquarters of the General Staff, the General Political Department, the General Logistics Department and the General Armament Department. The document has institutionalized political democracy, economic democracy and military democracy for grass-roots units in the new situation. The servicemen's committee is an organization through which the grass-roots military units practice democracy in political, economic and military affairs and through which the servicemen exercise their democratic rights and carry out mass activities.

It exercises the following functions too: to advise on combat readiness training, education and management, logistical support, and weaponry and equipment management of its own unit; to make recommendations on issues concerning the immediate interests of officers and men, such as the selection and promotion of non-commissioned officers (NCOs), selection of qualified enlisted men to enter military educational institutions either through examinations or directly, selection of enlisted men for technical training, and selection of servicemen for commendations and rewards; to supervise officers and men on the performance of their duties and observation of law and discipline; and to protect the collective interests of the unit, and the legitimate rights and interests of officers and men. Consisting of five to seven members chosen by the servicemen's assembly through election by secret ballot, the servicemen's committee works under the leadership of the unit Party branch (or grass-roots Party committee) and the guidance of the unit commanders.

ENHANCING THE COST-EFFECTIVENESS OF LOGISTICAL SUPPORT

The PLA vigorously promotes integration in logistical support system, outsourcing in logistical support method, informationization in logistical support means, and scientific approach in logistical support management, to build a modern logistics system. In December 2007 the CMC promulgated the Outline for Building a Modern Logistics System, specifying the guidelines, principles, objectives and tasks for the development of modern logistics.

Deepening logistics reform

The PLA persists in promoting re-forms in joint logistics. In April 2007 the Jinan Theater formally adopted the joint logistics system based on the integration of tri-service logistical support. To speed up the outsourcing process, the PLA out-sources the commercial and housing services of combat units stationed in large- and medium-sized cities, general-purpose materials storage, capital construction, logistical equipment production and logistical technical services.

To enhance budgeting reforms, it promotes the creation of databases for budget items, strengthens the investment assessment and evaluation of major projects, summarizes and popularizes such practices as the integration of assets management with budget management and the control of expenses concerning administrative consumables, and gradually adopts the practice of using work-related expenditure cards for payment and account settlement. It enlarges the scope of centralized procurement, increases the proportion of procurement through bidding, and extends centralized procurement to non-combat units.

Upgrading logistical support

The PLA has substantially increased funding for education and training, political work, health care, water and electricity supplies, heating, barracks maintenance, etc. It has increased allowances for aviators, sailors and astronauts.

It has increased post allowances for officers in grass-roots units and duty allowances for enlisted men. It has raised servicemen's injury and death insurance and board expenses.

It has set standards for the subsidies and fees for small, scattered, distant units and units directly under the headquarters. In August 2007 all PLA troops began to replace their old uniforms with the 07 series.

Regulating logistics management

To step up standardization, the PLA is redoubling its efforts in the standardized provision of maintenance funds and centrally allocated supplies, regulating the management of construction-related supplies, and creating step by step a system of logistical support standards and regulations covering supply, consumption and management.

It strengthens financial management, spends according to standards and within its budget, and carries out construction according to its financial strength. It pays close attention to the safe management of drinking water, food, medical care, medicine, petroleum, oils and lubricants, transportation and dangerous articles.

It is improving the mechanism to prevent and control public health hazards; standardizing the management of military vehicles; conducting a special review of housing for active officers at and above the corps level; imposing strict management on military housing and the lease of unoccupied real estate; and improving the system for the employment of civilians.

In January 2007 the CMC promulgated the newly revised Audit Regulations of the Chinese People's Liberation Army.

The PLA has launched an in-depth movement to conserve energy and resources by encouraging conservation-minded supply and consumption. It protects the ecological environment of military areas by initiating a grassland conservation project, a pilot project for preventing and alleviating sand storms affecting coastal military facilities, and efforts to harness pollution by military units stationed in the area known as the Bohai Sea rim.

BOOSTING INTEGRATED EQUIPMENT SUPPORT

Meeting the requirements of tri-service integration, joint operations, systems building and systems integration, the PLA is continually improving its weaponry and equipment system and elevating integrated equipment support. Accelerating the building of a modern weaponry and equipment system with Chinese characteristics.

Persisting in self-reliance and independent innovation, the PLA gives priority to developing informationized weapons and equipment which can meet the requirements of integrated joint operations, and carries out prioritized and selective retrofitting and upgrading of existing equipment. It has basically established an army equipment system featuring high mobility and three-dimensional assault, a naval equipment system with integrated sea-air capabilities for offshore defensive operations, an air force equipment system with integrated air-land capabilities for both offensive and defensive operations, a surface-to-surface missile equipment system for the Second Artillery Force comprising both nuclear and conventional missiles with different ranges, and an electronic information equipment system featuring systems integration and joint development.

Raising the level of equipment management and the capability of new equipment maintenance and support. The PLA is intensifying the scientific, institutionalized and regular management of equipment, and has adopted a system of accountability to improve weapon and equipment readiness. Emphasis is laid on cultivating the capability of equipment maintenance and support, the techniques and means of which are being gradually shifted from being applicable to equipment of the first and second generations to being applicable to the second and third generations. Overhaul and emergency support capabilities have been basically developed for the main equipment. The PLA has augmented equipment support forces and formed a preliminary system of such forces, with regular forces as the backbone, reserve forces as the reinforcement, and backup forces as the supplement. Equipment manufacturing units have been ordered to rehearse the mobilization of technical support forces, and approaches to civil-military integrated support have been explored.

Adjusting and reforming the equipment procurement system. In the past two years, the PLA has further expanded the scope of competitive, centralized and integrated procurement. In line with the demand to separate and balance planning, contract fulfillment, contract supervision and contract auditing, the PLA has adjusted and improved the organizational system for equipment procurement, and reformed the system of resident military representatives in factories.

SPEEDING UP INFORMATIONIZATION

Actively coping with the challenges presented by the worldwide RMA, the PLA extensively applies information technology, develops and utilizes information resources in various fields of military building, and strives to take a road of military informationization with Chinese characteristics which highlights the leading role of information, pursues composite development, promotes independent innovation and facilitates transformation. Starting with command automation in the 1970s, the PLA has shifted the focus of informationization from specific areas to trans-area systems integration, and is on the whole at the initial stage of comprehensive development.

Currently, aiming at integration, the PLA is persisting in combining breakthroughs in key sectors with comprehensive development, technological innovation with structural reform, and the development and building of new systems with the modification of existing ones to tap their potentials; enhancing systems integration; stepping up efforts to develop and utilize information resources; and gradually developing and improving the capability of fighting based on information systems. Achievements have been made in the building of military information systems, with the priority being given to command information systems.

The integrated military information network came into operation in 2006, resulting in the further improvement of the information infrastructure, basic information support and information security assurance. Progress has been made in the building of command and control systems for integrated joint operations, significantly enhancing the capability of battlefield information support. IT-based training methods have undergone considerable development; surveying and mapping, navigation, weather forecasting, hydrological observation and space environment support systems have been further optimized; a number of information systems for logistical and equipment support have been successfully developed and deployed; and full-scale efforts in building "digital campuses" have begun in PLA educational institutions.

Main battle weapon systems are being gradually informationized. The focus is to increase the capability of the main battle weapon systems in the areas of rapid detection, target location, friend-or-foe identification and precision strikes. Some tanks, artillery pieces, ships and aircraft in active service have been informationized, new types of highly informationized combat platforms have been successfully developed, and the proportion and number of precision-guided munitions are on the rise.

The conditions for informationization have been improved. A leadership, management and consultation system for informationization has been basically set up, and the centralized and unified leadership for informationization has been strengthened. Theoretical explorations and studies of key practical issues related to informationization have been continuously intensified, medium-and long-term plans and guidance for informationization of the military formulated and promulgated, technical standards revised and refined, and institutional education and personnel training catering to the requirements of informationization strengthened.

STEPPING UP PERSONNEL TRAINING

The PLA is further implementing the strategic project for talented people, improving its training system and laying stress on the training of commanding officers for joint operations and high-level technical experts in an effort to cultivate a large contingent of new-type and high-caliber military personnel.

In April 2008, the CMC issued Opinions on Strengthening and Improving the Officers Training Work of the Armed Forces, explicitly requiring the establishment and improvement of the service-long and all-personnel training system, which takes level-by-level training as the backbone and on-the-job training as the supplement, and matches training with assignment.

A situation is to be created in which institutional education is linked with training in units, education in military educational institutions is carried on in parallel with education through regular institutions of higher learning, and domestic training is combined with overseas training.

Strengthening the training of commanding officers for joint operation. Various measures are being taken to step up efforts to train commanding officers for joint operations, such as institutional education, on-the-job study and rotation of posts. Incorporating joint operations into the whole training process, the PLA carefully distinguishes between the training tasks of educational institutions of different levels and types, and couples institutional education with training in units, so as to establish a system for training joint operations commanding officers which emphasizes both institutional education and practice in units. The PLA has launched the Key Projects of Military Educational Institutions and made step-by-step progress in these projects.

SELECTING AND TRAINING OFFICER CANDIDATES

In October 2007 the CMC approved and the four general headquarters/departments jointly promulgated the Regulations of the Chinese People's Liberation Army on the Admission Work of Educational Institutions, regulating the admission of high-school graduates and enlisted men into military educational institutions. At the end of 2007 the Ministry of Education and the General Political Department of the PLA co-sponsored a conference on the issue of training PLA officers via regular institutions of higher learning. At present, there are117 colleges and universities with Defence students. The PLA has selected nearly 1,000 key middle schools in the various provinces and municipalities as the main sources of Defence students.

Creating a favorable environment for cultivating talented people. The PLA has established and improved a mechanism for rewarding and inspiring talented people, issuing high rewards to outstanding commanding officers, staff officers and technical experts, as well as teams which have made great contributions in scientific and technological innovation. Since 2007 additional funds amounting to RMB 700 million have been devoted to talent cultivation. In July 2007 the CMC promulgated the Provisions of the Armed Forces on Attracting and Retaining High-level Specialized Technical Personnel, specifying effective measures to attract and retain particularly leading scientists, first-rate personnel in specific disciplines and technical experts.

In March 2008 the Guideline of the Chinese People's Liberation Army for the Evaluation of Commanding Officers, the Implementation Measures of the Chinese People's Liberation Army on the Evaluation of Commanding Officers and the Standards of the Chinese People's Liberation Army for the Evaluation of Commanding Officers (Trial) were published, which marked the initial establishment of a system for the evaluation of commanding officers in accordance with the requirements of scientific development.

PERSISTING IN GOVERNING THE FORCES IN ACCORDANCE WITH THE LAW

The PLA persists in taking it as the basic requirement of the regularization drive to govern the armed forces in accordance with the law, and emphasizes scientific legislation and strict law enforcement to enhance its level of regularization. In the past 30 years of reform and opening-up the military legislative system has been improved step by step, and remarkable achievements have been made in military legislation. In 1988 the CMC set up a legal organ, and the general headquarters/departments, Navy, Air Force, Second Artillery Force and military area commands designated specific departments to be in charge of legal affairs. In 1997 the Law of the People's Republic of China on National Defence was promulgated, specifying that the CMC enacts military regulations in accordance with the Constitution and relevant laws.

The Law of the People's Republic of China on Legislation promulgated in 2000 further defined the legislative authority of the CMC, general headquarters/ departments, Navy, Air Force, Second Artillery Force, and military area commands. By October 2008, the National People's Congress (NPC) and its Standing Committee had made 15 laws and law-related decisions concerning national Defence and armed forces building; the State Council and the CMC had jointly formulated 94 military administrative regulations; the CMC had formulated 215 military regulations; and the general headquarters/departments, Navy, Air Force, Second Artillery Force, military area commands and People's Armed Police Force (PAPF) had enacted more than 3,000 military rules and regulations.

In June 2007 and December 2008, the NPC Standing Committee ratified respectively the Treaty on the Temporary Stay of the Army of One Party in the Territory of the Other Party during the Period of Joint Military Exercises between the People's Republic of China and the Russian Federation and the Agreement among the Member States of the Shanghai Cooperation Organization on Conducting Joint Military Exercises. The PLA persists in governing the forces strictly and in accordance with the law, and improves the mechanism for making decisions and providing guidance in accordance with the law in an effort to institutionalize and regularize military, political, logistical and equipment work.

It practices scientific management, strictly enforces rules and regulations, and incorporates the cultivation of proper style and strict discipline into the routine education and administration of the forces. Through strict training and daily cultivation, the PLA aims to build a force with a refined military posture, strict discipline and fine work style. Taking disseminating knowledge of the law as an important part of strengthening all-round building, the PLA places emphasis on disseminating legal knowledge, and is stepping up efforts to popularize knowledge of the law with a clear aim and in an active and effective way.

Units with security tasks in the 2008 Beijing Olympics and Paralympics organized officers and men to study relevant laws and regulations to enhance their legal awareness and their capability of dealing with emergencies in accordance with the law. Officers and men of units tasked with international peacekeeping missions and of naval ships making port calls have been organized to study the United Nations Charter, the United Nations Convention on the Law of the Sea, etc. In November 2007 the Chinese government established the National Committee for International Humanitarian Law, under the arrangement and coordination of which relevant military agencies disseminate knowledge of and implement international humanitarian law within the PLA.

11

Chinese Nationalism And Its Foreign Policy Implication

The importance of sovereignty and independence of action in Chinese foreign policy since 1949 has been closely related to Chinese nationalism. Just as Chinese national pride has been a natural outgrowth of China's long and rich historical tradition, the nationalism of Chinese leaders also has derived from the injustices China suffered in more recent history, in particular, China's domination by foreign powers from the nineteenth century until the end of World War II. During this time, which China refers to as "the century of shame and humiliation," the formerly powerful imperial government devolved to what China calls "semicolonial" status, as it was forced to sign unequal treaties and grant foreigners special privileges of extraterritoriality. Foreign powers divided China into spheres of influence.

Most debilitating and humiliating was the foreign military threat that overpowered China, culminating in Japan's invasion and occupation of parts of China in the late 1930s. The bitter recollection of China's suffering at the hands of foreign powers has continued to be a source of Chinese nationalistic sentiment since 1949. The suspicion of foreign powers, opposition to any implication of inferior status, and desire to reassert sovereignty and independence have strongly influenced Chinese foreign policy. Examples of this attitude are Mao Zedong's statement in 1949 that "the Chinese people have stood up" and Deng Xiaoping's 1982 pronouncement that "no foreign country can expect China to be its vassal or expect it to swallow any bitter fruit detrimental to its interests." A foreign policy goal closely related to nationalism has been the desire to achieve territorial integrity and to restore to Chinese sovereignty areas previously considered a part of China.

Although China as of 1987 had not resolved border disputes with several of its neighbors, including India, the Russia, and Vietnam (including islands in the South China Sea), Beijing had concluded boundary settlements with other nations, including Pakistan, Burma, Nepal, Afghanistan, the Democratic People's Republic of Korea (North Korea), and the Mongolian People's Republic (Mongolia). Negotiations on border issues, held intermittently with the Russia since 1949 and with India since the early 1980s, continued to be held in 1987. The difficulty of resolving these issues seemed to reflect their relation to sensitive questions of national pride both in China and in neighboring countries and sometimes to questions of China's perceived national security interests.

For example, Qing control over Outer Mongolia (present-day Mongolia) had lapsed long before 1949 and had been supplanted by Russian and then Soviet influence. Although it was most likely with reluctance and regret, China recognized Mongolia as a separate nation in 1949. By contrast, asserting sovereignty over another outlying area, Xizang (Tibet), was considered such an important strategic goal that military force was used to gain control there in 1950 and to reassert it in 1959.

Two other Chinese areas under the control of foreign powers are Hong Kong and Macao. According to Chinese statements, these "problems left over from history" were the result of imperialist aggression and the incompetence of Chinese rulers. Macao, the first European enclave on the Chinese coast, was occupied by Portugal in 1557 and ceded to Portugal under an 1887 treaty. Britain gained control of Hong Kong island and adjacent territory through three treaties with China in the nineteenth century. In the mid-1980s China concluded formal arrangements with Britain and Portugal for the return of these areas to Chinese sovereignty in 1997 (Hong Kong) and 1999 (Macao). Both agreements were made under a policy of "one country, two systems", giving the areas a high degree of autonomy as "special administrative regions" of China.

From the perspective of Chinese nationalism, negotiating the return of both Hong Kong and Macao to Chinese sovereignty before the end of the twentieth century was undoubtedly one of the major foreign policy accomplishments of Chinese leaders in the 1980s. The most crucial of the issues of national reunification, however, remained unresolved in the late 1980s: the issue of Taiwan. Chiang Kai-shek and his forces fled to Taiwan after the founding of the People's Republic of China in 1949. The government they established there, the "Republic of China," continued to claim authority as the government of the Chinese nation almost four decades after the founding of the People's Republic.

Although China's goal of reunifying Taiwan with the mainland remained unchanged, the previous, more militant Chinese policy of "liberating Taiwan" was replaced in the 1980s by the concept of reunification under the "one country, two systems" policy. The agreements on Hong Kong and Macao were considered by many observers as possible precedents for reunifying Taiwan with the mainland. Because of the legacy of mistrust between the leaders of the two sides and other complex factors, however, this difficult and longstanding problem did not appear close to resolution in the late 1980s. Since the early 1980s China has pursued a highly independent foreign policy, formally disavowing too close a relationship with any country or region. The stated goals of this policy were safeguarding world peace, opposing all forms of hegemony, and achieving economic modernization at home.

Chinese statements repeatedly emphasized the interrelation among these goals. In other words, China needed a peaceful international environment so that adequate resources could be devoted to its ambitious development plans. The goal of economic modernization was a driving force behind China's increasingly active participation in world affairs, exemplified by its policy of opening up to the outside world, which greatly expanded Chinese economic relations with foreign countries. As part of what it called an "independent foreign policy of peace," Beijing has joined numerous international organizations, and it has maintained diplomatic relations with more nations than at any time since the founding of the People's Republic of China in 1949.

By 2007, China has diplomatic relations with 157 nations, and—in contrast with earlier periods—has been willing to interact with governments of different social systems or ideologies on a basis of peaceful coexistence and mutual respect. Although Chinese foreign policy since 1949 has had distinctive characteristics, the forces that shape Beijing's foreign policy and many of its overall goals have been similar to those of other nations. China has sought to protect its sovereignty and territorial integrity and to achieve independence of action, while interacting with both more powerful and less powerful countries.

As with most other nations, Beijing's foreign relations have been conditioned by its historical experiences, nationalism and ideology, and the worldview of its leaders, as well as by the governmental structure and decision-making process. At times China's domestic policies have had wide-ranging ramifications for its foreign policy formulation. Another characteristic Chinese foreign policy has had in common with that of many other countries is that the actual conduct of foreign relations sometimes has been at odds with official policy. Beijing's stress on principles in its official statements at times makes the contrast between statements and actions particularly noticeable. In addition, a nation's leaders must often make decisions in reaction to events and circumstances, rather than simply formulating a rational foreign policy based on their goals.

The need to react to what has happened or what may happen adds an element of unpredictability to foreign policy decision making, as has been the case at several crucial junctures in Chinese foreign relation since 1949. In addition to the aspects of foreign policy formulation and implementation that China has in common with other countries, China's foreign policy from 1949 has had these characteristics: contrast between practicality and adherence to principles; fluctuation between militancy and peacefulness; tension between self-reliance and dependence on others; and contrast between China's actual and potential capabilities.

These contradictory characteristics have at times created a confusing picture of Chinese foreign policy: is Chinese foreign policy basically pragmatic or primarily based on principles? Is China peace-loving or intent on fomenting unrest? Is China's ultimate goal to be self-sufficient or economically interdependent with the rest of the world? And is China basically a poor, developing country that is at most a regional power or actually a nascent economic and military giant deserving of superpower status?

The response to these questions is that since 1949 Chinese foreign policy has reflected all of these contrasting features. Beijing had emphasized principles and ideology above everything else in foreign relations, especially during the 1950s and 1960s, but Chinese leaders at times have also shown a practical side that gave them the flexibility to change policies, sometimes drastically, when they deemed it in China's best interest.

One of the most dramatic changes was the shift from an alliance with the Russia against the United States and Japan in the 1950s to an explicitly anti-Soviet policy and rapprochement with Japan and the United States in the

1970s. Since 1949 Chinese foreign policy has fluctuated between periods of militancy, for example during the Cultural Revolution, when China called for worldwide revolution, and periods when Beijing has been a chief proponent of peaceful coexistence among nations, such as during the mid-1950s and again during the 1980s. How self-reliant or dependent on others China should become in order to modernize has been a constant dilemma in Chinese policy since the nineteenth century.

As this policy fluctuated, Chinese foreign relations have alternated between a tendency toward isolation and periods of openness to foreign assistance and influence. Finally, the contradiction between China's actual capabilities since 1949 and its perceived potential has been another salient and distinctive feature of its foreign relations. China's tremendous size, population, natural resources, military strength, and sense of history have placed it in the unusual position of being a developing country that has often been treated as a major global power having a special relationship with the United States and, Russia, previously, the Russia.

EVOLUTION OF FOREIGN POLICY

Understanding the origins and forces that have shaped China's foreign policy provides a framework in which to view both the changes and the continuities in Chinese foreign policy from 1949. The origins of China's foreign policy can be found in its size and population, historical legacy, worldview, nationalism, and Marxism-Leninism-Mao Zedong Thought. These factors have combined with China's economic and military capabilities, governmental structure, and decision-making processes to make certain foreign policy goals prominent: security, sovereignty and independence, territorial integrity and reunification, and economic development.

China's long and rich history as the world's oldest continuous civilization has affected Chinese foreign relations in various ways. For centuries the Chinese empire enjoyed basically unchallenged greatness and self-sufficiency. China saw itself as the cultural center of the universe, a view reflected in the concept of the Middle Kingdom (*Zhongguo*, the Chinese word for China). For the most part, it viewed non-Chinese peoples as uncivilized barbarians. Although China was occasionally overrun and ruled by these "barbarians," as during the Yuan and Qing (1644-1911) dynasties, the non-Chinese usually retained enough Chinese institutions to maintain a continuity of tradition. Because the Chinese emperor was considered the ruler of all mankind by virtue of his innate superiority, relations with other states or entities were tributary, rather than state-to-state relations between equals.

Traditionally, there was no equivalent of a foreign ministry; foreign relations included such activities as tributary missions to the emperor made by countries seeking trade with China and Chinese military expeditions against neighboring barbarians to keep them outside China's borders. The first Europeans who sought trade with China, beginning in the sixteenth century, were received as tributary missions and had to conform to the formalities and rituals of the tribute system at the Chinese court. China's view of itself as the undisputed center of civilization—a phenomenon called sinocentrism—remained basically unchanged until the nineteenth century, when the Qing dynasty began to deteriorate under Western pressure.

A traditional concept related to China's view of itself as the Middle Kingdom that continues to have relevance is the idea of "using barbarians to control barbarians." In modern times, this practice has taken the form of using relations with one foreign power as a counterweight to relations with another. Two examples are China's policy of "leaning to one side" in the Sino-Soviet alliance of the 1950s for support against the United States and Beijing's rapprochement with the United States in the 1970s to counteract the Soviet threat China perceived at the time. China's strong desire for sovereignty and independence of action, however, seems to have made Chinese alliances or quasi-alliances shortlived.

Another effect of China's historical legacy is its tendency toward isolationism and an ambivalence about opening up to the outside world. In imperial times, China's foreign relations varied from dynasty to dynasty—from cosmopolitan periods like the Tang dynasty (618-907) to isolationist periods such as the Ming dynasty (1368-1644), when few foreigners were allowed in the country. Overall, the sinocentric worldview and China's history of centuries of self-sufficiency favored isolation, which contributed to China's difficulty when confronted by expansionist Western powers in the nineteenth century. The debate over self-reliance and possible corruption by foreign influences or opening up to the outside world in order to modernize more quickly has continued for over a century and is still an issue today.

NATIONALISM

The importance of sovereignty and independence of action in Chinese foreign policy since 1949 has been closely related to Chinese nationalism. Just as Chinese national pride has been a natural outgrowth of China's long and rich historical tradition, the nationalism of Chinese leaders also has derived from the injustices China suffered in more recent history, in particular, China's domination by foreign powers from the nineteenth century until the end of World War II. During this time, which China refers to as "the century of shame and humiliation," the formerly powerful imperial government devolved to what China calls "semicolonial" status, as it was forced to sign unequal treaties and grant foreigners special privileges of extraterritoriality. Foreign powers divided China into spheres of influence.

Most debilitating and humiliating was the foreign military threat that overpowered China, culminating in Japan's invasion and occupation of parts of China in the late 1930s. The bitter recollection of China's suffering at the hands of foreign powers has continued to be a source of Chinese nationalistic sentiment since 1949.

The suspicion of foreign powers, opposition to any implication of inferior status, and desire to reassert sovereignty and independence have strongly influenced Chinese foreign policy. Examples of this attitude are Mao Zedong's statement in 1949 that "the Chinese people have stood up" and Deng Xiaoping's 1982 pronouncement that "no foreign country can expect China to be its vassal or expect it to swallow any bitter fruit detrimental to its interests."

A foreign policy goal closely related to nationalism has been the desire to achieve territorial integrity and to restore to Chinese sovereignty areas previously considered a part of China. Although China has not resolved many border disputes with several of its neighbors, including India, the Russia, and Vietnam (including islands in the South China Sea), Beijing has concluded boundary settlements with other nations, including Pakistan, Burma, Nepal, Afghanistan, the North Korea, and Mongolia. Negotiations on border issues, held intermittently with Russia since 1949 and with India since the early 1980s, continue to be held.

The difficulty of resolving these issues seem to reflect their relation to sensitive questions of national pride both in China and in neighboring countries and sometimes to questions of China's perceived national security interests. For example, Qing control over Outer Mongolia (present-day Mongolia) had lapsed long before 1949 and had been supplanted by Soviet influence.

Although it was most likely with reluctance and regret, China recognized Mongolia as a separate nation in 1949. By contrast, asserting sovereignty over another outlying area, Xizang (Tibet), was considered such an important strategic goal that military force was used to gain control there in 1950 and to reassert it in 1959.

Two other Chinese areas that had been under the control of foreign powers were Hong Kong and Macau.

According to Chinese statements, these "problems left over from history" were the result of imperialist aggression and the incompetence of Chinese rulers. Macau, the first European enclave on the Chinese coast, was occupied by Portugal in 1557 and ceded to Portugal under an 1887 treaty. Britain gained control of Hong Kong island and adjacent territory through three treaties with China in the nineteenth century.

In the mid-1980s China concluded formal arrangements with Britain and Portugal for the return of these areas to Chinese sovereignty in 1997 (Hong Kong) and 1999 (Macau). Both agreements were made under a policy of "one country, two systems", giving the areas a high degree of autonomy as "special administrative regions" of China. From the perspective of Chinese nationalism, negotiating the return of both Hong Kong and Macau to Chinese sovereignty before the end of the twentieth century was undoubtedly one of the major foreign policy accomplishments of Chinese leaders in the late twentieth century.

The most crucial of the issues of national reunification, however, remain unresolved: the issue of Taiwan. Chiang Kai-shek and his forces fled to Taiwan after the founding of the People's Republic of China in 1949. The government they established there, the "Republic of China," continued to claim authority as the government of the Chinese nation almost four decades after the founding of the People's Republic. Although China's goal of reunifying Taiwan with the mainland remained unchanged, the previous, more militant Chinese policy of "liberating Taiwan" was replaced in the 1980s by the concept of reunification under the "one country, two systems" policy.

The agreements on Hong Kong and Macau were considered by many observers as possible precedents for reunifying Taiwan with the mainland. Because of the legacy of mistrust between the leaders of the two sides and other complex factors, however, this difficult and longstanding problem does not appear close to resolution today.

INFLUENCE OF IDEOLOGY

An important influence on Chinese foreign policy that had especially affected China's interpretations of world events has been ideology, both Marxist-Leninist and Maoist. The ideological components of China's foreign policy, whose influence varied over time, had included a belief that conflict and struggle were inevitable; a focus on opposing imperialism; the determination to advance communism throughout the world, especially through the Chinese model; and the Maoist concept of responding with flexibility while adhering to fundamental principles.

One of the most basic aspects of China's ideological worldview had been the assumption that conflict, though not necessarily military conflict, was omnipresent in the world. According to Marxist-Leninist analysis, all historical development was the result of a process of struggle, between classes within a nation, between nations themselves, or between broader forces such as socialism and imperialism. A basic tenet of Chinese leaders held that the international situation is best understood in terms of the "principal contradictions" of the time.

Once these contradictions were understood, they could be exploited in order to, as Mao said, "win over the many, oppose the few, and crush our enemies one by one." China amplified the Leninist policy of uniting with some forces in order to oppose others more effectively in a united front. Chinese leaders urged the formation of various united fronts as they had perceived the contradictions in the world to change over time.

Perhaps because of the belief in struggle as necessary for progress, for most of its history after 1949 China considered world war inevitable. This changed in the 1980s, when Chinese leaders began to say that the forces for peace in the world had become greater than the forces for war. One reason for growing world stability was seen in "multipolarization," that is, the growth of additional forces, such as the Third World and Europe, to counterbalance the tension between the United States and the Russia. China's description of world events as a struggle between opposing forces, however, had remained unchanged until the early 1990s.

Opposition to imperialism—domination by foreign powers—is another major ideological component of Chinese foreign policy. The Leninist emphasis on the struggle against imperialism made sense to Chinese leaders, whose nationalism had evolved in part in reaction to China's exploitation by foreign powers during the nineteenth century. Although opposition to imperialism and hegemony has remained a constant, the specific target of the opposition has changed since 1949.

In somewhat oversimplified terms, China focused on opposing United States imperialism in the 1950s; on opposing collusion between United States imperialism and Soviet revisionism in the 1960s; on combating Soviet social-imperialism or hegemony in the 1970s; and on opposing hegemony by either superpower in the 1980s. The extent of China's determination to advance communism throughout the world had been another component of its foreign policy that has fluctuated since 1949. In the early 1950s and during the 1960s, Chinese leaders called for worldwide armed struggle against colonialism and "reactionary" governments.

China supplied revolutionary groups with rhetorical and, in some cases, material support. Central to support for leftist movements was the idea that they should take China as a model in their struggle for national liberation. Chinese leaders expressed the belief that China's experience was directly applicable to the circumstances in many other countries, but they also stressed the importance of each country's suiting its revolution to its own conditions— creating ambiguity about China's position on "exporting" revolution. For most of the time since 1949, China's dedication to encouraging revolution abroad has appeared to receive a lower priority than other foreign policy goals.

Militancy and support for worldwide revolution peaked during the Cultural Revolution, when China's outlook on liberation struggles seemed to take its cue from Lin Biao's famous 1965 essay "Long Live the Victory of People's War!" This chapter predicted that the underdeveloped countries of the world would surround and overpower the industrial nations and create a new communist world order. As a result of alleged Chinese involvement in subversive activities in Indonesia and several African countries in the late 1960s, those nations broke off diplomatic relations with Beijing. By the 1980s China had lessened or discontinued its support for revolutionary and liberation movements around the world, prominent exceptions being the Palestine Liberation Organization and resistance fighters in Cambodia and Afghanistan.

Despite its shift toward cultivating state-to-state relations with established governments, many other countries had continued to be suspicious of China's intentions. Especially in Asia, where Beijing previously supported many local communist parties, China's image as a radical power intent on fomenting world revolution continued to affect the conduct of its foreign relations into the late 1980s. One of the major characteristics of Chinese foreign policy since 1949 has been its claim of consistently adhering to principles while particular interpretations and policies have changed dramatically. A statement by Mao Zedong seems to summarize this apparent contradiction: "We should be firm in principle; we should also have all flexibility permissible and necessary for carrying out our principles."

Although claiming that, on the whole, China has never deviated from such underlying principles as independence and safeguarding peace, Chinese leaders have made major shifts in foreign policy based on their pragmatic assessment of goals and the international situation. Aiding this interpretation of the primacy of principles in Chinese foreign policy has been the emphasis on long-term goals.

According to Chinese leaders, China has pursued a long-term strategy is "definitely not swayed by expediency or anybody's instigation or provocation." In keeping with the view of Chinese foreign policy as constant and unvarying, Chinese pronouncements often describe their policy with words such as "always" and "never."

An example of how certain principles have provided a framework of continuity for Chinese foreign policy since 1949 has been found in the Five Principles of Peaceful Coexistence embodied in an agreement signed by China and India in 1954. The five principles played an important role in the mid-1950s, when China began to cultivate the friendship of newly independent nations of Asia and Africa.

By the time of the Cultural Revolution, however, China was involved in acrimonious disputes with many of these same nations, and their relations could have been described as anything but "peacefully coexistent." The Five Principles of Peaceful Coexistence were reemphasized in the 1980s, were considered the basis for relations with all nations regardless of their social systems or ideology, and were made a part of the 1982 party constitution.

DECISION MAKING AND IMPLEMENTATION

Understanding the intricate workings of a government can be difficult, especially in a country such as China, where information related to leadership and decision making is often kept secret.

Although it still was not possible to understand fully the structure of Chinese foreign policy-related governmental and nongovernmental organizations or how they made or implemented decisions, more was known about them by the late 1980s than at any time previously. After 1949 China's foreign relations became increasingly more complex as China established formal diplomatic relations with more nations, joined the United Nations (UN) and other international and regional political and economic organizations, developed ties between the Chinese

Communist Party and foreign parties, and expanded trade and other economic relations with the rest of the world. These changes had affected foreign relations in significant ways by the late 1980s.

The economic component of China's international relations increased dramatically from the late 1970s to the late 1980s; more ministries and organizations were involved in foreign relations than ever before; and the Chinese foreign policy community was more experienced and better informed about the outside world than it had been previously.

Despite the growing complexity of Chinese foreign relations, one fundamental aspect of foreign policy that has remained relatively constant since 1949 is that the decision-making power for the most important decisions has been concentrated in the hands of a few key individuals at the top of the leadership hierarchy.

In the past, ultimate foreign policy authority rested with such figures as Mao Zedong and Zhou Enlai, while in the 1980s major decisions were understood to have depended on Deng Xiaoping. By the late 1980s, Deng had initiated steps to institutionalize decision making and make it less dependent on personal authority, but this transition has not yet been fully completed.

In examining the workings of a nation's foreign policy, at least three dimensions can be discerned: the structure of the organizations involved, the nature of the decision-making process, and the ways in which policy is implemented.

These three dimensions are interrelated, and the processes of formulating and carrying out policy have often been more complex than the structure of organizations would indicate.

GOVERNMENT AND PARTY ORGANIZATIONS

By the late 1980s, more organizations were involved in China's foreign relations than at any time previously. High-level party and government organizations such as the Central Committee, Political Bureau, party Secretariat, party and state Central Military Commissions, National People's Congress, and State Council and such leaders as the premier, president, and party general secretary all were involved in foreign relations to varying degrees by virtue of their concern with major policy issues, both foreign and domestic. The party Secretariat and the State Council together carried the major responsibility for foreign policy decisions. By the 1980s, as China's contacts with the outside world grew, party and government leaders at all levels increasingly were involved in foreign affairs.

The president of the People's Republic fulfilled a ceremonial role as head of state and also was responsible for officially ratifying or abrogating treaties and agreements with foreign nations. In addition to meeting with foreign visitors, Chinese leaders, including the president, the premier, and officials at lower levels, traveled abroad regularly. In the late 1980s, the Political Bureau, previously thought of as the major decision-making body, was no longer the primary party organization involved in foreign policy decision making. Instead, the State Council referred major decisions to the Secretariat for resolution and the Political Bureau for ratification.

Under the party Secretariat, the International Liaison Department had primary responsibility for relations between the Chinese Communist Party and a growing number of foreign political parties. Other party organizations whose work was related to foreign relations were the United Front Work Department, responsible for relations with overseas Chinese, the Propaganda Department, and the Foreign Affairs Small Group. Of the Chinese government institutions, the highest organ of state power, the National People's Congress, appeared to have only limited influence on foreign policy. In the 1980s the National People's Congress was becoming more active on the international scene by increasing its contacts with counterpart organizations in foreign countries.

Through its Standing Committee and its Foreign Affairs Committee, the National People's Congress had a voice in foreign relations matters and occasionally prepared reports on foreign policy-related issues for other party and government bodies. As the primary governmental organization under the National People's Congress, the State Council had a major role in foreign policy, particularly with regard to decisions on routine or specific matters, as opposed to greater questions of policy that might require party involvement.

As in the past, the Ministry of Foreign Affairs was the most important institution involved in conducting day-to-day foreign relations, but by the 1980s many other ministries and organizations under the State Council had functions related to foreign affairs as well. These included the Ministry of Foreign Economic Relations and Trade, Ministry of Finance, Ministry of National Defence, Bank of China, People's Bank of China, and China Council for the Promotion of International Trade. In addition, over half of the ministries, overseeing such disparate areas as aeronautics, forestry, and public health, had a bureau or department concerned explicitly with foreign affairs. These offices presumably handled contacts between the ministry and its foreign counterparts.

MINISTRY OF FOREIGN AFFAIRS

Since 1949 the Ministry of Foreign Affairs has been one of China's most important ministries. Each area of foreign relations, divided either geographically or functionally, is overseen by a vice minister or assistant minister. For example, one vice minister's area of specialty was the Russia and Eastern Europe, while another was responsible for the Americas and Australia. At the next level, the Ministry of Foreign Affairs was divided into departments, some geographical and some functional in responsibility. The regionally oriented departments included those concerned with Africa, the Americas and

Oceania, Asia, the Middle East, the Russia and Eastern Europe, Western Europe, Taiwan, and Hong Kong and Macau.

The functional departments were responsible for administration, officials, consular affairs, finance, information, international laws and treaties, international organizations and affairs, personnel, protocol, training and education, and translation. Below the department level were divisions, such as the United States Affairs Division under the Department of American and Oceanian Affairs. A recurring problem for the foreign ministry and the diplomatic corps had been a shortage of qualified personnel. In the first years after the founding of the People's Republic, there were few prospective diplomats with international experience.

Premier Zhou Enlai relied on a group of young people who had served under him in various negotiations to form the core of the newly established foreign ministry, and Zhou himself held the foreign ministry portfolio until 1958. In the second half of the 1960s, China's developing foreign affairs sector suffered a major setback during the Cultural Revolution, when higher education was disrupted, foreign-trained scholars and diplomats were attacked, all but one Chinese ambassador (to Egypt) were recalled to Beijing, and the Ministry of Foreign Affairs itself practically ceased functioning.

Since the early 1970s, the foreign affairs establishment has been rebuilt, and by the late 1980s, foreign affairs personnel were recruited from such specialized training programs as the ministry's Foreign Affairs College, College of International Relations, Beijing Foreign Languages Institute, and international studies departments at major universities. Foreign language study still was considered an important requirement, but it was increasingly supplemented by substantive training in foreign relations.

Foreign affairs personnel benefited from expanded opportunities for education, travel, and exchange of information with the rest of the world. In addition, specialists from other ministries served in China's many embassies and consulates; for example, the Ministry of National Defence provided military attaches, the Ministry of Foreign Economic Relations and Trade provided commercial officers, and the Ministry of Culture and the State Education Commission provided personnel in charge of cultural affairs.

MINISTRY OF FOREIGN ECONOMIC RELATIONS AND TRADE

Since the late 1970s, economic and financial issues have become an increasingly important part of China's foreign relations. In order to streamline foreign economic relations, the Ministry of Foreign Economic Relations and Trade was established in 1982 through the merger of two commissions and two ministries. By the late 1980s, this ministry was the second most prominent ministry involved in the routine conduct of foreign relations. The ministry had an extremely broad mandate that included foreign trade, foreign investment, foreign aid, and international economic cooperation. Through regular meetings with the Ministry of Foreign Affairs, the Ministry of Foreign Economic Relations and Trade participated in efforts to coordinate China's foreign economic policy with other aspects of its foreign policy. It was unclear how thoroughly this was accomplished.

MINISTRY OF NATIONAL DEFENCE

In any nation, the interrelation of the political and military aspects of strategy and national security necessitates some degree of military involvement in foreign policy. The military's views on Defence capability, deterrence, and perceptions of threat are essential components of a country's global strategy. As of the late 1980s, however, little information was available on foreign policy coordination between the military and foreign policy establishments. The most important military organizations with links to the foreign policy community were the Ministry of National Defence and the party and state Central Military Commissions.

The Ministry of National Defence provides military attaches for Chinese embassies, and, as of 1987, its Foreign Affairs Bureau dealt with foreign attaches and military visitors. Working-level coordination with the Ministry of Foreign Affairs was maintained when, for example, high-level military leaders traveled abroad. In addition, the Ministry of National Defence's strategic research arm, the Beijing Institute for International Strategic Studies, carried out research on military and security issues with foreign policy implications.

In the late 1980s, the most important link between the military and foreign policy establishments appeared to be at the highest level, particularly through the party and state Central Military Commissions and through Deng Xiaoping, who was concurrently chairman of both commissions. The views of the commissions' members on major foreign policy issues were almost certainly considered in informal discussions or in meetings of other high-level organizations they also belonged to, such as the Political Bureau, the Secretariat, or the State Council. It was significant, though, that compared with earlier periods fewer military leaders served on China's top policy-making bodies since the 1980s.

"PEOPLE-TO-PEOPLE" DIPLOMACY

Since 1949 a significant forum for Chinese foreign relations has been cultural or "people-to-people" diplomacy. The relative isolation of the People's Republic during its first two decades increased the importance of cultural exchanges and informal ties with people of other countries through mass organizations and friendship societies. In some cases, activities at this level have signaled important diplomatic breakthroughs, as was the case with the American-Chinese ping-pong exchange in 1971.

In addition to educational and cultural institutions, many other organizations, including the media, women's and youth organizations, and academic and professional societies, have been involved in foreign relations. Two institutes responsible for this aspect of Chinese diplomacy were associated with the Ministry of Foreign Affairs and staffed largely by former diplomats: the Chinese People's Association for Friendship with Foreign Countries and the Chinese People's Institute of Foreign Affairs.

THE DECISION-MAKING PROCESS

The most crucial foreign policy decisions in the mid-1980s were made by the highest-level leadership, with Deng Xiaoping as the final arbiter. A shift was underway, however, to strengthen the principles of collective and institutional decision making and, at the same time, to reduce party involvement in favor of increased state responsibility. In line with this trend, the State Council made foreign policy decisions regarding routine matters and referred only major decisions either to the party Secretariat or to informal deliberations involving Deng Xiaoping for resolution.

When called upon to make decisions, the Secretariat relied largely on the advice of the State Council and members of China's foreign affairs community. The importance of the Political Bureau appeared to have lessened. Although individual members of the Political Bureau exerted influence on the shaping of foreign policy, the Political Bureau's role as an institution seemed to have become one of ratifying decisions, rather than formulating them. The division between party and government functions in foreign affairs as of the mid-1980s could therefore be summarized as party supremacy in overall policy making and supervision, with the government's State Council and ministries under it responsible for the daily conduct of foreign relations.

These high-level decision-making bodies comprised the apex of an elaborate network of party and government organizations and research institutes concerned with foreign policy. To support the formulation and implementation of policy, especially in a bureaucracy as complex and hierarchical as China's, there existed a network of small advisory and coordination groups. These groups functioned to channel research, provide expert advice, and act as a liaison between organizations. Perhaps the most important of these groups was the party Secretariat's Foreign Affairs Small Group.

This group comprised key party and government officials, including the president, the premier, state councillors, the ministers of foreign affairs and foreign economic relations and trade, and various foreign affairs specialists, depending on the agenda of the meeting. The group possibly met weekly, or as required by circumstances. Liaison and advisory functions were provided by other groups, including the State Council's Foreign Affairs Coordination Point, the staff of the premier's and State Council's offices, and bilateral policy groups, such as one composed of ministers and vice ministers of the Ministry of Foreign Affairs and the Ministry of Foreign Economic Relations and Trade, which met at least every few months.

In the late 1980s, the decision-making process for foreign policy matters followed a fairly hierarchical pattern. If a particular ministry was unable to make a decision because the purview of other ministries was involved, it would attempt to resolve the issue through informal discussion or through an interagency group. If that was not successful or if higher-level consideration was needed, the problem might be referred to the Foreign Affairs Coordination Point or to select members of the State Council for review. Certain major decisions would then be discussed by the Foreign Affairs Small Group before consideration by the party Secretariat itself. If the issue was extremely controversial or important, the final decision would be directed to the highest-level leadership.

RELATIONS BY REGION AND COUNTRY

Affected by the confluence of a myriad of factors, including its historical legacy, worldview, nationalism, ideology, the decision-making process in Beijing, and the international situation, China's foreign relations have had a rich and varied development in the years since 1949. Two aspects of Chinese foreign policy that have led to wide fluctuations over time are the degree of militancy or peacefulness Beijing has espoused and its ambivalence in choosing between self-reliance and openness to the outside world.

Although dividing something as complex as foreign policy into time periods necessarily obscures certain details, Chinese foreign relations can be examined roughly by decades: the Sino-Soviet alliance of the 1950s, isolationism and radicalism in the 1960s, increased international involvement in the 1970s, and the independent foreign policy since 1980s. During each of these periods, China's relations with the rest of the world underwent significant changes.

SINO-SOVIET RELATIONS

After the founding of the People's Republic, the Chinese leadership was concerned above all with ensuring national security, consolidating power, and developing the economy. The foreign policy course China chose in order to translate these goals into reality was to form an international united front with the Russia and other socialist nations against the United States and Japan. Although for a time Chinese leaders may have considered trying to balance Sino-Soviet relations with ties with Washington, by mid-1949 Mao Zedong declared that China had no choice but to "lean to one side"—meaning the Soviet side.

Soon after the establishment of the People's Republic, Mao traveled to Moscow to negotiate the 1950 Sino-Soviet Treaty of Friendship, Alliance, and Mutual Assistance. Under this agreement, China gave the Russia certain rights, such as the continued use of a naval base at Luda, Liaoning Province, in return for military support, weapons, and large amounts of economic and technological assistance, including technical advisers and machinery. China acceded, at least initially, to Soviet leadership of the world communist movement and took the Russia as the model for development.

China's participation in the Korean War (1950-53) seemed to strengthen Sino-Soviet relations, especially after the UN-sponsored trade embargo against China. The Sino-Soviet alliance appeared to unite Moscow and Beijing, and China became more closely associated with and dependent on a foreign power than ever before. During the second half of the 1950s, strains in the Sino-Soviet alliance gradually began to emerge over questions of ideology, security, and economic development. Chinese leaders were disturbed by the Russia's moves under Nikita Khrushchev toward de-Stalinization and peaceful coexistence with the West.

Moscow's successful earth satellite launch in 1957 strengthened Mao's belief that the world balance was in the communists' favor—or, in his words, "the east wind prevails over the west wind"—leading him to call for a more militant policy toward the noncommunist world in contrast to the more conciliatory policy of the Russia. In addition to ideological disagreements, Beijing was dissatisfied with several aspects of the Sino-Soviet security relationship: the insufficient degree of support Moscow showed for China's recovery of Taiwan, a Soviet proposal in 1958 for a joint naval arrangement that would have put China in a subordinate position, Soviet neutrality during the 1959 tension on the Sino-Indian border, and Soviet reluctance to honor its agreement to provide nuclear weapons technology to China.

And, in an attempt to break away from the Soviet model of economic development, China launched the radical policies of the Great Leap Forward (1958-60), leading Moscow to withdraw all Soviet advisers from China in 1960.

In retrospect, the major ideological, military, and economic reasons behind the Sino-Soviet split were essentially the same: for the Chinese leadership, the strong desire to achieve self-reliance and independence of action outweighed the benefits Beijing received as Moscow's junior partner. During the 1960s the Sino-Soviet ideological dispute deepened and spread to include territorial issues, culminating in 1969 in bloody armed clashes on their border.

In 1963 the boundary dispute had come into the open when China explicitly raised the issue of territory lost through "unequal treaties" with tsarist Russia. After unsuccessful border consultations in 1964, Moscow began the process of a military buildup along the border with China and in Mongolia, which continued into the 1970s. The Sino-Soviet dispute also was intensified by increasing competition between Beijing and Moscow for influence in the Third World and the international communist movement. China accused the Russia of colluding with imperialism, for example by signing the Partial Nuclear Test Ban Treaty with the United States in 1963. Beijing's support for worldwide revolution became increasingly militant, although in most cases it lacked the resources to provide large amounts of economic or military aid.

The Chinese Communist Party broke off ties with the Communist Party of the Soviet Union in 1966, and these had not been restored by mid-1987. During the Cultural Revolution, China's growing radicalism and xenophobia had severe repercussions for Sino-Soviet relations. In 1967 Red Guards besieged the Soviet embassy in Beijing and harassed Soviet diplomats. Beijing viewed the Soviet invasion of Czechoslovakia in 1968 as an ominous development and accused the Russia of "social imperialism." The Sino-Soviet dispute reached its nadir in 1969 when serious armed clashes broke out at Zhenbao Island on the northeast border. Both sides drew back from the brink of war, however, and tension was defused when Zhou Enlai met with Aleksey Kosygin, the Soviet premier, later in 1969.

In the 1970s Beijing shifted to a more moderate course and began a rapprochement with Washington as a counterweight to the perceived threat from Moscow. Sino-Soviet border talks were held intermittently, and Moscow issued conciliatory messages after Mao's death in 1976, all without substantive progress. Officially, Chinese statements called for a struggle against the hegemony of both superpowers, but especially against the Soviet Union, which Beijing called "the most dangerous source of war." In the late 1970s, the increased Soviet military buildup in East Asia and Soviet treaties with Vietnam and Afghanistan heightened China's awareness of the threat of Soviet encirclement.

In 1979 Beijing notified Moscow it would formally abrogate the long-dormant Sino-Soviet Treaty of Friendship, Alliance, and Mutual Assistance but proposed bilateral talks. China suspended the talks after only one round, however, following the Soviet invasion of Afghanistan in 1979. In the 1980s China's approach toward the Soviet Union shifted once more, albeit gradually, in line with China's adoption of an independent foreign policy and the opening up economic policy.

Another factor behind the shift was the perception that, although the Russia still posed the greatest threat to China's security, the threat was long-term rather than immediate. Sino-Soviet consultations on normalizing relations were resumed in 1982 and held twice yearly, despite the fact that the cause of their suspension, the Soviet presence in Afghanistan, remained unchanged. Beijing raised three primary preconditions for the normalization of relations, which it referred to as "three obstacles" that Moscow had to remove: the Soviet presence in of Afghanistan, Soviet support for Vietnam's invasion of Cambodia, and the presence of Soviet forces along the Sino-Soviet border and in Mongolia.

For the first half of the 1980s, Moscow called these preconditions "third country issues" not suitable for bilateral discussion, and neither side reported substantial progress in the talks. Soviet leadership changes between 1982 and 1985 provided openings for renewed diplomacy, as high-level Chinese delegations attended the funerals of Soviet leaders Leonid Brezhnev, Yuriy Andropov, and Konstantin Chernenko.

During this time, Sino-Soviet relations improved gradually in many areas: trade expanded, economic and technical exchanges were resumed (including the renovation of projects originally built with Soviet assistance in the 1950s), border points were opened, and delegations were exchanged regularly. The Soviet position on Sino-Soviet relations showed greater flexibility in 1986 with General Secretary Mikhail Gorbachev's July speech at Vladivostok.

Among Gorbachev's proposals for the Asia-Pacific region were several directed at China, including the announcement of partial troop withdrawals from Afghanistan and Mongolia, the renewal of a concession pertaining to the border dispute, and proposals for agreements on a border railroad, space cooperation, and joint hydropower development. Further, Gorbachev offered to hold discussions with China "at any time and at any level." Although these overtures did not lead to an immediate high-level breakthrough in Sino-Soviet relations, bilateral consultations appeared to gain momentum, and border talks were resumed in 1987. Even though Sino-Soviet relations improved remarkably when compare with the two previous decades, China and the Russia would never to resume a formal alliance.

SINO-AMERICAN RELATIONS

China's relations with the other superpower, the United States, have like that with the Russia followed an uneven course. Chinese leaders expressed an interest in possible economic assistance from the United States during the 1940s, but by 1950 Sino-American relations could only be described as hostile. During its first two decades the People's Republic considered the United States "imperialist" and "the common enemy of people throughout the world." The Korean War was a major factor responsible for setting relations between China and the United States in a state of enmity and mistrust, as it contributed to the United States policy of "containing" the Chinese threat through a trade embargo and travel restrictions, as well as through military alliances with other Asian nations.

An important side effect of the Korean War was that Washington resumed military aid to Taiwan and throughout the 1950s became increasingly committed to Taiwan's Defence, making the possibility of Chinese reunification more remote. After the United States-Taiwan Mutual Defence Treaty was signed in 1954, Taiwan became the most contentious issue between the United States and China, and remained so in the late 1980s, despite the abrogation of the treaty and the subsequent normalization of relations between Beijing and Washington in 1979. In 1955 Premier Zhou Enlai made a conciliatory opening toward the United States in which he said the Chinese people did not want war with the American people.

His statement led to a series of official ambassadorial-level talks in Geneva and Warsaw that continued fairly regularly for the next decade and a half. Although the talks failed to resolve fundamental conflicts between the two countries, they served as an important line of communication. Sino-American relations remained at a stalemate during most of the 1960s. Political considerations in both countries made a shift toward closer relations difficult, especially as the United States became increasingly involved in the war in Vietnam, in which Washington and Beijing supported opposite sides.

China's isolationist posture and militancy during the Cultural Revolution precluded effective diplomacy, and Sino-American relations reached a low point with seemingly little hope of improvement. Several events in the late 1960s and early 1970s, however, led Beijing and Washington to reexamine their basic policies toward each other. After the Soviet Union's invasion of Czechoslovakia in 1968 and the Sino-Soviet border clashes in 1969, China saw its major threat as clearly coming from the Soviet Union rather than the United States and sought a closer relationship with Washington as a counterweight to Moscow. When President Richard M. Nixon assumed office in 1969, he explored rapprochement with China as part of his doctrine of reduced United States military involvement in Asia.

Moves in this direction resulted in an American ping-pong team's trip to China and Henry A. Kissinger's secret visit, both in 1971, followed by Nixon's dramatic trip to China in 1972. The Shanghai Communique, a milestone document describing the new state of relations between the two countries, and signed by Nixon and Zhou Enlai, included a certain degree of ambiguity that allowed China and the United States to set aside differences, especially on the Taiwan issue, and begin the process of normalizing relations. After the signing of the Shanghai Communique, however, movement toward United States-China normalization during the 1970s saw only limited progress.

The United States and China set up liaison offices in each other's capitals in 1973, and bilateral trade grew unevenly throughout the decade. "People's diplomacy" played an important role, as most exchanges of delegations were sponsored by friendship associations. Chinese statements continued to express the view that both superpowers were theoretically adversaries of China, but they usually singled out the Soviet Union as the more "dangerous" of the two. In the second half of the 1970s, China perceived an increasing Soviet threat and called more explicitly for an international united front against Soviet hegemony. In addition, rather than strictly adhering to the principle of self-reliance, China adopted an economic and technological modernization program that greatly increased commercial links with foreign countries.

These trends toward strategic and economic cooperation with the West gave momentum to Sino-United States normalization, which had been at an impasse for most of the decade. Ties between China and the United States began to strengthen in 1978, culminating in the December announcement that diplomatic relations would be established as of January 1, 1979. In establishing relations, Washington reaffirmed its agreement that the People's Republic was the sole legal government of China and that Taiwan was an inalienable part of China. Deng Xiaoping's visit to the United States the following month was symbolic of the optimism felt in Beijing and Washington concerning their strategic alignment and their burgeoning commercial, technical, and cultural relations.

In the 1980s United States-China relations went through several twists and turns. By late 1981 China appeared to pull back somewhat from the United States as it asserted its independent foreign policy. Beijing began to express increasing impatience with the lack of resolution on the Taiwan issue. One of the main issues of contention was the Taiwan Relations Act, passed by the United States Congress in 1979, which provided for continuing unofficial relations between Washington and Taipei. In late 1981 China began to make serious demands that the United States set a firm timetable for terminating American arms sales to Taiwan, even threatening to retaliate with the possible downgrading of diplomatic relations.

In early 1982 Washington announced it would not sell Taiwan more advanced aircraft than it had already provided, and in August, after several months of intense negotiations, China and the United States concluded a joint communique that afforded at least a partial resolution of the problem. Washington pledged to increase neither the quality nor the quantity of arms supplied to Taiwan, while Beijing affirmed that peaceful reunification was China's fundamental policy. Although the communique forestalled further deterioration in relations, Beijing and Washington differed in their interpretations of it.

The Taiwan issue continued to be a "dark cloud" (to use the Chinese phrase) affecting United States-China relations to varying degrees into the late 1980s. In addition to the question of Taiwan, other aspects of United States-China relations created controversy at times during the 1980s: Sino-American trade relations, the limits of American technology transfer to China, the nature and extent of United States-China security relations, and occasional friction caused by defections or lawsuits. Difficulties over trade relations have included Chinese displeasure with United States efforts to limit imports such as textiles and a degree of disappointment and frustration within the American business community over the difficulties of doing business in China.

The issue of technology transfer came to the fore several times during the 1980s, most often with Chinese complaints about the level of technology allowed or the slow rate of transfer. China's dissatisfaction appeared to be somewhat abated by the United States 1983 decision to place China in the "friendly, nonaligned" category for technology transfer and the conclusion of a bilateral nuclear energy cooperation agreement in 1985.

Determining the nature and limits of security relations between China and the United States had been a central aspect of their relations in the 1980s. After a period of discord during the first years of the decade, Beijing and Washington renewed their interest in security-related ties, including military visits, discussions of international issues such as arms control, and limited arms and weapons technology sales.

Beginning in 1983, Chinese and United States Defence ministers and other high-level military delegations exchanged visits, and in 1986 United States Navy ships made their first Chinese port call since 1949. The United States approved certain items, such as aviation electronics, for sale to China, restricting transfers to items that would contribute only to China's defensive capability. As of the late 1980s, it appeared that American assistance in modernizing China's arms would also be limited by China's financial constraints and the underlying principle of self-reliance.

Despite the issues that have divided them, relations between the United States and China continued to develop during the 1980s through a complex network of trade ties, technology-transfer arrangements, cultural exchanges, educational exchanges (including thousands of Chinese students studying in the United States), military links, joint commissions and other meetings, and exchanges of high-level leaders.

By the second half of the 1980s, China had become the sixteenth largest trading partner of the United States, and the United States was China's third largest; in addition, over 140 American firms had invested in China. High-level exchanges, such as Premier Zhao Ziyang's visit to the United States and President Ronald Reagan's trip to China, both in 1984, and President Li Xiannian's 1985 tour of the United States demonstrated the importance both sides accorded their relations.

RELATIONS WITH THE DEVELOPING WORLD

Although committed to good relations with the nations of the Middle East, Africa, and Latin America, in the twenty-first century China finds perhaps the greatest value in these areas as markets and sources of raw materials. The years of solidarity with revolutionary movements in these regions have long been replaced by efforts to cultivate normal diplomatic and economic relations.

RELATIONS WITH THE DEVELOPED WORLD

Since 1949 China's overriding concerns have been security and economic development. In working toward both of these goals, China has focused on its relations with the superpowers. Because most of the developed world, with the exception of Japan, was relatively distant from

China and was aligned formally or informally with either the Soviet Union or the United States, China's relations with the developed world often have been subordinate to its relations with the superpowers. In the 1950s China considered most West European countries "lackeys" of United States imperialism, while it sided with Eastern Europe and the Soviet Union.

As China's relations with the superpowers have changed, so have its ties with other developed nations. An example of this is that more than a dozen developed countries, including the Germany, Spain, Japan, Australia, and New Zealand, all established diplomatic relations with China after the Sino-American rapprochement in the early 1970s. The developed nations have been important to China for several reasons: as sources of diplomatic recognition, as alternative sources of trade and technology to reduce reliance on one or the other superpower, and as part of China's security calculations. In the 1980s China stressed the role of developed nations in ensuring peace in an increasingly multipolar world. Australia and Canada were important trading partners for China, but Beijing's most important relations with the developed world were with Japan and Europe.

JAPAN

Japan has been by far the most important to China of the developed nations. Among the reasons for this are geographical proximity and historical and cultural ties, China's perception of Japan as a possible resurgent threat, Japan's close relations with the United States since the end of World War II, and Japan's role as the second-ranked industrialized power in the world. Japan's invasion and occupation of parts of China in the 1930s was a major component of the devastation China underwent during the "century of shame and humiliation." After 1949 Chinese relations with Japan changed several times, from hostility and an absence of contact to cordiality and extremely close cooperation in many fields. One recurring Chinese concern in Sino-Japanese relations has been the potential remilitarization of Japan.

At the time of the founding of the People's Republic, Japan was defeated and Japanese military power dismantled, but China continued to view Japan as a potential threat because of the United States presence there. The Sino-Soviet Treaty of Friendship, Alliance, and Mutual Assistance included the provision that each side would protect the other from an attack by "Japan or any state allied with it," and China undoubtedly viewed with alarm Japan's role as the principal United States base during the Korean War.

At the same time, however, China in the 1950s began a policy of attempting to influence Japan through trade, "people's diplomacy," contacts with Japanese opposition political parties, and through applying pressure on Tokyo to sever ties with Taipei. Relations deteriorated in the late 1950s when Chinese pressure tactics escalated. After the Sino-Soviet break, economic necessity caused China to reconsider and revitalize trade ties with Japan.

Sino-Japanese ties declined again during the Cultural Revolution, and the decline was further exacerbated by Japan's growing strength and independence from the United States in the late 1960s. China was especially concerned that Japan might remilitarize to compensate for the reduced United States military presence in Asia brought about under President Nixon. After the beginning of Sino-American rapprochement in 1971, however, China's policy toward Japan immediately became more flexible. By 1972 Japan and China had established diplomatic relations and agreed to conclude a separate peace treaty. The negotiations for the peace treaty were protracted and, by the time it was concluded in 1978, China's preoccupation with the Soviet threat led to the inclusion of an "anti-hegemony" statement. In fewer than three decades, China had signed an explicitly anti-Japanese treaty with the Soviet Union and a treaty having an anti-Soviet component with Japan.

From the 1970s into the 1980s, economic relations were the centerpiece of relations between China and Japan. Japan has been China's top trading partner since the 1960s. Despite concern in the late 1980s over a trade imbalance, the volume of Sino-Japanese trade showed no sign of declining. Relations suffered a setback in 1979 and 1980, when China canceled or modified overly ambitious plans made in the late 1970s to import large quantities of Japanese technology, the best-known example involving the Baoshan iron and steel complex in Shanghai. Lower expectations on both sides seemed to have created a more realistic economic and technological partnership by the late 1980s.

Chinese relations with Japan during the 1980s were generally close and cordial. Tension erupted periodically, however, over trade and technology issues, Chinese concern over potential Japanese military resurgence, and controversy regarding Japan's relations with Taiwan, especially Beijing's concern that Tokyo was pursuing a "two Chinas" policy. China joined other Asian nations in criticizing Japanese history textbooks that deemphasized past Japanese aggression, claiming that the distortion was evidence of the rise of militarism in Japan. By the late 1980s, despite occasional outbreaks of tension, the two governments held regular consultations, high-level leaders frequently exchanged visits, Chinese and Japanese military leaders had begun contacts, and many Chinese and Japanese students and tourists traveled back and forth.

EUROPE

Although it had been the European powers that precipitated the opening of China to the West in the nineteenth century, by 1949 the European presence was limited to Hong Kong and Macau. Europe exerted a strong intellectual influence on modern Chinese leaders (Marxism and Leninism of course originated in Europe), and some leaders, including Zhou Enlai and Deng Xiaoping, studied in Europe early in their careers.

Nevertheless, China's geographic distance from Europe, its preoccupation with the superpowers, and the division of Europe after World War II meant that China's relations with European nations usually were subordinate to its relations with the Soviet Union and the United States. East European nations were the first countries to establish diplomatic relations with China in 1949, following the Soviet Union's lead. In the early 1950s, through the Sino-Soviet alliance, China became an observer in the Council for Mutual Economic Assistance (Comecon), and Chinese relations with Eastern Europe included trade and receipt of limited amounts of economic and technical aid.

The Sino-Soviet dispute was manifested in China's relations with certain East European countries, especially China's support for Albania's break with the Soviet Union in the late 1950s. After the Sino-Soviet split in the 1960s, the only East European nations maintaining significant ties with China until the late 1970s were Albania, Romania, and Yugoslavia.

By the late 1980s, however, as Beijing's relations with Moscow improved and relations with governments and parties on the basis of "mutual respect and peaceful coexistence" were renewed, China's ties with the other nations of Eastern Europe also had improved noticeably, to include communist party ties.

China's ties with Western Europe were minimal for the first two decades of the People's Republic. Several West European nations, mostly in Scandinavia, established diplomatic relations with China in the early 1950s, and Britain and the Netherlands established ties with China at the charge d'affaires level in 1954.

In the late 1950s, Britain became the first Western nation to relax the trade embargo against China imposed during the Korean War. The establishment of diplomatic relations between China and France in 1964 also provided an opening for trade and other limited Chinese contacts with Western Europe until the 1970s.

China's relations with Western Europe grew rapidly in the 1970s, as more nations recognized China and diplomatic relations were established with the European Economic Community in 1975. In the second half of the 1970s, China's emphasis on an international united front against Soviet hegemony led to increased Chinese support for West European unity and for the role of the North Atlantic Treaty Organization. Ties with Western Europe also were featured prominently in Beijing's independent foreign policy of the 1980s. Furthermore, China's opening up to foreign trade, investment, and technology beginning in the late 1970s greatly improved Sino-European ties. One of the few major problems in China's relations with Western Europe in the post-Mao era was the downgrading of diplomatic ties with the Netherlands from 1981 to 1984 over the latter's sale of submarines to Taiwan.

ROLE IN INTERNATIONAL ORGANIZATIONS

Participation in international organizations is perceived as an important measure of a nation's prestige as well as a forum through which a nation can influence others and gain access to aid programs and sources of technology and information. The People's Republic was precluded from participating actively in most mainstream international organizations for the first two decades of its existence because of its subordinate position in the Sino-Soviet alliance in the 1950s and the opposition of the United States after China's involvement in the Korean War. China repeatedly failed to gain admission to the UN.

In 1971 Beijing finally gained China's seat when relations with the United States changed for the better. Taipei's representatives were expelled from the UN and replaced by Beijing's. After becoming a member of the UN, China also joined most UN-affiliated agencies, including, by the 1980s, the World Bank and the International Monetary Fund. China's willingness, under the policy of opening up to the outside world beginning in the late 1970s, to receive economic and technical assistance from such agencies as the UN Development Program was a significant departure from its previous stress on self-reliance. In 1986 China renewed its application to regain its seat as one of the founding members of the General Agreement on Tariffs and Trade.

By the late 1980s, China had become a member of several hundred international and regional organizations, both those of major significance to world affairs, including the International Atomic Energy Agency, the World Intellectual Property Organization, and the International Olympic Committee, and associations or societies focused on such narrow subjects as acrobatics or the study of seaweed. Besides providing China a forum from which to express its views on various issues, membership in the 1970s and 1980s in increasing numbers of international groups gave Chinese foreign affairs personnel wider knowledge and valuable international experience. It is notable that by the late 1980s Beijing had not sought formal membership in several important international organizations representative of Third World interests: the Group of 77, the Non-Aligned Movement, and the Organization of Petroleum Exporting Countries.

Despite the emphasis China placed on Third World relations, China's independent foreign policy and special position as a somewhat atypical Third World nation made it seem unlikely in the late 1980s that China would seek more than observer status in these groups. By the second half of the 1980s, China's participation in international organizations reflected the two primary goals of its independent foreign policy: furthering domestic economic development through cooperation with the outside world and promoting peace and stability by cultivating ties with other nations on an equal basis. As expressed by Zhao Ziyang in a 1986 report to the National People's Congress, "China is a developing socialist country with a population of over 1 billion. We are well aware of our obligations and responsibilities in the world. We will therefore continue to work hard on both fronts, domestic and international, to push forward the socialist modernization of our country and to make greater contributions to world peace and human progress."

Bibliography

1. Aalto, Pentti. "The Horse in Central Asian Nomadic Cultures. " *Studia Orientalia* 46 (1975): 1–9.
2. Academy of Sciences MPR. *Information Mongolia*. Oxford: Pergamon Press, 1990.
3. Alekseev, Valery P. "Some Aspects of the Study of Productive Forces in the Empire of Chengiz Khan." In *Rulers from the Steppe*, ed. Gary Seaman and Daniel Marks. Los Angeles: Ethnographics Press/The University of Southern California, 1991, pp. 186–98.
4. Alekshin, V. A. "Problème de l'origin des cultures archéologiques du néolithique et de l'Âge du Bronze en Asie centrale (d'après les rites funéraires). In *L'Asie centrale et ses rapports avec les civilisations orientales des origines a l'Age du Fer*. Paris: Diffusion de Boccard, 1988, pp. 255–64.
5. Ames, Roger T. *The Art of Rulership: A Study in Ancient Chinese Political Thought*. Honolulu: University of Hawaii Press, 1983.
6. Askarov, A., V. Volkov, and N. Ser-Odjav. "Pastoral and Nomadic Tribes at the Beginning of the First Millennium B. C. " In *History of Civilizations of Central Asia*. Vol. 1: *The Dawn of Civilization: Earliest Times to 700 B. C.*, ed. A. H. Dani and V. M. Masson. Paris: Unesco, 1992, pp. 459–75.
7. Bacon, Elisabeth. *Obok: A Study of Social Structure in*

Eurasia. New York: WennerGren Foundation, 1958.

8. Bagley, Robert. "Shang Archaeology. " In *Cambridge History of Ancient China*, ed. Michael Loewe and Edward L. Shaughnessy. Cambridge: Cambridge University Press, 1999, pp. 124–231.

9. Bailey, H. W. *Indo-Scythian Studies. Khotanese Texts VII*. Cambridge: Cambridge University Press, 1985.

10. Balazs, Etienne. "L'histoire comme guide de la pratique bureaucratique. " In *Historians of China and Japan*, ed. W. G. Beasley and E. G. Pulleyblank. London: Oxford University Press, 1961, pp. 78–94. [Trans. as "History as a Guide to Bureaucratic Practice, " in Etienne Balazs, *Chinese Civilization and Bureaucracy*. New Haven: Yale University Press, 1964.]

11. Barfield, Thomas. "The Hsiung-nu Imperial Confederacy: Organization and Foreign Policy. " *Journal of Asian Studies* 41.1 (November 1981): 45–61.

12. Chang Ch'ang-ming. "Shih-lun Hsi Han te Han Hsiung kuan-hsi chi ch'i kuan-hsi chi ho-ch'in cheng-ts'e. " *Chiang-huai lun-t'an* 1983.6: 83–88.

13. Chang Chun-shu. "Military Aspects of Han Wu-ti's Northern and Northwestern Campaigns. " *Harvard Journal of Asiatic Studies* 21 (1966): 68–173.

14. Chao Hua-ch'eng. "Chung-kuo tsao-ch'i ch'ang-ch'eng te k'ao-ku tiao-ch'a yü yenchiu. " In *Ch'ang-ch'eng kuo-chi hsüeh-shu yen-t'ao-hui lun-wen*, ed. Chungkuo ch'ang-ch'eng hsüeh-hui. Chi-lin-shih: Chi-lin Jen-min, 1994.

15. Chao Shan-t'ung. "Hei-lung-chiang kuan-ti yi-chih fa-hsien de mu-tsang. " *K'ao-ku* 1965.1: 45–6. *Ch'ao Ts'o chi chu-yi*. Shanghai: Jen-min, 1976.

16. David, T. "Peuples mobiles de l'eurasie: contacts d'une périphérie 'barbare' avec le monde 'civilisé', à la fin de l'Age du Bronze et au 1er Age du Fer. " In *L'Asie centrale et ses rapports avec les civilisations orientales des origines a l'Age du Fer*. Paris: Diffusion de Boccard, 1988, pp. 159–68.

17. Davydova, A. V. "The Ivolga Gorodishche. A Monument of the Hsiung-nu Culture in the Trans-Baikal Region. " *Acta Orientalia Academiae Scientiarum Hungaricae* 20 (1968): 209–45. *Ivolginskii kompleks (gorodishche i mogil'nik) — pamiatnik khunnu v Zabaikal'e.* Leningrad: Izd-vo Leningradskogo Universiteta, 1985.

18. Davydova A. V., and V. P. Shilov. "K voprosy o zemledelii y gunnov. " *Vestnik drevnei istorii* 2.44 (1983): 193–201.

19. Egami, Namio. "The Kuai ti, the Tao you, and the Dao xi: The Strange Animals of the Xiongnu. " *Memoirs of the Research Department of Toyo Bunko* 13 (1951): 87–123.

20. Enoki, Kazuo. "On the Relationship between the *Shih-chi*, Bk. 123 and the *Hanshu*, Bks. 61 and 96. " *Memoirs of the Research Department of the Toyo Bunko* 41 (1983): 1–31.

21. Erdy, Miklos. "Hun and Xiongnu Type Cauldron Finds throughout Eurasia. " *Eurasian Studies Yearbook* (1995): 5–94.

22. Erkes, Edouard. "Das Pferd im Alten China. " *T'oung Pao* 36 (1942): 26–63.

23. Falkenhausen, Lothar von. "On the Historiographical Orientation of Chinese Archaeology. " *Antiquity* 67 (1993): 839–49.

24. Fraser, Everard D. H., and James H. S. Lockhart. *Index to the Tso Chuan.* London: Oxford University Press, 1930.

25. Gale, Esson M. *Discourses on Salt and Iron.* Leiden: Brill, 1931; rpt. Taipei: Ch'engwen, 1967.

26. Gardiner-Gardner, J. R. "Chang Ch'ien and Central Asian Ethnography. " *Papers of Far Eastern History* 33 (1986): 23–79.

27. Gardiner-Garden, John. *Apollodoros of Artemita and the Central Asian Skythians.* Papers on Inner Asia no. 3. Bloomington: Research Institute for Inner Asian Studies, 1987.

28. *Greek Conceptions on Inner Asian Geography and Ethnography from Ephoros to Eratosthenes.* Papers on Inner Asia no. 9. Bloomington: Research Institute for Inner Asian Studies, 1987.

29. *Herodotos' Contemporaries on Skythian Geography and Ethnography.* Papers on Inner Asia no. 10. Bloomington: Research Institute for Inner Asian Studies, 1987.

30. *Ktesias on Central Asian History and Ethnography.* Papers on Inner Asia no. 6. Bloomington: Research Institute for Inner Asian Studies, 1987.

31. Heine-Geldern, R. "Das Tocharenproblem und die Pontische Wanderung. " *Saeculum* 2 (1951): 225–55.

32. Hervouet, Yves. *Un poéte de cour sous les Han: Sseu-ma Siang-jou.* Paris: Presses universitaires de France, 1964. "Le valeur relative de textes du Che-Ki et du Han-chou. " In *Melanges de Sinologie offérts a Monsieur Paul Demieville, part II.* Paris: Bibliotheque de l'Istitute des Hautes Etudes Chinoises, 1974, vol. 20, pp. 55–76.

33. Hiebert, Fredrik T. "Pazyryk Chronology and Early Horse Nomads Reconsidered. " *Bulletin of the Asia Institute,* n.s. 6 (1992): 117–29.

34. Irincin. "Dumdatu ulus-un umaradakin-u uãsaãatan nuãud bolon monggolèud-un uãsaãan ijaãur. " In *Monggol teüke-yin tuqai ügülel-üd.* Huhhot: Öbör Monggol-un Arad-un Keblel-un Qoriy-a, 1981, pp. 4–12.

35. Itina, Mariana A. "The Steppes of the Aral Sea in Pre- and Early Scythian Times. " In *Foundations of Empire: Archaeology and Art of the Eurasian Steppes,* ed. Gary Seaman. Los Angeles: Ethnographics Press/University of Southern California, 1992, pp. 49–58.

36. Janhunen, Juha. "The Horse in East Asia: Reviewing the Linguistic Evidence. " In *The Bronze Age and Early Iron Age Peoples of Eastern Central Asia,* ed. Victor H. Mair. Washington: Institute for the Study of Man, 1998, vol. 1, pp. 415– 30.

37. Jen Chi-yu. "Ssu-ma Ch'ien te che-hsüeh ssu-hsiang. "In *Ssu-ma Ch'ien yü 0Shih Chi   0 lun-chi*, ed. Li-shih yen-chiu pien-chi-pu. Hsi-an: Shaansi jen-min ch'u-pan-she, 1982, pp. 105–18.

38. Jettmar, Karl. *Art of the Steppes*. New York: Crown Publishers, 1967.

39. Johnson, David. "Epic and History in Early China: The Matter of Wu Tzu-hsü. " *Journal of Asian Studies* 40.2 (1981): 255–71.

40. Kai Shan-lin. "Nei Meng-ku tzu-chih-ch'ü Chun-ke-erh-ch'i Su-chi-kou ch'u-t'u yi-pi t'ung-ch'i. " *Wen-wu* 1965.2: 44–45.

41. Lattimore, Owen. *The Mongols of Manchuria*. New York: The John Day Company, 1934.

Inner Asian Frontiers of China. Boston: Beacon Press, 1962 [1940]. "Herders, Farmers, Urban Culture. " In *Pastoral Production and Society. Proceedings of the International Meeting on Nomadic Pastoralism, Paris 1–3 Dec. 1976*, ed. L'Equipe écologie et anthropologie des sociétés pastorales. Cambridge: Cambridge University Press, 1979, pp. 479–90.

42. Laufer, Berthold. *Chinese Clay Figures. Part I: Prolegomena on the History of Defensive Armor*. Chicago: Field Museum of Natural History Publication no. 177, 1914.

43. Le Blanc, Charles. *Huai-nan Tzu. Philosophical Synthesis in Early Han Thought*. Hong Kong: Hong Kong University Press, 1985.

44. Moshkova, Marina. "Sarmatians, Concluding Remarks. " In *Nomads of the Eurasian Steppes in the Early Iron Age*, ed. Jeannine Davis-Kimball et al. Berkeley: Zinat Press, 1995, pp. 185–88.

45. Myroshnikov, L. I. "Appendix: A Note on the Meaning of 'Central Asia' as Used in This Book. " In *History of Civilizations of Central Asia*. Vol. 1: *The Dawn of Civilization: Earliest Times to 700 B. C.*, ed. A. H. Dani and V. M. Masson. Paris: Unesco, 1992, pp. 477–80.

46. Nakayama, Shigeru. *Academic and Scientific Traditions in China, Japan and the West.* Tokyo: University of Tokyo Press, 1984.

47. Needham, Joseph. *Science and Civilization in China.* Vol. 2: *History of Scientific Thought.* Cambridge, Cambridge University Press, 1956.

48. O'Donoghue, Diane M. "Reflection and Reception: The Origins of the Mirror in Bronze Age China. " *Bulletin of the Museum of Far Eastern Antiquities* 62 (1990): 5–183.

49. Ohama, Akira. *Chûgoku. rekishi. unmei: Shiki to Shitsu.* Tokyo: Keiso Shobo, 1975.

50. Pumpelly, Raphael, ed. *Explorations in Turkestan. Expedition of 1904. Prehistoric Civilizations of Anau: Origins, Growth, and Influence of Environment.* 2 vols. Washington: Carnegie Institution, 1908.

51. Rachewiltz, Igor de. "Some Remarks on the Ideological Foundations of Chingis Khan's Empire. " *Papers on Far Eastern History* 7 (March 1973): 21–36.

52. Raschke, Manfred. "New Studies in Roman Commerce with the East. " In *Aufstieg und Niedergang der römischen Welt, II Principat,* ed. Hildegard Temporini and W. Haase, vol. 9.2. Berlin: W. de Gruyter, 1978, pp. 614–1361.

53. Salzman, Philip Carl. "Introduction. " In *When Nomads Settle: Processes of Sedentarization as Adaptation and Response,* ed. Philip Carl Salzman. New York: Praeger, 1980.

54. Samolin, W. "Hsiung-nu, Hun, Turk. " *Central Asiatic Journal* 3 (1957–58): 143– 50.

55. Sargent, C. B. "Subsidized History. " *Far Eastern Quarterly* 3.1 (1943): 134–38.

56. Saunders, J. J. "The Nomad as Empire-Builder: A Comparison of the Arab and Mongol Conquests. " In *Muslims and Mongols: Essays on Medieval Asia by J. J. Saunders,* ed. G. W. Rice. Christchurch: University of Canterbury, 1977, pp. 36–66.

57. Suzuki, Chusei. "China's Relations with Inner Asia:

The Hsiung-nu, Tibet. " In *The Chinese World Order,* ed. John K. Fairbank. Cambridge: Harvard University Press, 1968, pp. 180–97.

58. Swann, Nancy Lee. *Food and Money in Ancient China. The Earliest Economic History of China to A. D. 25. Han Shu 24 with Related Texts, Han Shu 91 and Shih Chi 129.* Princeton: Princeton University Press, 1950.

59. T'a La, and Liang Chin-ming. "Hu-lu-ssu-t'ai Hsiung-nu mu. " *Wen-wu* 1980.7: 11–12.

60. Taaffe, Robert N. "The Geographic Setting. " *The Cambridge History of Early Inner Asia,* ed. Denis Sinor. Cambridge: Cambridge University Press, 1990, pp. 19–40.

61. Turan, Osman. "The Ideal of World Dominion among the Medieval Türks. " *Studia Islamica* 4 (1955): 77–90.

62. Vainshtein, S. *Nomads of South Siberia. The Pastoral Economies of Tuva.* Cambridge: Cambridge University Press, 1980.

63. Van der Loon, Piet. "The Ancient Chinese Chronicles and the Growth of Historical Ideals. " In *Historians of China and Japan,* ed. W. G. Beasley and E. G. Pulleyblank. London: Oxford University Press, 1961, pp. 24–30.

64. Vandermeersch, Leon. *Wangdao ou, La voie royale. Recherches sur l'esprit des institutions de la Chine archaique.* 2 vols. Paris: Ecole Française d'Extreme-Orient, 1977–80.

65. Vreeland, Herbert. *Mongol Community and Kinship Structure.* New Haven: Human Relations Area Files, 1957.

66. Waldron, Arthur. *The Great Wall of China: From History to Myth.* Cambridge: Cambridge University Press, 1990.

67. Waley, Arthur. *The Analects of Confucius.* London: Allen and Unwin, 1938.

Index